NFPA® 79

Electrical Standard for

Industrial Machinery

2021 Edition

This edition of NFPA 79, *Electrical Standard for Industrial Machinery*, was prepared by the Technical Committee on Electrical Equipment of Industrial Machinery and released by the Correlating Committee on National Electrical Code®. It was issued by the Standards Council on October 5, 2020, with an effective date of October 25, 2020, and supersedes all previous editions.

This edition of NFPA 79 was approved as an American National Standard on October 25, 2020.

Origin and Development of NFPA 79

This standard was first submitted at the 1961 NFPA Annual Meeting under the title *Electrical Standard for Machine Tools* and was tentatively adopted subject to comments. It was extensively revised and resubmitted at the 1962 NFPA Annual Meeting, where it was officially adopted. In 1965 a revised edition was adopted, reconfirmed in 1969, and in 1970, 1971, 1973, 1974, 1977, 1980, 1985, 1987, 1991, 1994, 1997, 2002 and 2007, revised editions were adopted.

In September 1941, the metalworking machine tool industry wrote its first electrical standard to make machine tools safer to operate, more productive, and less costly to maintain, and to improve the quality and performance of their electrical components. That particular standard served as an American "War Standard."

To study the special electrical problems involved with machine tools, in 1941 the Electrical Section of the National Fire Protection Association sanctioned a Special Subcommittee on Wiring, Overcurrent Protection, and Control of Motor-Operated Machine Tools. This subcommittee, cooperating with machine tool builders, manufacturers of control equipment, and Underwriters Laboratories Inc., conducted tests and investigated the peculiar conditions involved with machine tools that might warrant exception to certain specific *National Electrical Code* requirements. This investigation resulted, on August 4, 1942, in a Tentative Interim Amendment and first appeared in a 1943 supplement to the 1940 edition of *NFPA 70®, National Electrical Code (NEC)*, as Article 670, "Machine Tools." It remained essentially unchanged through the 1959 edition.

Meanwhile, manufacturers of other types of industrial equipment erroneously began to follow the specialized practices permitted by Article 670. Late in 1952, a Technical Subcommittee on Fundamentals of Electrically Operated Production Machinery and Material Handling and Processing Equipment for Fixed Locations was organized to attempt to group the special requirements of this broad field into one article. The extremely broad scope introduced so many problems that, in December 1956, this technical subcommittee was reorganized into an NFPA committee whose scope was limited to machine tools and whose objective was the preparation of this NFPA standard with corresponding revisions in Article 670 in the *National Electrical Code*.

Modern machine tool electrical equipment may vary from that of single-motor machines, such as drill presses, that perform simple, repetitive operations, to that of very large, multimotored automatic machines that involve highly complex electrical control systems, including electronic and solid-state devices and equipment. Generally these machines are specially designed, factory wired, and tested by the builder and then erected in the plant in which they will be used. Because of their importance to plant production and their usually high cost, they are customarily provided with many safeguards and other devices not often incorporated in the usual motor and control application as contemplated by the *National Electrical Code*.

Although these machines may be completely automatic, they are constantly attended, when operating, by highly skilled operators. The machine usually incorporates many special devices to protect the operator, protect the machine and building against fires of electrical origin, protect the machine and work in process against damage due to electrical failures, and protect against loss of production due to failure of a machine component. To provide these safeguards, it may be preferable to deliberately sacrifice a motor or some other component, rather than to chance injury to the operator, the work, or the machine. It is because of such considerations that this standard varies from the basic concepts of motor protection as contained in the *National Electrical Code*.

As NFPA 79 evolved, it became apparent that certain classes of light industrial machinery (e.g., small drill presses, bench grinders, sanders) were not appropriately covered. The 1977 edition of the standard recognized this problem and purposely excluded tools powered by 2 hp or less.

Subsequent to publication of the 1977 standard, a light industrial machinery standard development activity was initiated by the Power Tool Institute. The 1985 edition of NFPA 79 reflects this activity, and appropriate requirements are now included in the standard.

In 1975, the Society of the Plastics Industry requested that this standard be enlarged in scope to include plastics machinery. A formal request was received by NFPA in September 1978, and, through the combined efforts of the NFPA 79 committee and representatives of the Society of the Plastics Industry, the scope was broadened to include such machinery in the 1980 edition.

In June 1981, the Joint Industrial Council (JIC) Board of Directors acknowledged the dated state of the electrical and electronic standards and requested that NFPA 79 incorporate into its standard the material and topics covered by the JIC electrical (EMP-1-67, EGP-1-67) and electronic (EL-1-71) standards with the intention that the JIC standards eventually would be declared superseded. The NFPA Standards Council approved the request with the stipulation that the material and topics incorporated from the JIC standards be limited to areas related to electrical shock and fire hazards. The 1985 edition reflected the incorporation of the appropriate material from the JIC electrical (EMP-1-67, EGP-1-67) standards not previously covered. The 1991, 1994, and 1997 editions included additional references to international standards and reflected the committee's efforts in harmonization.

The 2002 edition was a major rewrite and represented a significant and historic effort in harmonizing an existing NFPA standard with an existing IEC standard. Major changes for this edition included renumbering section and chapter numbers to align with IEC 60204–1. A new chapter was added to address testing.

The 2007 edition continued to be aligned with IEC 60204–1. Because so much electrical equipment today contains both electrical and electronic equipment, Chapter 11, Electronic Equipment, was deleted, and any sections that remained applicable were dispersed to the appropriate chapters. The deletion of Chapter 11 caused all chapters after Chapter 11 to be renumbered to one less than in previous editions. A new Chapter 19, entitled "Servo Drives and Motors," was added to the end of the standard. This new chapter addressed some of the user concerns that are arising as servo drives and servo motors are integrated into industrial machinery. Other changes include further defining of cables and cords, clarifying emergency stop functions, permitting system isolation equipment, clarifying short-circuit current markings, and refining requirements associated with software- and firmware-based control systems performing safety-related functions.

Changes to the 2012 edition continued to align the standard with IEC 60204–1. Due to the continued advancement and expansion of wireless and cableless technology, major changes for this edition included a revised definition for the term cableless control and a new definition for the term *cableless control* and a new definition for the term *cableless operator control station*, along with revisions to Chapter 9, which aligned with IEC 60204-1. The title of Chapter 6 was changed, to recognize that there are other hazards (such as arc flash and stored energy) besides electrical shock. New sections were added to Chapters 6 and 16 to recognize these hazards and correlate with *NFPA 70E*. Furthermore, the sections on the hazards from stored energy in Chapter 7 were moved to Chapter 6 for clarity and proper location of those rules in the document. To align with the *NEC*, the requirements in 7.2.10 were changed for selecting overcurrent devices for motors. Chapter 12 received a new section to address user concerns permitting the use of appliance wiring material (AWM) as special cables, with clarifications on determining suitability for use under specific conditions. An important addition of a 90°C (194°F) temperature column to the conductor ampacity table in Chapter 12 was included to correlate with the *NEC*.

Other changes included adding the definition for short-circuit current rating (SCCR), extracted from the *NEC*; revising the definition for equipment grounding conductor; and adding a new definition for safety-related function specific to industrial machines to harmonize with IEC and ISO standards. Further changes to Chapter 19 addressed some of the user concerns arising from servo drives and servo motors being more commonly used in industrial machinery. Finally, adding an American Wire Gauge (AWG) to the metric conductor cross-reference table in Annex I provided the user and enforcement officials a means to judge AWG versus metric wire sizes required by the standard.

As in previous editions, the 2015 edition aligned with IEC 60204–1, and the alignment was made more intuitive and informative. Parenthetical terms that aligned with IEC terms throughout the main body of the document without explanation reside in Annex J with further explanation for their use. Global changes of the editorial type were accepted to comply with the *Manual of Style for NFPA Technical Committee Documents*. Two definitions were added — *industrial control panel* and *overcurrent protective device, branch circuit*. Seven definitions were deleted — *cable trunking systems* (3.3.16), *duct* (3.3.33), *earth* (3.3.34), *positive opening operation* (of a contact element) (3.3.74), *protective bonding circuit* (3.3.77), *protective conductor* (3.3.78), and *subassembly* (3.3.98). The title of Section 6.6 was revised to Arc Flash Hazard Warning to clarify that the requirement is to warn qualified individuals of, not to protect them from, a potential arc flash hazard. This change aligned with the 2014 *NEC* revision to 110.16, which added "or factory" to allow the required arc-flash warning label to be applied at the factory as well as in the field — a change that was more conducive to industrial machinery and industrial control panels.

The conditions for emergency stop on Category 1 and Category 0 were revised, as well as those for emergency switching off. Working space rules for enclosures that contain supply conductors were revised to clarify that 110.26 of the *NEC* applies, and an exhibit was added to Annex A to illustrate the requirement. The requirement for width of the working space was also revised to specify the opening into the control cabinet and to consider situations where there were devices involved with industrial machine control cabinets. Table 12.5.5(a) was revised to add 60 degree and 90 degree columns to correlate with the addition of a 90 degree column to 12.5.1 in the 2012 edition and in the *NEC*. Finally, language was revised to clarify the rules for separate supply sources; the standard to use for warning signs; how to calculate SCCR marking where there are multiple control panels; that overcurrent protection is required for servo drives; and that conveyors, conveying machines, and material handling machines are within the scope of NFPA 79.

In the 2018 edition, "600 volts" was replaced with "1000 volts" to align with the NEC. Three definitions were revised — *adjustable speed drive, liquidtight flexible metal conduit,* and *wet location.* Four definitions were added — *basic protection, effective ground-fault current path, fault protection,* and *machine supply circuit.* Four definitions were deleted — *attachment plug (plug cap) (plug), receptacle, socket,* and *visible.* The title of Chapter 5 was revised to Disconnecting Means to clarify that Chapter 5 covers all the supply circuit conductor terminations on the machine.

The 2018 edition also revised Section 5.1 to remove "incoming" and add "machine" to align with the newly added definition. The main disconnecting means must be marked "main disconnecting means" if it supplies multiple disconnecting means on the machine. The machine supply circuit disconnecting means, by Exception No. 2 to 5.3.1.3, is permitted to be externally mounted up to 20 ft (6 m) away. Finally, language was revised to allow adjustable speed drives marked "suitable for output conductor protection" to have the rating of the short-circuit protective device (SCPD) determined by the drive's rated input current.

A requirement was added to 7.8.1 to require a surge-protection device (SPD) to correlate with 670.6 of the *NEC*; the title of Chapter 8 for grounding added "bonding"; clarification was added on connection of the grounded conductor to the equipment grounding conductor; and clarification that all parts of effective ground-fault current path is capable of withstanding the highest thermal and mechanical stress that can be caused by fault currents. Further enhancements to Chapter 11 were added to clarify the peculiar working space condition of industrial machines and machine tools.

In the 2021 edition, the inconsistent use of text involving voltages has been resolved and the use of the term *safety related control systems* has been updated. In Chapter 3, terms extracted from *NFPA 70* have been updated and the definition of *safety circuit* has been revised. In Chapter 4, references to voltage dips have been revised, cable types for power conversion equipment have been removed, and electromagnetic compatibility (EMC) involving transients has been revised. Requirements involving supply circuit disconnecting means, access, operations, and markings in Chapter 5 have been enhanced; in 5.2.4, the term *isolation devices* has been replaced with *disconnecting means.*

Chapter 6 requirements on enclosure access and interlocking have been changed, and voltage limitations and rejection capabilities for attachment plugs in protective extra low voltage (PELV) systems have been revised. In Chapter 7, language requiring surge-protection devices (SPDs) has been updated. Control system grounding requirements in Chapter 8 have been updated, and the exception to 8.3.2 involving insulation monitoring for Class 2 circuits has been changed.

In Chapter 9, an exception has been added to 9.4.2.1. In Chapter 10, 10.7.1.3 has been revised, requiring emergency stop devices to be listed. Revisions to Chapter 15 deleted "in the machine area" in 15.2.2.1. In Chapter 19, Section 19.1 has been determined as redundant to 19.1.1 and 19.1.2 and was deleted. Duplicate material in the annexes has also been deleted, and A.9.2.5.4 added a reference to ISO 12100.

The technical committee for this standard reports to NFPA through the Correlating Committee of the National Electrical Code. The primary reason is to correlate this standard and *NFPA 70*, especially with respect to Article 670.

Correlating Committee on National Electrical Code®

Lawrence S. Ayer, *Chair*
Biz Com Electric, Inc., OH [IM]
Rep. Independent Electrical Contractors, Inc.

James E. Brunssen, Telcordia Technologies (Ericsson), NJ [UT]
Rep. Alliance for Telecommunications Industry Solutions

Palmer L. Hickman, Electrical Training Alliance, MD [L]
Rep. International Brotherhood of Electrical Workers

Richard A. Holub, The DuPont Company, Inc., DE [U]
Rep. American Chemistry Council

Michael J. Johnston, National Electrical Contractors Association, MD [IM]

John R. Kovacik, UL LLC, IL [RT]

Alan Manche, Schneider Electric, KY [M]

Roger D. McDaniel, Georgia Power Company, GA [UT]
Rep. Electric Light & Power Group/EEI

Christine T. Porter, Intertek Testing Services, WA [RT]

George A. Straniero, AFC Cable Systems, Inc., NJ [M]
Rep. National Electrical Manufacturers Association

David A. Williams, Delta Charter Township, MI [E]
Rep. International Association of Electrical Inspectors

Alternates

Derrick L. Atkins, Minneapolis Electrical JATC, MN [L]
(Alt. to Palmer L. Hickman)

Donald R. Cook, Shelby County Department of Development Services, AL [E]
(Alt. to David A. Williams)

Roland E. Deike, Jr., CenterPoint Energy, Inc., TX [UT]
(Alt. to Roger D. McDaniel)

William T. Fiske, Intertek Testing Services, NY [RT]
(Alt. to Christine T. Porter)

Ernest J. Gallo, Telcordia Technologies (Ericsson), NJ [UT]
(Alt. to James E. Brunssen)

David L. Hittinger, Independent Electrical Contractors of Greater Cincinnati, OH [IM]
(Alt. to Lawrence S. Ayer)

David H. Kendall, ABB Inc., TN [M]
(Alt. to George A. Straniero)

Robert D. Osborne, UL LLC, NC [RT]
(Alt. to John R. Kovacik)

Timothy James Schultheis, T.S.B. Inc., Schultheis Electric, PA [IM]
(Alt. to Michael J. Johnston)

Nonvoting

Timothy J. Pope, Canadian Standards Association, Canada [SE]
Rep. CSA/Canadian Electrical Code Committee

Rodger Reiswig, Johnson Controls, FL [M]

William R. Drake, Fairfield, CA [M]
(Member Emeritus)

D. Harold Ware, Libra Electric Company, OK [IM]
(Member Emeritus)

Jeffrey S. Sargent, NFPA Staff Liaison

This list represents the membership at the time the Committee was balloted on the final text of this edition. Since that time, changes in the membership may have occurred. A key to classifications is found at the back of the document.

NOTE: Membership on a committee shall not in and of itself constitute an endorsement of the Association or any document developed by the committee on which the member serves.

Committee Scope: This Committee shall have primary responsibility for documents on minimizing the risk of electricity as a source of electric shock and as a potential ignition source of fires and explosions. It shall also be responsible for text to minimize the propagation of fire and explosions due to electrical installations.

Technical Committee on Electrical Equipment of Industrial Machinery

Luis M. Bas, *Chair*
Intertek Testing Services, FL [RT]

William Brungs, Honeywell Intelligrated Systems, OH [M]
David R. Carpenter, City of Florence, Alabama, AL [E]
Jim Couch, Mazak Corporation, KY [M]
Rep. The Association for Manufacturing Technology
Frank C. DeFelice, Jr., Allnex, Inc., CT [U]
Paul Dobrowsky, Innovative Technology Services, NY [SE]
Stephen W. Douglas, QPS Evaluation Services Inc., Canada [RT]
Matt Egloff, Montana Tech, University of Montana, MT [SE]
Heath Garrison, National Renewable Energy Laboratory, CO [E]
Bobby J. Gray, Hoydar/Buck, Inc., WA [IM]
Rep. National Electrical Contractors Association
Robert Gruendel, Amazon, MI [U]
Palmer L. Hickman, Electrical Training Alliance, MD [L]
Rep. International Brotherhood of Electrical Workers
Mark R. Hilbert, MR Hilbert Electrical Inspections & Training, NH [E]
Rep. International Association of Electrical Inspectors
John R. Kovacik, UL LLC, IL [RT]

Dino Mariuz, Pilz Automation Safety L.P., MI [M]
Terrance L. McKinch, Mortenson Construction, MI [IM]
Daleep C. Mohla, DCM Electrical Consulting Services, Inc., TX [U]
Rep. Institute of Electrical & Electronics Engineers, Inc.
Sean Mulherrin, EPLAN Software & Services LLC, MI [U]
Daniel R. Neeser, Eaton's Bussmann Division, MO [M]
Rep. National Electrical Manufacturers Association
John A. Piller, J Piller Design and Consulting, IN [SE]
George M. Schreck, Komatsu America Industries, LLC, IL [M]
Mike Soter, SDK Engineering, LLC, MI [SE]
Andras Szende, TUV Rheinland of North America, Inc., NY [RT]
Marco Tacchini, GT Engineering, Italy [SE]
Jay Tamblingson, Rockwell Automation, WI [M]
Richard S. Trainor, TUV SUD America Inc., MA [RT]
Stephen J. Ziegeweid, Ashley Furniture Industries, WI [M]
Rep. Woodworking Machinery Manufacturers of America

Alternates

Ron Borowski, Eaton Corporation, WI [M]
(Alt. to Daniel R. Neeser)
Jacob Bradley Chouinard, Quality Electric Inc., ID [IM]
(Alt. to Bobby J. Gray)
Michael J Duta, Rockwell Automation, OH [M]
(Alt. to Jay Tamblingson)
Glyn R. Garside, Pilz Automation Safety L.P., WI [M]
(Alt. to Dino Mariuz)
Adam Gilbert, Intertek, GA [RT]
(Alt. to Luis M. Bas)
Paul Goleniak, EPLAN Software & Services LLC, MI [U]
(Alt. to Sean Mulherrin)

Douglas Johanneman, Toyota Motor Engineering & Manufacturing North America, Inc., KY [U]
(Voting Alt.)
James H. Maxfield, City of Dover Fire & Rescue, NH [E]
(Alt. to Mark R. Hilbert)
Jim Morrison, QPS Evaluation Services Inc., Canada [RT]
(Alt. to Stephen W. Douglas)
Thi Nguyen, The Boeing Company, WA [U]
(Voting Alt.)
Ivan Obelar, TUV Rheinland of North Amercia, CT [RT]
(Alt. to Andras Szende)

Mike McCabe, NFPA Staff Liaison

This list represents the membership at the time the Committee was balloted on the final text of this edition. Since that time, changes in the membership may have occurred. A key to classifications is found at the back of the document.

NOTE: Membership on a committee shall not in and of itself constitute an endorsement of the Association or any document developed by the committee on which the member serves.

Committee Scope: This Committee shall have primary responsibility for documents intended to minimize the potential hazard of electric shock and electrical fire hazards of industrial metalworking machine tools, woodworking machinery, plastics machinery and mass production equipment, not portable by hand. This Committee shall report to Correlating Committee of the National Electrical Code.

Contents

NFPA 79

Electrical Standard for

Industrial Machinery

2021 Edition

IMPORTANT NOTE: This NFPA document is made available for use subject to important notices and legal disclaimers. These notices and disclaimers appear in all publications containing this document and may be found under the heading "Important Notices and Disclaimers Concerning NFPA Standards." They can also be viewed at www.nfpa.org/disclaimers or obtained on request from NFPA.

UPDATES, ALERTS, AND FUTURE EDITIONS: New editions of NFPA codes, standards, recommended practices, and guides (i.e., NFPA Standards) are released on scheduled revision cycles. This edition may be superseded by a later one, or it may be amended outside of its scheduled revision cycle through the issuance of Tentative Interim Amendments (TIAs). An official NFPA Standard at any point in time consists of the current edition of the document, together with all TIAs and Errata in effect. To verify that this document is the current edition or to determine if it has been amended by TIAs or Errata, please consult the National Fire Codes® Subscription Service or the "List of NFPA Codes & Standards" at www.nfpa.org/docinfo. In addition to TIAs and Errata, the document information pages also include the option to sign up for alerts for individual documents and to be involved in the development of the next edition.

NOTICE: An asterisk (*) following the number or letter designating a paragraph indicates that explanatory material on the paragraph can be found in Annex A.

A reference in brackets [ ] following a section or paragraph indicates material that has been extracted from another NFPA document. Extracted text may be edited for consistency and style and may include the revision of internal paragraph references and other references as appropriate. Requests for interpretations or revisions of extracted text should be sent to the technical committee responsible for the source document.

Information on referenced and extracted publications can be found in Chapter 2 and Annex K.

Chapter 1   Administration

1.1* Scope.

1.1.1 The provisions of this standard shall apply to the electrical/electronic equipment, apparatus, or systems of industrial machines supplied from a nominal voltage of 1000 volts or less, and commencing at the point of connection of the supply circuit conductors to the electrical equipment of the machine.

1.1.2* This standard does not include the additional requirements for machines intended for use in hazardous (classified) locations.

1.2 Purpose. This standard shall provide detailed information for the application of electrical/electronic equipment, apparatus, or systems supplied as part of industrial machines that will promote safety to life and property.

1.3 Application.

1.3.1 This standard is not intended to be applied retroactively.

1.3.2 When changes other than repairs are made to machines that do not comply with the provisions of this standard, the changes shall conform to the provisions of this standard.

1.3.3 This standard shall not apply to the following:

(1)   Fixed or portable tools judged under the requirements of a testing laboratory acceptable to the authority having jurisdiction
(2)   Machines used in dwelling units

1.4 Specific Provisions Other Than NFPA 79. The size and overcurrent protection of the supply conductors to a machine shall be covered by Article 670 of *NFPA 70*. The wiring between component machines of an industrial manufacturing system shall be covered by *NFPA 70*.
Exception: Wiring of component machines of an industrial manufacturing system that is supplied by the manufacturer and is an integral part of the system, is adequately protected and supported, and meets the requirements of this standard.

1.5* Specific Provisions Not Made in Relation to NFPA 70. On any point for which specific provisions are not made in this standard the provisions of *NFPA 70* shall be observed.

1.6 State of the Art. This standard shall not limit or inhibit the advancement of the state of the art. Each type of machine has unique requirements that shall be accommodated to provide adequate safety.

Chapter 2   Referenced Publications

2.1 General. The documents or portions thereof listed in this chapter are referenced within this standard and shall be considered part of the requirements of this document.

2.2 NFPA Publications. National Fire Protection Association, 1 Batterymarch Park, Quincy, MA 02169-7471.

NFPA 70®, National Electrical Code®, 2020 edition.
NFPA 70E®, Standard for Electrical Safety in the Workplace®, 2021 edition.

2.3 Other Publications.

2.3.1 ANSI Publications. American National Standards Institute, Inc., 25 West 43rd Street, 4th Floor, New York, NY 10036.

ANSI Z535.4, *Product Safety Signs and Labels*, 2011, reaffirmed 2017.

2.3.2 ASTM Publications. ASTM International, 100 Barr Harbor Drive, P.O. Box C700, West Conshohocken, PA 19428-2959.

ASTM B8, *Standard Specification for Concentric-Lay-Stranded Copper Conductors, Hard, Medium-Hard, or Soft*, 2011, reapproved 2017.

ASTM B174, *Standard Specification for Bunch-Stranded Copper Conductors for Electrical Conductors*, 2017.

ASTM B286, *Standard Specification for Copper Conductors for Use in Hookup Wire for Electronic Equipment*, 2007, reapproved 2017.

2.3.3 IEC Publications. International Electrotechnical Commission, 3, rue de Varembé, P.O. Box 131, CH-1211 Geneva 20, Switzerland.

IEC 60072-1, *Dimensions and output series for rotating electrical machines — Part 1: Frame numbers 56 to 400 and flange numbers 55 to 1080*, 1991.

IEC 60072-2, *Dimensions and output series for rotating electrical machines — Part 2: Frame numbers 355 to 1000 and flange numbers 1180 to 2360*, 1990.

2.3.4 IEEE Publications. IEEE, 3 Park Avenue, 17th Floor, New York, NY 10016-5997.

IEEE 315, *Graphic Symbols for Electrical and Electronics Diagrams (Including Reference Designation Letters)*, 1993.

2.3.5 NEMA Publications. National Electrical Manufacturers Association, 1300 North 17th Street, Suite 900, Arlington, VA 22209.

NEMA ICS 2, *Industrial Control and Systems: Controllers, Contactors, and Overload Relays Rated 600 Volts*, 2000, errata 2008.

NEMA MG-1, *Motors and Generators*, 2016.

NEMA 250, *Enclosures for Electrical Equipment (1000 Volts Maximum)*, 2014.

Δ **2.3.6 UL Publications.** Underwriters Laboratories Inc., 333 Pfingsten Road, Northbrook, IL 60062-2096.

UL 50, *Enclosures for Electrical Equipment, Non-Environmental Considerations*, 2015.

UL 50E, *Enclosures for Electrical Equipment, Environmental Considerations*, 2015.

UL 508, *Industrial Control Equipment*, 2018.

UL 508A, *Industrial Control Panels*, 2018.

UL 870, *Wireways, Auxiliary Gutters,, and Associated Fittings*, 2016.

UL 1063, *Machine-Tool Wires and Cables*, 2017, revised 2018.

UL 1581, *Electrical Wires, Cables, and Flexible Cords*, 2001, revised 2017.

2.3.7 US Government Publications. US Government Publishing Office, 732 North Capitol Street, NW, Washington, DC 20401-0001.

Title 29, Code of Federal Regulations, Part 1910.331–335, "Safety-Related Work Practices."

2.3.8 Other Publications.

Merriam-Webster's Collegiate Dictionary, 11th edition, Merriam-Webster, Inc., Springfield, MA, 2003.

2.4 References for Extracts in Mandatory Sections.

NFPA 70®, National Electrical Code®, 2020 edition.
NFPA 70E®, Standard for Electrical Safety in the Workplace®, 2018 edition.

Chapter 3 Definitions

3.1 General. The definitions contained in this chapter shall apply to the terms used in this standard. Where terms are not defined in this chapter or within another chapter, they shall be defined using their ordinarily accepted meanings within the context in which they are used. *Merriam-Webster's Collegiate Dictionary*, 11th edition, shall be the source for the ordinarily accepted meaning.

3.2 NFPA Official Definitions.

3.2.1* Approved. Acceptable to the authority having jurisdiction.

3.2.2* Authority Having Jurisdiction (AHJ). An organization, office, or individual responsible for enforcing the requirements of a code or standard, or for approving equipment, materials, an installation, or a procedure.

3.2.3 Labeled. Equipment or materials to which has been attached a label, symbol, or other identifying mark of an organization that is acceptable to the authority having jurisdiction and concerned with product evaluation, that maintains periodic inspection of production of labeled equipment or materials, and by whose labeling the manufacturer indicates compliance with appropriate standards or performance in a specified manner.

3.2.4* Listed. Equipment, materials, or services included in a list published by an organization that is acceptable to the authority having jurisdiction and concerned with evaluation of products or services, that maintains periodic inspection of production of listed equipment or materials or periodic evaluation of services, and whose listing states that either the equipment, material, or service meets appropriate designated standards or has been tested and found suitable for a specified purpose.

3.2.5 Shall. Indicates a mandatory requirement.

3.2.6 Should. Indicates a recommendation or that which is advised but not required.

3.2.7 Standard. An NFPA Standard, the main text of which contains only mandatory provisions using the word "shall" to indicate requirements and that is in a form generally suitable for mandatory reference by another standard or code or for adoption into law. Nonmandatory provisions are not to be considered a part of the requirements of a standard and shall be located in an appendix, annex, footnote, informational note, or other means as permitted in the NFPA Manuals of Style. When used in a generic sense, such as in the phrase "standards development process" or "standards development activities," the term "standards" includes all NFPA Standards, including Codes, Standards, Recommended Practices, and Guides.

3.3 General Definitions.

3.3.1 Accessible (as applied to equipment). Admitting close approach; not guarded by locked doors, elevation, or other effective means. [**70:**100]

3.3.2 Accessible, Readily (Readily Accessible). Capable of being reached quickly for operation, renewal, or inspections, without requiring those to whom ready access is requisite to climb over or remove obstacles or to resort to portable ladders, and so forth.

3.3.3* Actuator. The part of the actuating system to which an external actuating force is applied.

3.3.4* Actuator, Machine. A power mechanism used to effect motion of the machine.

3.3.5* Adjustable Speed Drive. Power conversion equipment that provides a means of adjusting the speed of an electric motor. [**70**:100]

3.3.6 Adjustable Speed Drive System. A combination of an adjustable speed drive, its associated motor(s), and auxiliary equipment. [**70**:100]

3.3.7* Ambient Temperature. The temperature of the air or other medium where the equipment is to be used.

3.3.8 Ampacity. The maximum current, in amperes, that a conductor can carry continuously under the conditions of use without exceeding its temperature rating. [**70**:100]

N **3.3.9 Attachment Plug (Plug Cap) (Plug).** A device that, by insertion in a receptacle, establishes a connection between the conductors of the attached flexible cord and the conductors connected permanently to the receptacle. [**70**:100]

3.3.10 Barrier. A physical obstruction that is intended to prevent contact with equipment or energized electrical conductors and circuit parts or to prevent unauthorized access to a work area. [**70E**:100]

3.3.11* Basic Protection. Protection against electric shock under fault-free conditions.

3.3.12 Bonding (Bonded). Connected to establish electrical continuity and conductivity. [**70**:100]

3.3.13 Branch Circuit. The circuit conductors between the final overcurrent device protecting the circuit and the outlet(s). [**70**:100]

3.3.14* Cable. A combination of conductors insulated from one another with a common covering that is not a cord.

3.3.14.1* *Cable with Flexible Properties.* A cable or special cable that is malleable but without flexing or constant flexing properties.

3.3.14.2* *Flexible Cable.* A cable or special cable manufactured with flexing or constant flexing properties.

3.3.14.3* *Special Cable.* A cable intended for specific limited purposes.

3.3.15 Cable Tray System. A unit or assembly of units or sections and associated fittings forming a structural system used to securely fasten or support cables and raceways. [**70**:392.2]

3.3.16 Cableless Control. Control devices employing wireless (e.g., radio, infrared) techniques for transmitting commands and signals between a machine control system and operator control station(s).

3.3.17* Cableless Operator Control Station. An operator control station that is capable of using wireless (e.g., radio, infrared) techniques to communicate with one or more machines and that incorporates a self-contained power source, such as a battery.

3.3.18* Circuit Breaker. A device designed to open and close a circuit by nonautomatic means and to open the circuit automatically on a predetermined overcurrent without damage to itself when properly applied within its rating. [**70**:100]

3.3.19* Color Graphic Interface Device. An interface between the operator and the machine, where a color video display and either a touch screen or touch pad or keyboard or mouse are used to initiate machine action by the selection of on-screen icons.

3.3.20 Concurrent. Acting in conjunction; used to describe a situation wherein two or more control devices exist in an actuated condition at the same time (but not necessarily simultaneously).

3.3.21 Conduit.

3.3.21.1 *Flexible Metal Conduit (FMC).* A raceway of circular cross section made of helically wound, formed, interlocked metal strip. [**70**:348.2]

3.3.21.2 *Intermediate Metal Conduit (IMC).* A steel threadable raceway of circular cross section designed for the physical protection and routing of conductors and cables when installed with its integral or associated coupling and appropriate fittings.

3.3.21.3 *Liquidtight Flexible Metal Conduit (LFMC).* A raceway of circular cross section having an outer liquidtight, nonmetallic, sunlight-resistant jacket over an inner flexible metal core with associated couplings, connectors, and fittings for the installation of electric conductors. [**70**:350.2]

3.3.21.4* *Liquidtight Flexible Nonmetallic Conduit (LFNC).* A raceway of circular cross section of various types as follows: (1) A smooth seamless inner core and cover bonded together and having one or more reinforcement layers between the core and covers, designated as Type LFNC-A; (2) A smooth inner surface with integral reinforcement within the raceway wall, designated as Type LFNC-B; (3) A corrugated internal and external surface without integral reinforcement within the raceway wall, designated as LFNC-C. [**70**:356.2]

3.3.21.5 *Rigid Metal Conduit (RMC).* A threadable raceway of circular cross section designed for the physical protection and routing of conductors and cables when installed with its integral or associated coupling and appropriate fittings. RMC is generally made of steel (ferrous) with protective coatings or aluminum (nonferrous). Special use types are silicon bronze and stainless steel.

3.3.21.6 *Rigid Nonmetallic Conduit (RNC).* A nonmetallic raceway of circular cross section, with integral or associated couplings, connectors, and fittings for the installation of electrical conductors and cables.

3.3.22 Contact.

3.3.22.1 *Direct Contact.* Contact of persons with live parts.

3.3.22.2 *Indirect Contact.* Contact of persons with exposed conductive parts that have become live under fault conditions.

3.3.23* Control Circuit (of a machine). The circuit of a control apparatus or system that carries the electric signals directing the performance of the controller but does not carry the main power current.

3.3.24 Control Circuit Transformer. A voltage transformer utilized to supply a voltage suitable for the operation of control devices.

Shaded text = Revisions. Δ = Text deletions and figure/table revisions. • = Section deletions. *N* = New material.

3.3.25 Control Circuit Voltage. The voltage utilized for the operation of control devices.

3.3.26 Control Device. A device connected into the control circuit and used for controlling the operation of the machine (e.g., position sensor, manual control switch, relay, magnetically operated valve).

3.3.27 Control Equipment. Operating elements, such as relays, contactors, circuit breakers, switches, solenoids, brakes, and similar types of components, intended to govern or perform a given function in the operation, including measuring, sensing, monitoring, protecting, and regulating of machinery.

3.3.28 Controller. A device or group of devices that serves to govern, in some predetermined manner, the electric power delivered to the apparatus to which it is connected. [**70:**100]

3.3.29 Cord. Two or more flexible insulated conductors enclosed in a flexible covering that provides mechanical protection.

3.3.30 Device. A unit of an electrical system, other than a conductor, that carries or controls electric energy as its principal function. [**70:**100]

3.3.31 Digital. Operated by the use of discrete signals to represent data in the form of numbers or other characters.

3.3.32 Direct Opening Operation. Achievement of contact separation as the direct result of a specified movement of the switch actuator through nonresilient members (e.g., not dependent upon springs).

3.3.33 Disconnecting Means. A device, or group of devices, or other means by which the conductors of a circuit can be disconnected from their source of supply. [**70:**100]

3.3.34 Dwelling Unit. A single unit, providing complete and independent living facilities for one or more persons, including permanent provisions for living, sleeping, cooking, and sanitation. [**70:**100]

3.3.35 Effective Ground-Fault Current Path. An intentionally constructed, low-impedance electrically conductive path designed and intended to carry current under ground-fault conditions from the point of a ground fault on a wiring system to the electrical supply source and that facilitates the operation of the overcurrent protective device or ground-fault detectors. [**70:**100]

3.3.36 Electromechanical. Any device in which electrical energy is used to magnetically cause mechanical movement.

3.3.37 Electronic Equipment. That part of electrical equipment containing circuitry mainly based on electronic devices and components.

3.3.38 Emergency Switching Off. An emergency operation intended to switch off the supply of the electrical energy to all or part of an installation.

3.3.39 Enabling Device. Manually operated control device used in conjunction with a start control, that when continuously actuated, will allow a machine to function.

3.3.40 Enclosure. The case or housing of apparatus, or the fence or walls surrounding an installation to prevent personnel from accidentally contacting energized parts or to protect the equipment from physical damage. [**70:**100]

3.3.41 Energized. Electrically connected to, or is, a source of voltage. [**70:**100]

3.3.42 Equipment. A general term including material, fittings, devices, appliances, luminaires, apparatus, and the like.

3.3.43 Exposed (as applied to live parts). Capable of being inadvertently touched or approached nearer than a safe distance by a person. It is applied to parts not suitably guarded, isolated, or insulated.

3.3.44* Failure (of equipment). The termination of the ability of an item to perform a required function.

3.3.45* Fault. The state of an item characterized by inability to perform a required function, excluding the inability, during preventive maintenance or other planned actions, or due to lack of external resources.

3.3.46 Fault Current. The current delivered at a point on the system during a short-circuit condition. [**70:**100]

N **3.3.47* Fault Current, Available (Available Fault Current).** The largest amount of current capable of being delivered at a point on the system during a short-circuit condition. [**70:**100]

3.3.48* Fault Protection. Protect against electric shock under single-fault conditions.

3.3.49 Feeder. All circuit conductors between the service equipment, the source of a separately derived system, or other power supply source and the final branch-circuit overcurrent device. [**70:**100]

3.3.50 Flame Retardant. So constructed or treated that it will not support flame.

3.3.51 Ground. The earth. [**70:**100]

N **3.3.52 Ground Fault.** An unintentional, electrically conductive connection between an ungrounded conductor of an electrical circuit and the normally non-current-carrying conductors, metallic enclosures, metallic raceways, metallic equipment, or earth. [**70:**100]

3.3.53 Grounded (Grounding). Connected (connecting) to ground or to a conductive body that extends the ground connection. [**70:**100]

3.3.54 Grounded Conductor. A system or circuit conductor that is intentionally grounded. [**70:**100]

3.3.55 Grounding Conductor, Equipment (EGC). The conductive path(s) that provides a ground-fault current path and connects normally non–current-carrying metal parts of equipment together and to the system grounded conductor or to the grounding electrode conductor, or both. [**70:**100]

3.3.56* Guard. Part of a machine specifically used to provide protection by means of a physical barrier.

3.3.57 Hazard. A source of possible injury or damage to health.

3.3.58 Hazardous Condition. A circumstance in which a person is exposed to a hazard(s) that has the potential to result in harm immediately or over a long period of time.

3.3.59* Identified (as applied to equipment). Recognizable as suitable for the specific purpose, function, use, environment, application, and so forth, where described in a particular code or standard requirement. [**70:**100]

3.3.60 Industrial Control Panel. An assembly of two or more components consisting of one of the following: (1) power circuit components only, such as motor controllers, overload relays, fused disconnect switches, and circuit breakers; (2) control circuit components only, such as pushbuttons, pilot lights, selector switches, timers, switches, and control relays; (3) a combination of power and control circuit components. These components, with associated wiring and terminals, are mounted on, or contained within, an enclosure or mounted on a subpanel. The industrial control panel does not include the controlled equipment. [**70**:100]

3.3.61 Industrial Machinery (Machine). A power-driven machine (or a group of machines working together in a coordinated manner), not portable by hand while working, that is used to process material by cutting; forming; pressure; electrical, thermal, or optical techniques; lamination; or a combination of these processes. It can include associated equipment used to transfer material or tooling, including fixtures, to assemble/disassemble, to inspect or test, or to package. [The associated electrical equipment, including the logic controller(s) and associated software or logic together with the machine actuators and sensors, are considered as part of the industrial machine.] [**70**:670.2]

3.3.62 Industrial Manufacturing System. A systematic array of one or more industrial machines that is not portable by hand and includes any associated material handling, manipulating, gauging, measuring, or inspection equipment.

3.3.63 Input. The terminals where current, voltage, power, or driving force may be applied to a circuit or device; the state or sequence of states occurring on a specific input channel; or the device or collective set of devices used for bringing data into another device.

3.3.64 Inrush Current (Solenoid). The inrush current of a solenoid is the steady-state current taken from the line at rated voltage and frequency with the plunger blocked in the rated maximum open position.

3.3.65 Inrush Locked Rotor Current (Motor). See 3.3.72, Locked Rotor Current.

3.3.66 In Sight From (Within Sight From, Within Sight). Where this standard specifies that one equipment shall be "in sight from," "within sight from," or "within sight of," and so forth, of another equipment, the specified equipment is to be visible and not more than 15 m (50 ft) distant from the other. [**70**:100]

3.3.67 Interlock (for safeguarding). An arrangement that interconnects guard(s) or device(s) with the control system or all or part of the electrical energy distributed to the machine.

3.3.68* Interrupting Rating. The highest current at rated voltage that a device is identified to interrupt under standard test conditions. [**70**:100]

3.3.69 Jogging (Inching). The quickly repeated closure of the circuit to start a motor from rest for the purpose of accomplishing small movements of the driven machine.

3.3.70 Live Parts. Energized conductive components. [**70**:100]

3.3.71 Location.

3.3.71.1 *Dry Location.* A location not normally subject to dampness or wetness. A location classified as dry may be temporarily subject to dampness or wetness, as in the case of a building under construction. [**70**:100]

3.3.71.2 *Wet Location.* Installations underground or in concrete slabs or masonry in direct contact with the earth; in locations subject to saturation with water or other liquids, such as vehicle washing areas; and in unprotected locations exposed to weather. [**70**:100]

3.3.72 Locked Rotor Current. The steady-state current taken from the line with the rotor locked and with rated voltage (and rated frequency in the case of alternating-current motors) applied to the motor.

3.3.73 Machine Supply Circuit. The conductors between the premises wiring and the machine supply circuit disconnecting means or terminals.

3.3.74 Marking. Signs or inscriptions attached by the manufacturer, for the identification of the type of a component or device.

3.3.75 Obstacle. A part preventing unintentional direct contact, but not preventing direct contact by deliberate action.

3.3.76 Output. The terminals where current, voltage, power, or driving force may be delivered by a circuit or device; the state or sequence of states occurring on a specific output channel; or the device or collective set of devices used for taking data out of another device.

3.3.77* Overcurrent. Any current in excess of the rated current of equipment or the ampacity of a conductor. It may result from overload, short circuit, or ground fault. [**70**:100]

3.3.78 Overcurrent Protective Device, Branch-Circuit. A device capable of providing protection for service, feeder, and branch circuits and equipment over the full range of overcurrents between its rated current and its interrupting rating. Such devices are provided with interrupting ratings appropriate for the intended use but no less than 5000 amperes. [**70**:100]

3.3.79* Overcurrent Protective Device, Supplementary. A device intended to provide limited overcurrent protection for specific applications and utilization equipment such as found within industrial machines. This limited protection is in addition to the protection provided in the required branch circuit by the branch circuit overcurrent protective device.

3.3.80* Overload. Operation of equipment in excess of normal, full-load rating, or of a conductor in excess of rated ampacity that, when it persists for a sufficient length of time, would cause damage or dangerous overheating. A fault, such as a short circuit or a ground fault, is not an overload. [**70**:100]

3.3.81 Point of Operation. The location in the (machine) where the material or workpiece is positioned and work is performed.

3.3.82 Power Circuit. A circuit used for supplying power from the supply network to units of equipment used for productive operation and to transformers supplying control circuits.

3.3.83* Programmable Electronic System (PES). A system based on one or more central processing units (CPUs), connected to sensors or actuators, or both, for the purpose of control or monitoring.

3.3.84* Qualified Person. One who has skills and knowledge related to the construction and operation of the electrical equipment and installations and has received safety training to recognize and avoid the hazards involved. [**70**:100]

3.3.85 Raceway. An enclosed channel of metal or nonmetallic materials designed expressly for holding wires, cables, or busbars, with additional functions as permitted in this standard. Raceways include, but are not limited to, rigid metal conduit, rigid nonmetallic conduit, intermediate metal conduit, liquidtight flexible conduit, flexible metallic tubing, flexible metal conduit, electrical nonmetallic tubing, electrical metallic tubing, underfloor raceways, cellular concrete floor raceways, cellular metal floor raceways, surface raceways, wireways, and busways.

_N_ **3.3.86 Receptacle.** A contact device installed at the outlet for the connection of an attachment plug, or for the direct connection of electrical utilization equipment designed to mate with the corresponding contact device. A single receptacle is a single contact device with no other contact device on the same yoke. A multiple receptacle is two or more contact devices on the same yoke or strap. [**70**:100]

3.3.87 Redundancy. The application of more than one device or system, or part of a device or system, with the objective of ensuring that in the event of one failing to perform its function another is available to perform that function.

3.3.88 Reference Designation. A distinctive code that serves to identify an item in a diagram, list, or chart, and on the equipment.

3.3.89 Relative Humidity. The ratio between the amount of water vapor in the gas at the time of measurement and the amount of water vapor that could be in the gas when condensation begins, at a given temperature.

3.3.90* Risk. A combination of the probability and the degree of possible injury or damage to health in a hazardous situation.

3.3.91 Risk Assessment. The process by which the intended use of the machine, the tasks and hazards, and the level of risk are determined.

3.3.92 Safe Working Procedure. A method of working that reduces risk.

3.3.93 Safeguard. A guard or protective device used as a safety measure to protect persons from a present or impending hazard.

3.3.94 Safeguarding. Those safety measures consisting of the use of specific means called safeguards to protect persons from hazards that cannot reasonably be removed or are not sufficiently limited by design.

_N_ **3.3.95* Safety Circuit.** The part of a control system containing one or more devices that perform a safety-related function.

3.3.96 Safety-Related Function. A function which is intended to maintain the safe condition of the machine, or prevent or reduce hazardous situations.

3.3.97 Servicing Level. Location on which persons normally stand when operating or maintaining the electrical equipment.

3.3.98* Servo Drive System. A system consisting of a controller, servo amplifier, motor, and feedback device(s) providing for the positioning control of a motion axis through the use of velocity, acceleration, and deceleration.

3.3.99* Short-Circuit Current Rating. The prospective symmetrical fault current at a nominal voltage to which an apparatus or system is able to be connected without sustaining damage exceeding defined acceptance criteria. [**70**:100]

3.3.100 Special Permission. The written consent of the authority having jurisdiction. [**70**:100]

3.3.101 Stop.

    3.3.101.1 _Controlled Stop._ The stopping of machine motion, while retaining power to the machine actuators during the stopping process.

    3.3.101.2 _Uncontrolled Stop._ The stopping of machine motion by removing power to the machine actuators, all brakes and/or other mechanical stopping devices being activated.

3.3.102 Subplate (Subpanel). An internal metal surface separate from the walls of an enclosure or controller on which various component parts of the controller are mounted and wired.

3.3.103* Supplier. An entity (e.g., manufacturer, contractor, installer, integrator) that provides equipment or services associated with the machine.

3.3.104 Surge-Protective Device (SPD). A protective device for limiting transient voltages by diverting or limiting surge current; it also prevents continued flow of follow current while remaining capable of repeating these functions and is designated as follows: Type 1: Permanently connected SPDs intended for installation between the secondary of the service transformer and the line side of the service disconnect overcurrent device. Type 2: Permanently connected SPDs intended for installation on the load side of the service disconnect overcurrent device, including SPDs located at the branch panel. Type 3: Point of utilization SPDs. Type 4: Component SPDs, including discrete components, as well as assemblies. [**70**:100]

3.3.105 Switching Device. A device designed to make or break the current in one or more electric circuits.

3.3.106 System Isolation Equipment. A redundantly monitored, remotely operated contactor-isolating system, packaged to provide the disconnecting/isolation function, capable of verifiable operation from multiple remote locations by means of lockout switches, each having the capability of being padlocked in the "off" (open) position. [**70**:430.2]

3.3.107 Tap Conductors. As used in this standard, a tap conductor is defined as a conductor, other than a service conductor, that has overcurrent protection ahead of its point of supply that exceeds the value permitted for similar conductors that are protected as described elsewhere in this standard. [**70**:240.2]

3.3.108 Terminal. A conductive part of a device provided for electrical connection to circuits external to the device.

3.3.109 Tight (suffix). So constructed that the specified material is excluded under specified conditions.

3.3.110* Undervoltage Protection. The effect of a device that operates on the reduction or failure of voltage to cause and maintain the interruption of power.

3.3.111 User. An entity that utilizes the machine and its associated electrical equipment.

3.3.112 Ventilated. Provided with a means to permit circulation of air sufficient to remove excess heat, fumes, or vapors. [**70:**100]

3.3.113 Voltage, Nominal. A nominal value assigned to a circuit or system for the purpose of conveniently designating its voltage class (e.g., 120/240 volts, 480Y/277 volts, 600 volts). The actual voltage at which a circuit operates can vary from the nominal within a range that permits satisfactory operation of equipment.

3.3.114 Wireway. A sheet-metal or flame-retardant nonmetallic trough with hinged or removable covers for housing and protecting electric wires and cable and in which conductors are laid in place after the wireway has been installed as a complete system.

Chapter 4   General Requirements and Operating Conditions

4.1* General Considerations. This chapter describes the general requirements and conditions for the operation of the electrical equipment of the machine. The risks associated with the hazards relevant to the electrical equipment shall be assessed as part of the overall requirements for risk assessment of the machine. The risks associated with the hazards identified by the risk assessment shall be reduced such that the safety performance determined by the risk assessment is met.

4.2* Electrical Components and Devices. Electrical components and devices shall be installed and used assuming the operating conditions of ambient temperature, altitude, humidity, and supply voltage outlined in this chapter, and within their design ratings, taking into account any derating stipulated by the component or device manufacturer. Listed or labeled equipment shall be permitted to be used without modifications, on or with industrial machines, where approved for the location and use.

4.3 Installation and Use of Listed or Labeled Equipment. Listed or labeled equipment shall be installed and used in accordance with any instructions included in the listing or labeling.

4.4 Electrical Supply.

4.4.1* General. The electrical equipment shall be designed to operate correctly with the conditions of the supply as specified according to one of the following:

(1)   The requirements in 4.4.2, 4.4.3, and 4.4.4
(2)   The requirements specified by the user
(3)   The requirements specified by the supplier

4.4.2* Alternating Current (ac) Supplies.

4.4.2.1 Voltage. The electrical equipment shall be designed to operate correctly where the steady-state supply voltage is from 90 percent to 110 percent of the nominal voltage.

4.4.2.2 Frequency. The electrical equipment shall be designed to operate correctly where the supply frequency is from 99 percent to 101 percent of the nominal frequency

continuously. For short periods of time, the supply frequency shall be permitted to be from 98 percent to 102 percent of the nominal frequency.

4.4.2.3 Harmonics. The electrical equipment shall be designed to operate correctly where the harmonic distortion from the electric supply does not exceed 10 percent of the total voltage (rms value) between ungrounded conductors for the sum of the second through fifth harmonic. An additional 2 percent of the total voltage (rms value) between ungrounded conductors for the sum of the sixth through thirtieth harmonic shall be permitted.

4.4.2.4 Voltage Unbalance (in 3-Phase Supplies). The electrical equipment shall be designed to operate correctly where neither the voltage of the negative sequence component nor the voltage of the zero sequence component in 3-phase supplies exceeds 2 percent of the voltage of the positive sequence component.

4.4.2.5 Voltage Impulses. The electrical equipment shall be designed to operate correctly where the supply voltage impulses do not exceed 1.5 milliseconds in duration with a rise/fall time between 500 nanoseconds and 500 microseconds. A peak supply voltage impulse shall not exceed more than 200 percent of the rated supply voltage (rms value).

4.4.2.6 Voltage Interruption. The electrical equipment shall be designed to operate correctly where the supply voltage is interrupted at zero voltage for not more than 3 milliseconds at any random time in the supply cycle. The time interval between successive voltage interruptions shall be more than 1 second.

4.4.2.7 Voltage Dips. The electrical equipment shall be designed to operate correctly where the supply voltage dips do not exceed 20 percent of the peak voltage of the supply for more than one cycle. The time interval between successive dips shall be more than 1 second.

4.4.2.8* Circuits Supplied from Power Conversion Equipment. Electrical conductors and equipment supplied by power conversion equipment as part of adjustable speed drive systems and servo drive systems shall be identified as suitable for the electrical power characteristics and in accordance with any instructions provided by the manufacturer(s).

4.4.3 Direct Current (dc) Supplies from Batteries.

4.4.3.1 Voltage. The electrical equipment shall be designed to operate correctly where the dc supply voltage of batteries is from 85 percent to 115 percent of the nominal voltage. A supply voltage from 70 percent to 120 percent of the nominal voltage shall be permitted for dc supplies to battery-operated vehicles.

4.4.3.2 Voltage Interruption. The electrical equipment shall be designed to operate correctly where the dc supply voltage of batteries is interrupted for a time interval not exceeding 5 milliseconds.

4.4.4 Direct Current (dc) Supplies from Converting Equipment.

4.4.4.1 Voltage. The electrical equipment shall be designed to operate correctly where the dc supply voltage of converting equipment is from 90 percent to 110 percent of the nominal voltage.

4.4.4.2 Voltage Interruption. The electrical equipment shall be designed to operate correctly where the dc supply voltage of converting equipment is interrupted for a time interval not exceeding 20 milliseconds. The time interval between successive voltage interruptions shall be more than 1 second.

4.4.4.3 Ripple (Peak-to-Peak). The electrical equipment shall be designed to operate correctly where the dc supply voltage ripple (peak-to-peak value) of converting equipment does not exceed 0.05 of the nominal voltage.

4.5 Physical Environment and Operating Conditions.

4.5.1* General. The electrical equipment shall be suitable for use in the physical environment and operating conditions specified in 4.5.3 through 4.5.6 and 4.5.8. When the physical environment or the operating conditions are outside those specified, an agreement between the supplier and the user shall be considered.

4.5.2* Electromagnetic Compatibility (EMC). Transient suppression, isolation, or other appropriate means shall be provided where necessary to ensure that the expected level of electromagnetic interference or electrical transients in the machine supply circuit(s) or generated by the electrical equipment of the machine does not lead to the loss of the safety-related control function(s) of the industrial machine.

4.5.3* Ambient Operating Temperature. Electrical equipment shall be capable of operating correctly in the intended ambient air temperature. The ambient operating temperatures for correct operation of the electrical equipment shall be between air temperatures of 5°C and 40°C (41°F and 104°F).

4.5.4* Relative Humidity. The electrical equipment shall be capable of operating correctly within a relative humidity range of 20 to 95 percent (noncondensing). Harmful effects of relative humidity outside the permitted range shall be avoided by design of the equipment or, where necessary, by additional measures (e.g., built-in heaters, air conditioners, humidifiers).

4.5.5* Altitude. Electrical equipment shall be capable of correct operation at altitudes up to 1000 m (3300 ft) above mean sea level.

4.5.6* Contaminants. Electrical equipment shall be adequately protected against the ingress of solid bodies and liquids *(see Section 11.3)*. Equipment shall be suitable for the environment where contaminants (e.g., dust, acids, corrosive gases, salt) are present.

4.5.7* Nonionizing Radiation.

4.5.8 Vibration, Shock, and Bump. Undesirable effects of vibration, shock, and bump, including those generated by the machine and its associated equipment and those created by the physical environment, shall be avoided by the selection of suitable equipment, by mounting it away from the machine, or by the use of antivibration mountings.

4.6 Transportation and Storage. The electrical equipment shall be designed to withstand storage and transportation temperatures within the range of −25°C to 55°C (−13°F to 131°F) and up to 70°C (158°F) for short periods not exceeding 24 hours. Suitable means shall be provided to prevent damage from excessive moisture, vibration, stress, and mechanical shock during shipment.

4.7 Provisions for Handling. Heavy and bulky electrical equipment that has to be removed from the machine for transport or that is independent of the machine shall be provided with suitable means for handling by cranes or similar equipment.

4.8 Installation and Operating Conditions. The electrical equipment shall be installed and operated in accordance with the conditions outlined in the manufacturer's instructions. Any conditions that are outside the operating conditions specified in Chapter 4 shall be permitted where acceptable to both the manufacturer and the user.

4.9 Available Fault Current. The available fault current at each machine supply circuit disconnecting means shall not be greater than the corresponding short-circuit current rating marked on the machine industrial control panel nameplate.

Chapter 5 Disconnecting Means

5.1 Machine Supply Circuit and Disconnecting Means.

5.1.1* Machine Supply Circuit. Where practicable, the electrical equipment of a machine shall be connected to a single power supply circuit. Where it is necessary to use another supply circuit for certain parts of the equipment (e.g., electronic circuits, electromagnetic clutches), that supply circuit shall, as far as is practicable, be derived from devices (e.g., transformers, converters) forming part of the electrical equipment of the machine.

5.1.2 Machine Supply Circuit Conductor Separation. Each set of machine supply circuit conductors on the line side of the machine supply circuit disconnecting means shall be separated from all other internal conductors, including conductors of other circuits, by either of the following:

(1) Mounting the machine supply circuit disconnect as near as practicable to the top of the enclosure with dedicated wire bending space as required in 5.1.5
(2) Mounting the machine supply circuit disconnect other than at the top of the enclosure and by separating the machine supply circuit conductors from other internal conductors with a barrier

Δ **5.1.3 Machine Supply Circuit Conductor Terminations.** The machine supply circuit conductors shall be terminated at the machine supply circuit disconnecting means, where practicable. Connections to terminal blocks ahead of the machine supply circuit disconnecting means shall be permitted for excepted circuits according to 5.1.13 or where the machine supply circuit conductors are other than those identified for the disconnecting means. Terminals for more than one conductor shall be so identified.

5.1.3.1 Marking. All terminals for each machine supply circuit shall be legibly marked (e.g., L1, L2, L3) and shall correspond with markings on the technical documentation.

N **5.1.4 Back-Fed Terminations.**

N **5.1.4.1** The connections to the machine supply circuit disconnecting means shall not be back-fed or reversed with the load side if it is marked line and load.

N **5.1.4.2** A machine supply circuit disconnecting means that is not marked line and load shall be permitted to be back-fed provided there is a marking on or adjacent to the disconnecting means identifying the line and load terminations.

Δ **5.1.5 Wire-Bending Space.** The wire-bending space provided between the terminals of a supply circuit disconnecting means or terminals described in 5.1.3 and the wall of the enclosure shall not be less than what is required by 430.10(B) of *NFPA 70.* The wire-bending space shall either be determined by the maximum wire size of the supply circuit conductors or be equal to or larger than the conductors required by 670.4(A) of *NFPA 70.* When the wire-bending space is based on more than one conductor per phase, the intended conductor size and number shall be so identified on interconnection diagrams as required in 17.5.7.

5.1.6 Protection of Line Side Live Parts. All live parts on the line side of the machine supply circuit disconnecting means shall be protected from unintentional direct contact by use of insulation or obstacle(s) when the machine supply circuit disconnecting means is in the open (off) position and the enclosure door is open.

Δ **5.1.7* Grounded Conductor.** Where a grounded conductor is used, it shall be indicated in the technical documentation of the machine, such as in the installation diagram and in the circuit diagram. A separate insulated terminal shall be provided for the grounded conductor.

5.1.8* Equipment Grounding Conductor Terminal. A grounding terminal shall be provided for each machine supply circuit equipment grounding conductor.

Δ **5.1.9 Machine Supply Circuit Disconnecting Means.** The requirements in 5.1.9.1 through 5.1.9.8 apply to 5.1.10 through 5.1.13.

Δ **5.1.9.1** A machine supply circuit disconnecting means shall be provided for the following:

(1) Each machine supply circuit
(2) Each machine supply circuit to a machine or a number of machines connecting to a feeder system using collector wires, collector bars, slip-ring assemblies, or flexible cable systems (reeled, festooned)
(3) Each on-board power source (e.g., generators, uninterruptible power supplies)

Exception: Communication, remote control, and signaling circuits of less than 50 volts rms ac or 60 volts dc shall not be required to be provided with a machine supply circuit disconnecting means.

Δ **5.1.9.2*** Each machine supply circuit disconnecting means shall be legibly marked to indicate the equipment it disconnects.

5.1.9.3 A machine supply circuit disconnecting means shall be marked as "Machine Supply Circuit Disconnect" if additional disconnecting means are supplied from the supply circuit disconnecting means.

5.1.9.4 Where a machine is supplied by more than one supply circuit, a marking shall be installed at each machine supply circuit disconnect location denoting the location of all other machine supply circuit disconnects.

Δ **5.1.9.5** The machine supply circuit disconnecting means shall disconnect the electrical equipment of the machine, including all control circuits, from the machine supply circuit when required (e.g., for work on the machine, including the electrical equipment). Circuits that are not required to be disconnec-

ted by the machine supply circuit disconnecting means shall comply with 5.1.13.

Δ **5.1.9.6** Each machine supply circuit disconnecting means other than attachment plugs and receptacles shall be mounted within the control enclosure it supplies or immediately adjacent thereto.

Exception: Externally mounted machine supply circuit disconnecting means shall be permitted to be mounted up to 6 m (20 ft) away from the control enclosure, provided the control enclosure is marked to indicate the location of the machine supply circuit disconnecting means and the machine supply circuit disconnecting means complies with all the following:

(1) Is in sight of the control enclosure it supplies
(2) Is readily accessible
(3) Is marked in accordance with 5.1.9.2

Δ **5.1.9.7** Access to enclosures containing the machine supply circuit disconnecting means shall be in accordance with 6.2.3.1.

5.1.9.8 Where two or more machine supply circuit disconnecting means are provided within the same control enclosure for multiple machine supply circuits, they shall be grouped in one location where practicable. Protective interlocks for their correct operation shall be provided where a hazardous condition or damage to the machine or to the work in progress can occur.

5.1.10 Type. The machine supply circuit disconnecting means shall be one of the following types:

(1) A listed motor circuit switch rated in horsepower
(2) A listed molded case circuit breaker
(3) A listed molded case switch
(4) An instantaneous trip circuit breaker that is part of a listed combination motor controller limited to single motor applications
(5) A listed self-protected combination controller limited to single motor applications
(6) An attachment plug and receptacle for cord connection

5.1.11 Requirements.

Δ **5.1.11.1*** Where the machine supply circuit disconnecting means is one of the types in 5.1.10(1) through 5.1.10(5), it shall fulfill all of the following requirements:

(1) Disconnect the electrical equipment from the machine supply circuit and have one off (open) and one on (closed) position only. Circuit breakers, instantaneous trip circuit breakers, molded-case switches, and self-protected combination motor controllers are permitted to have a reset (tripped) position between off (open) and on (closed).
(2) Have an external operating means (e.g., handle) that complies with 5.1.12.

    Exception: Power-operated switchgear need not be operable from outside the enclosure where there are other means to open it.
(3) Be provided with a permanent means permitting it to be locked in the off (open) position only (e.g., by padlocks), independent of the enclosure door or enclosure cover position. When so locked, remote as well as local closing into the on position shall be prevented.
(4) Simultaneously disconnect all ungrounded conductors of the supply circuit.

(5) Be operable by qualified persons independent of the enclosure door or enclosure cover position without the use of accessory tools or devices.

(6) Be rated for the application as follows:

   (a) With an ampere rating at least 115 percent of the sum of the full-load currents required for all equipment that is in operation at the same time under normal conditions of use

   (b) Where rated in horsepower, with a horsepower rating at least equal to that which is defined by Table 430.251(B) of *NFPA 70* for a locked rotor current equal to the largest sum resulting from the locked rotor currents of any combination of motors that can be started simultaneously and the full-load currents of the remaining motor and non-motor loads that can be operated at that time

   (c) With a voltage rating at least equal to the nominal supply circuit voltage

(7) Be of a type that indicates whether it is in the off (open) or on (closed) position.

Δ **5.1.11.2*** When the machine supply circuit disconnecting means is an attachment plug and receptacle, it shall fulfill all of the following requirements:

(1) Have a load-break rating or be interlocked with a switching device that is load-break rated and complies with 5.1.11.1(6)

(2) Be listed as a switch-rated plug and receptacle rated greater than 20 amperes or 2 hp

(3) Be of such a type and be so installed to prevent unintended contact with live parts at any time, even during insertion or removal of the connectors

(4) Have a first-make, last-break electrical grounding contact

(5) Have a retaining means to prevent unintended or accidental disconnection where rated at more than 20 amperes

(6) Be located within sight from the operator station and be readily accessible

5.1.11.3 In addition to the requirements in 5.1.11.2, an additional switching device on the machine shall be provided for routine power switching operations of the machine on and off.

5.1.12 Operating Handle.

Δ **5.1.12.1** The center of the grip of the operating handle of a supply circuit disconnecting means, when in its highest position, shall be not more than 2.0 m (6 ft 7 in.) above the servicing level. A permanent operating platform, readily accessible by means of a permanent stair(s) or ladder, shall be considered the servicing level.

Δ **5.1.12.2** An operating handle of a machine supply circuit disconnecting means shall meet the following criteria:

(1) Be readily accessible with the enclosure door(s) in the open or closed position

(2) Maintain the environmental rating of the enclosure to the degree necessary for the application when installed through the control enclosure

(3) Not be restricted by the enclosure door(s) when the door is in the open or closed position

5.1.13 Excepted Circuits.

5.1.13.1 The following circuits shall not be required to be disconnected by the machine supply circuit disconnecting means:

(1) Lighting circuits for lighting needed during maintenance or repair

(2) Attachment plugs and receptacles for the exclusive connection of repair or maintenance tools and equipment (e.g., hand drills, test equipment)

(3) Undervoltage protection circuits that are only used for automatic tripping in the event of supply circuit failure

(4) Circuits supplying equipment that need to remain energized for satisfactory operation [e.g., temperature-controlled measuring devices, product (work in progress) heaters, program storage devices, inputs, non-motion outputs, displays, and safety interlocks]

Δ **5.1.13.2** Excepted circuits shall be provided with all of the following:

(1) A disconnecting means, isolating transformer, and over-current protection mounted in an enclosure adjacent to or within the control enclosure containing the machine supply circuit disconnecting means

(2) Line side (of the machine supply circuit disconnecting means) supply circuit conductors, when internal to the control enclosure, that are separate from and do not share a raceway with other conductors and that are encased in rigid or flexible conduit if longer than 460 mm (18 in.)

5.1.13.3 The control interlocking circuits shall be capable of being disconnected at the control panel from which they are sourced.

Δ **5.1.13.4** Where the excepted circuits are not disconnected by the machine supply circuit disconnecting means, all of the following requirements shall be met:

(1) A permanent safety sign(s) shall be placed adjacent to the machine supply circuit disconnecting operating handle(s), indicating that it does not de-energize all exposed live parts when it is in the open (off) position as in 16.2.4.

(2) A statement containing the information from 16.2.4 shall be included in the machine documentation.

(3) A permanent safety sign shall be placed on a nonremovable part inside the control enclosure in proximity to each excepted circuit, or shall be identified by color as defined in 13.2.4.

5.2 Additional Disconnecting Means.

Δ **5.2.1** In addition to the machine supply circuit disconnecting means, devices shall be permitted to be provided for disconnecting electrical equipment to enable work to be performed on individual portions of the machine.

Δ **5.2.2** The following devices shall be permitted to fulfill the function of 5.2.1:

(1) Devices described in 5.1.10

(2) A manual motor controller marked "suitable as motor disconnect" and in compliance with UL 508 where located on the load side of the last short-circuit protective device in the branch

---

(3) System isolation equipment that incorporates control lockout stations and is listed for disconnection purposes where located on the load side of the machine supply circuit disconnecting means and overcurrent protection

5.2.3 An operating means of the additional disconnecting means in 5.2.2 shall be as follows:

(1) Readily accessible and complies with 5.1.12

Exception: Switches and circuit breakers installed adjacent to motors, appliances, or other equipment that they supply shall be permitted to be accessible by portable means.

(2) Within sight of the part of the machine requiring disconnection
(3) Readily identifiable as a disconnecting means and marked to identify the equipment that is disconnected
(4) For other than attachment plugs, provided with permanent means for locking in the off position only

N **5.2.4 Enclosure Access.** Access to enclosures containing disconnecting means shall be in accordance with 6.2.3.1.

5.3 Means for Removal of Power for Prevention of Unexpected Start-Up.

5.3.1 Means for removal of power shall be provided when prevention of unexpected start-up is required (e.g., during maintenance where the unexpected start-up of a machine or part of the machine results in a hazardous situation) and shall be as follows:

(1) Appropriate for the intended use
(2) Conveniently located
(3) Readily identifiable as to their function and purpose
(4) Provided with permanent means for locking in the off position only

△ **5.3.2** Removal of power shall be accomplished by one of the following:

(1) The machine supply circuit disconnecting means
(2) Additional devices conforming to 5.1.10 or 5.2.2
(3) Other means (e.g., a contactor switched off by a control circuit) that meet the requirements of 5.3.3 and 5.3.4

5.3.3* Where other means of removal of power are used, a single failure of any of its components shall not result in an inadvertent or unexpected start-up.

5.3.4 Other means of removal of power shall be employed only for situations that include the following:

(1) Routine exchange of work pieces, fixtures, and tools requiring no significant dismantling of the machine
(2) Work on the electrical equipment where all of the following conditions exist:

(a) There is no hazard arising from electric shock and burn.
(b) The switching off means cannot be negated by the work.
(c) The work is of a minor nature (e.g., replacement of plug-in devices without disturbing existing wiring).
(d) There is no hazard arising from the unexpected energizing or de-energizing of circuits.

Chapter 6 Protection from Electrical Hazards

6.1* General. Electrical equipment shall provide basic protection *(see Sections 6.2 and 6.4)* and fault protection *(see Sections 6.3 and 6.4)* to persons from electric shock.

△ **6.2 Basic Protection.** Live parts operating at or above 50 volts rms ac or 60 volts dc shall be guarded against contact.

△ **6.2.1 General.** The basic protection *(see 3.3.11)* requirements of 6.2.2 or 6.2.3 shall be applied to live parts operating at or above 50 volts rms ac or 60 volts dc.

6.2.2 Protection by Insulation of Live Parts.

6.2.2.1 Live parts protected by insulation shall be completely covered with insulation that is removable only by destruction.

6.2.2.2 Such insulation as described in 6.2.2.1 shall be capable of withstanding the mechanical, chemical, electrical, and thermal stresses to which the insulation is subjected under normal operating conditions.

6.2.2.3 Paints, varnishes, lacquers, and similar products shall not be considered protection against electric shock under normal operating conditions.

△ **6.2.3 Protection by Enclosures.** Equipment enclosures, enclosure openings, and observation windows shall meet the requirements of UL 508, UL 508A, UL 50, or NEMA 250.

Exception: If an enclosure is not rated, its suitability shall be permitted to be determined by using a test finger as described in Figure 6.2.3. The test finger shall not be able to contact live parts in any direction by applying minimal force in every opening in the enclosure, including openings created by removal of parts mounted through the enclosure walls, doors, or covers.

△ **6.2.3.1* Enclosure Access.** Opening an enclosure (e.g., door, lid, cover) that contains live parts operating at or above 50 volts rms ac or 60 volts dc shall be permitted only under one or more of the following conditions:

(1) The use of a key or tool is necessary for access to live parts operating at or above 50 volts rms ac or 60 volts dc. All live parts mounted on the inside of doors or covers that are operating at or above 50 volts rms ac or 60 volts dc shall be protected from unintentional direct contact by the inherent design of components or the application of barriers or obstacles such that a 50 mm (2 in.) sphere cannot contact any live parts. A safety sign shall be provided in accordance with 16.2.4.
(2) The disconnecting means supplying the enclosure is interlocked with the enclosure door(s) in accordance with 6.2.3.2.
(3) Opening without the use of a key or a tool and without disconnection of live parts shall be permitted only when all live parts inside that are operating at or above 50 volts rms ac or 60 volts dc are separately enclosed or guarded such that there cannot be any contact with live parts. A safety sign shall be provided in accordance with 16.2.4.

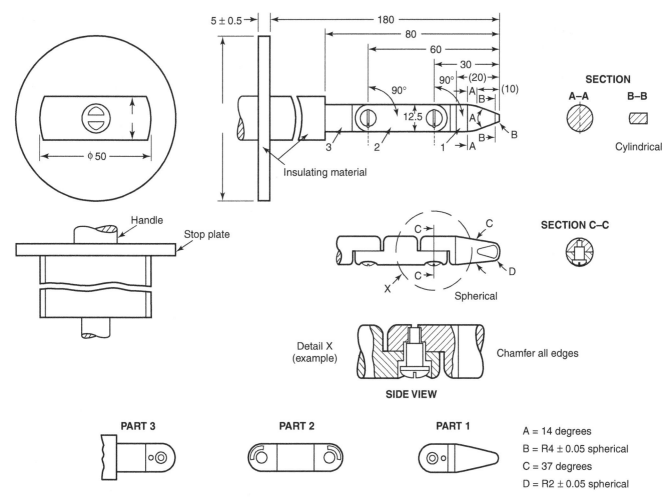

PART 3   **PART 2**   **PART 1**

A = 14 degrees
B = R4 ± 0.05 spherical
C = 37 degrees
D = R2 ± 0.05 spherical

Dimensions in millimeters

Tolerances on dimensions without specific tolerance:

On angles: $^{0}_{-10'}$

On linear dimensions:

up to 25 mm: $^{0}_{-0.05}$ mm

over 25 mm: ± 0.2 mm

Material of finger: heat-treated steel, etc.

Both joints of this finger may be bent through an angle of $(90\,^{+10}_{0})°$ but in one and the same direction only.

Using the pin and groove solution is only one of the possible approaches in order to limit the bending angle to 90°. For this reason, dimensions and tolerances of these details are not given in the drawing. The actual design must ensure a $(90\,^{+10}_{0})°$ bending angle.

△ **FIGURE 6.2.3 Jointed Test Finger.**

△ **6.2.3.2 Enclosure Interlocking.** If 6.2.3.1(2) is used to limit enclosure access, none of the interlocked enclosure door(s) shall open unless the power is disconnected and, upon closing the door(s), the interlock is automatically restored. Access shall be permitted without removing power if all of the following conditions are met:

(1) It is possible at all times while the interlock is defeated to open the disconnecting means without the use of tools and lock the disconnecting means in the OFF (open) position.

(2) Closing of the disconnecting means while the door of the enclosure containing the disconnecting means is open shall be prevented unless an interlock is operated by deliberate action.

(3) All live parts mounted on the inside of the doors that are operating at or above 50 volts rms ac or 60 volts dc shall be protected from unintentional direct contact by the inherent design of components or the application of barriers of obstacles such that a 50 mm (2 in.) sphere cannot contact any live parts.

(4) Relevant information about the procedures for the defeat of the interlock is provided with the instructions for use of the electrical equipment.

N **6.2.3.3 Excepted Circuits.** All parts operating at or above 50 volts rms ac or 60 volts dc that are still energized after switching off the machine supply circuit disconnecting means *(see 5.1.13)* shall be protected from unintentional contact by the inherent design of components or the application of barriers or obstacles such that a 50 mm (2 in.) sphere cannot contact any live parts.

6.3 Fault Protection.

6.3.1* General. Fault protection *(see 3.3.48)* preventing hazardous conditions to continue in the event of an insulation fault between live and exposed conductive parts shall be provided.

6.3.1.1 For each circuit part or part of the electrical equipment, at least one of the following measures shall be applied:

(1) Measures to prevent the occurrence of a hazardous touch voltage by means of double insulation *(see 6.3.2)*
(2) Automatic disconnection of the supply (interruption of one or more of the ungrounded conductors affected by the automatic operation of a protective device in case of a fault) *(see 6.3.2.3)*

△ **6.3.2 Protection by Double Insulation.**

△ **6.3.2.1** Measures to prevent the occurrence of a hazardous touch voltage shall be by use of double insulation to prevent the occurrence of hazardous touch voltages on the accessible parts through a failure in the basic insulation.

6.3.2.2 When the means described in 6.3.2.1 is used to prevent a hazardous touch voltage, the equipment shall be distinctively marked and shall be listed to be protected by a system of double insulation or its equivalent.

6.3.2.3 Protection by Automatic Disconnection of Supply. Automatic disconnection of the supply of any circuit affected by the particular circuit overcurrent protective device in the event of a fault shall prevent an exposure to a continuous hazardous touch voltage with the following protective measures:

(1) Protective bonding of exposed conductive parts *(see 8.2.3)*
(2) The use of overcurrent protection devices for the automatic disconnection of the supply in the event of a fault

6.4 Protection by the Use of Protective Extra Low Voltage (PELV) or Class 2 Circuits.

6.4.1 General Requirements.

6.4.1.1 The use of PELV, as described in Section 6.4, shall protect persons against electric shock from indirect contact and limited area direct contact.

6.4.1.2 Class 2 circuits, as covered in 13.1.1 and Article 725 of *NFPA 70* (NEC), shall be permitted to be used to provide protection from electric shock and other hazards.

6.4.2 PELV circuits shall satisfy all of the following conditions:

(1) The nominal voltage shall not exceed the following:

(a) 30 volts ac (rms value) or 60 volts dc (ripple-free) when the equipment is used in normally dry locations and when large area contact of live parts with the human body is not expected
(b) 6 volts ac (rms value) or 15 volts dc (ripple-free) in all other cases

(2) One side of the circuit or one point of the source of the supply of that circuit shall be connected to the equipment grounding circuit.
(3) Live parts of PELV circuits shall be electrically separated from other live circuits. Electrical separation shall be not less than that required between the primary and secondary circuits of a safety isolating transformer.
(4) Conductors of each PELV circuit shall be physically separated from those of any other circuit. When this requirement is impracticable, the insulation provisions of 13.1.3 shall apply.
(5) Attachment plugs and receptacles for a PELV circuit shall conform to the following:

(a) Attachment plugs shall not be able to enter receptacles of other voltage systems.
(b) Receptacles shall not admit plugs of other voltage systems.

6.4.3 Sources for PELV. The source for PELV shall be one of the following:

(1) A safety isolating transformer
(2) A source of current providing a degree of safety equivalent to that of the safety isolating transformer (e.g., a motor generator with winding providing equivalent isolation)
(3) An electrochemical source (e.g., a battery) or another source independent of a higher voltage circuit (e.g., a diesel-driven generator)
(4) An identified electronic power supply conforming to standards specifying measures to be taken to ensure that, even in the case of an internal fault, the voltage at the outgoing terminals does not exceed the values specified in 6.4.2(1)

6.5 Protection Against Residual Voltages.

6.5.1 Live parts having a residual voltage greater than 60 volts after the supply has been disconnected shall be reduced to 60 volts or less within 5 seconds of disconnecting the supply voltage.

Exception No. 1: Components having a stored charge of 60 microcoulombs or less shall be exempt from this requirement.

Exception No. 2: Where such a provision would interfere with the functioning of the equipment, a durable safety sign that draws attention to the hazard and states the delay required before entry to the enclosure is allowed shall be displayed at a visible location on or immediately adjacent to the enclosure containing the capacitance.

6.5.2 The withdrawal of plugs or similar devices, which results in the exposure of conductors (e.g., pins), shall have a discharge time that does not exceed 1 second.

Exception No. 1: Exempted from this requirement are components having a stored charge of 60 microcoulombs or less.

Exception No. 2: Exempted from this requirement are conductors that are protected against direct contact.

△ **6.5.3 Discharge of Stored Energy.** Capacitors shall be provided with a means of discharging stored energy.

Δ **6.5.3.1 Time of Discharge.** The residual voltage of a capacitor shall be reduced to 50 volts, nominal, or less, within 1 minute after the capacitor is disconnected from the source of supply.

Exception: Where the requirement would interfere with the functioning of the equipment, a safety sign that draws attention to the hazard and states the delay required before entry to the enclosure shall be permitted to be displayed at a visible location on or immediately adjacent to the enclosure containing the capacitor(s).

Δ **6.5.3.2 Means of Discharge.** The discharge circuit shall be either permanently connected to the terminals of the capacitor or capacitor bank, or provided with automatic means of connecting it to the terminals of the capacitor bank on removal of voltage from the line. Manual means of switching or connecting the discharge circuit shall not be used.

Exception: Where conductors in the main power circuit are protected against direct contact and where the capacitor is being used as an energy storage device in accordance with the manufacturer's instructions, a manual means of switching or connecting the discharge circuit shall be permitted.

6.6 Arc Flash Hazard Warning. A safety sign shall be provided in accordance with 16.2.3.

Chapter 7 Protection of Equipment

7.1 General. Chapter 7 shall detail the measures to be taken to protect equipment against the effects of the following:

(1) Overcurrent arising from a short circuit
(2) Overload or loss of cooling of motors
(3) Ground faults
(4) Overvoltages due to lightning and switching surges
(5) Abnormal temperatures
(6) Loss of or reduction in the supply voltage
(7) Overspeed of machines/machine elements
(8) Incorrect phase sequence

7.2 Overcurrent Protection.

7.2.1* General.

7.2.1.1 Overcurrent protection shall be provided where the current in a machine circuit can exceed either the rating of any component in the circuit or the current-carrying capacity of the conductors in the circuit, whichever is the lesser value.

7.2.1.2 All overcurrent protective devices shall be selected and applied with proper consideration being given to, but not limited to, the following:

(1) System maximum available fault current at the point of application
(2) Interrupting rating of the overcurrent protective device
(3) Voltage rating of the system
(4) Load and circuit characteristics

    (a) Normal operating current
    (b) Inrush characteristics
    (c) Thermal withstand capability (I^2t)
    (d) Magnetic withstand capability (I_p)

(5) Current-limiting ability of the overcurrent protective device
(6) Coordination of the overcurrent protective devices to each other

7.2.1.3 Supplementary overcurrent protective devices shall not be used as a substitute for branch-circuit overcurrent protective devices.

7.2.1.4 A circuit breaker, self-protected combination motor controller, or a manual motor controller suitable as tap conductor protection in group installations marked with a slash rating, such as 120/240V or 480Y/277V, shall be applied in a solidly grounded circuit where the nominal voltage of any conductor to ground does not exceed the lower voltage rating and the nominal voltage between any two conductors does not exceed the higher voltage rating. When slash-rated devices are connected to the supply circuit of the machine, the nameplate voltage rating in 16.4.1(3) shall not exceed the lower voltage rating or shall include the complete slash rating. When slash rated devices are connected to the secondary of a transformer forming part the electrical equipment of the machine, the transformer secondary shall be grounded such that the line-to-line voltage for each phase and voltage to ground for any pole do not exceed the respective slash ratings.

7.2.2* Supply Conductors. Unless otherwise specified by the user, the supplier of the electrical equipment shall not be responsible for providing the overcurrent protective device for the supply conductors to the electrical equipment. The supplier of the electrical equipment shall state on the installation diagram the data necessary for selecting this overcurrent protective device.

Δ **7.2.3 Power Circuits.** Feeder and branch-circuit conductors shall be protected against overcurrent in accordance with their ampacities as specified in Section 12.5. In power circuits for motors, devices for detection and interruption of overcurrent, selected in accordance with 7.2.10, shall be applied to each ungrounded phase conductor. The grounded conductor shall not be disconnected unless (1) all ungrounded and grounded conductors open with no pole operating independently, or (2) the overcurrent protection is additionally relied upon for motor overload protection in accordance with 430.36 and 430.37 of *NFPA 70*.

7.2.4 Control Circuit Protection.

7.2.4.1 General. A control circuit tapped from the load side of the branch-circuit short-circuit and ground-fault protective device(s) and functioning to control the load(s) connected to that branch circuit shall be protected against overcurrent in accordance with 7.2.4.2. Such a tapped control circuit shall not be considered to be a branch circuit and shall be permitted to be protected by either a supplementary or branch-circuit overcurrent protective device(s).

7.2.4.2 Control Circuit Conductor Protection.

7.2.4.2.1 Control circuit conductors, other than flexible cords and fixture wires, shall be protected against overcurrent in accordance with their ampacities as specified in Section 12.5, unless otherwise permitted in 7.2.4.2.2 through 7.2.4.2.6.

7.2.4.2.2 Control circuit conductors sizes of 18, 16, and 14 AWG shall be considered as protected by an overcurrent device(s) of not more than a 20-ampere rating.

7.2.4.2.3 Control circuit conductors that do not extend beyond the control cabinet enclosure shall be considered protected by the load branch-circuit short-circuit and ground-fault protective device(s) where the rating of the protective device(s) is not more than 400 percent of the ampacity of the control circuit conductor for conductors 14 AWG and larger, or not more than 25 amperes for 18 AWG and 40 amperes for 16 AWG.

7.2.4.2.4 Control circuit conductors of 14 AWG and larger that extend beyond the enclosure shall be considered protected by the load branch-circuit short-circuit and ground-fault protective device(s) where the rating of the protective device(s) is not more than 300 percent of the ampacity of the control circuit conductors.

7.2.4.2.5 Control circuit conductors supplied by the secondary side of a single-phase transformer having a 2-wire (single-voltage) secondary shall be considered protected by overcurrent protection provided on the primary (supply) side of the transformer, if this protection is in accordance with 7.2.7 and does not exceed the value determined by multiplying the secondary conductor ampacity by the secondary-to-primary voltage ratio. Transformer secondary conductors (other than 2-wire) shall not be considered to be protected by the primary overcurrent protective device.

7.2.4.2.6 Control circuits conductors shall be considered protected by the motor branch-circuit short-circuit and ground-fault protective device(s) where the opening of the control circuit would create a hazard (e.g., the control circuit of a magnetic chuck).

7.2.5 Receptacle Outlets and Their Associated Conductors for Accessory Circuits.

7.2.5.1 Overcurrent protection shall be provided for the circuits feeding general purpose receptacle outlets intended primarily for supplying power to maintenance equipment.

7.2.5.2 Overcurrent protective devices shall be provided in the ungrounded phase conductors of each circuit feeding receptacle outlets. Overcurrent protection for these receptacle outlets shall not exceed 15 amperes.

7.2.6 Lighting Circuits. Overcurrent protection for lighting branch circuits shall not exceed 15 amperes.

7.2.7 Transformers. Transformers for motor control circuits shall be protected in accordance with Article 430, Part VI, of *NFPA 70*. Transformers for other than motor control circuits shall be protected in accordance with Article 450, Part I, of *NFPA 70*.

7.2.8 Location of Overcurrent Protective Devices. An overcurrent protective device shall be located at the point where the conductor to be protected is connected to the supply except as follows:

(1) Overcurrent protection at the supply shall not be required if all of the following conditions are met:
   (a) The current-carrying capacity of each of the conductors is at least equal to that required for their respective load, in accordance with Section 12.5.
   (b) Each connecting conductor to the overcurrent protective devices is no longer than 3 m (10 ft).
   (c) The conductor is suitably protected from physical damage.
   (d) The conductor does not extend beyond the control panel enclosure.
   (e) The conductor terminates in a single branch circuit overcurrent protective device.

(2) Overcurrent protection at the supply shall not be required if all of the following conditions are met:
   (a) The conductor has an ampacity of at least one-third that of the conductor from which it is supplied.
   (b) The conductor is suitably protected from physical damage.
   (c) The conductor is not over 7.5 m (25 ft) long, and the conductor terminates in a single branch circuit overcurrent protective device.

7.2.9* Short-Circuit Current Rating or Interrupting Rating. The short-circuit current rating or interrupting rating shall be at least equal to the available fault current at the point of application. Where the fault current to an overcurrent protective device includes additional currents other than from the supply (e.g., from motors, from power factor correction capacitors), these shall be taken into consideration.

7.2.10 Rating and Setting of Overcurrent Protective Devices.

7.2.10.1* Each motor controller and its associated wiring shall be protected as an individual branch circuit by a short-circuit protective device (SCPD) as specified by the controller manufacturer. The maximum rating of the designated SCPD shall be as shown in Table 7.2.10.1.

Exception No. 1: Table 7.2.10.1 shall not apply to Design B energy efficient motor circuits. The provisions of NFPA 70 shall be observed for Design B energy efficient motor circuits.

Exception No. 2: Where the controller is an adjustable speed drive that is listed and marked "Suitable for Output Motor Conductor Protection," the maximum rating of the designated SCPD shall be permitted to be determined by replacing the full-load current in Table 7.2.10.1 with the drive's rated input current. The SCPD shall not exceed the rating marked on the adjustable speed drive or in the manufacturer's instructions.

7.2.10.1.1 A listed self-protected combination controller shall be permitted in lieu of the devices specified in Table 7.2.10.1 for branch circuit and overload protection of a single motor circuit.

7.2.10.1.2 Where a listed self-protected combination controller has an adjustable, instantaneous trip setting, the setting shall not exceed 1300 percent of full-load motor current for other than Design B energy efficient motors and not more than 1700 percent of full-load motor current for Design B energy efficient motors.

7.2.10.2 Several motors, each not exceeding 1 hp in rating, shall be permitted on a nominal 120-volt branch circuit protected at not over 20 amperes or a 1000-volt nominal or less branch circuit, protected at not over 15 amperes, where all of the following conditions are met:

(1) The full-load rating of each motor does not exceed 6 amperes.
(2) The rating of the branch-circuit short-circuit and ground-fault protective device marked on any of the controllers is not exceeded. The short-circuit and ground-fault protection is provided by a single inverse time circuit breaker or single set of fuses.
(3) Individual overload protection conforms to Section 7.3.

7.2.10.3 Where the branch-circuit short-circuit and ground-fault protective device is selected not to exceed that allowed by 7.2.10.1 for the smallest rated motor, two or more motors or

Table 7.2.10.1 Maximum Rating or Setting of Fuse and Circuit Breakers: Motor, Motor Branch Circuit, and Motor Controller

Fuse Class with Non–Time Delay	Full-Load Current (%)		
	AC-2	AC-3	AC-4
R	300	300	300
CF or J	300	300	300
CC	300	300	300
T	300	300	300
Fuse Class with Time Delay[b]	Type of Application[a]		
	AC-2	AC-3	AC-4
RK-5[c]	150	175	175
RK-1	150	175	175
CF or J	150	175	225
CC	150	300	300
Instantaneous trip circuit breaker[d]	800	800	800
Inverse trip circuit breaker[e]	150	250	250

Note: Where the values determined by this table do not correspond to the standard sizes or ratings, the next higher standard size, rating, or possible setting shall be permitted.
[a] Types of starting duty are as follows:
(1) AC-2: All light-starting duty motors, including slip-ring motors; starting, switching off
(2) AC-3: All medium starting duty motors including squirrel-cage motors; starting, switching off while running, occasional inching, jogging, or plugging but not to exceed 5 operations per minute or 10 operations per 10 minutes and all wye-delta and two-step autotransformer starting motors
(3) AC-4: All heavy starting duty motors including squirrel-cage motors; starting, plugging, inching, jogging
[b] Where the rating of a time-delay fuse (other than CC type) specified by the table is not sufficient for the starting of the motor, it shall be permitted to be increased but shall in no case be permitted to exceed 225 percent. The rating of a time-delay Class CC fuse and non–time-delay Class CC, J, CF, or T fuse shall be permitted to be increased but shall in no case exceed 400 percent of the full-load current.
[c] Unless a motor controller is listed for use with RK-5 fuses, Class RK-5 fuses shall be used only with NEMA-rated motor controllers.
[d] Instantaneous trip circuit breakers shall be permitted to be used only if they comply with all of the following:
(1) They are adjustable.
(2) Part of the combination controller has motor-running protection, short-circuit protection, and ground-fault protection in each conductor.
(3) The combination is especially identified for use.
(4) It is installed per any instructions included in its listing or labeling.
(5) They are limited to single motor applications; circuit breakers with adjustable trip settings are to be set at the controller manufacturer's recommendation, but not greater than 1300 percent of the motor full-load current.
[e] Where the rating of an inverse time circuit breaker specified in this table is not sufficient for the starting current of the motor, it shall be permitted to be increased but in no case exceed 400 percent for full-load currents of 100 amperes or less or 300 percent for full-load currents greater than 100 amperes.

one or more motors and other loads, with each motor having individual overload protection, shall be permitted to be connected to a branch circuit where it can be determined that the branch-circuit short-circuit and ground-fault protective device will not open under severe normal conditions of service that might be encountered. The short-circuit and ground-fault protection shall be provided by a single inverse time circuit breaker or single set of fuses.

7.2.10.4 Two or more motors, or one or more motors and other loads, and their control equipment shall be permitted to be connected to a single branch circuit where short-circuit and ground-fault protection is provided by a single inverse time circuit breaker or a single set of fuses, provided the following conditions under 7.2.10.4(1) and either 7.2.10.4(2) or 7.2.10.4(3) are met:

(1) Each motor controller and overload device is either listed for group installation with specified maximum branch-circuit protection or selected such that the ampere rating of the motor branch short-circuit and ground-fault protective device does not exceed that permitted by 7.2.10.1 for that individual motor controller or overload device and corresponding motor load.

(2) The rating or setting of the branch short-circuit and ground-fault protection device does not exceed the values in Table 7.2.10.4 for the smallest conductor in the circuit.

Exception: Where a controller is an adjustable speed drive that is listed and marked "Suitable for Output Motor Conductor Protection," the conductors from the drive to the motor shall not be required to be used when determining the smallest conductor in the circuit. The conductors from the drive to the motor shall have an ampacity in accordance with Sections 12.5 and 12.6.

(3) The rating or setting of the branch short-circuit and ground-fault protection does not exceed the value specified in 7.2.10.1 for the highest rated motor connected to

the branch circuit plus an amount equal to the sum of the full-load current ratings of all other motors and the ratings of other loads connected to the circuit. Where this calculation results in a rating less than the ampacity of the branch circuit conductors, it shall be permitted to increase the maximum rating of the fuses or circuit breaker to a value not exceeding that permitted by Sections 12.5 and 12.6. Overcurrent protection for loads other than motor loads shall be in accordance with 7.2.3, 7.2.4, and 7.2.11. Where 16 AWG or 18 AWG conductors are used for branch circuit conductors or tap conductors under 7.2.10.5, the rating and type of the branch short-circuit and ground-fault protection shall be in accordance with 12.6.1.

7.2.10.5 For group installations described in 7.2.10.4(3), the conductors of any tap supplying a single motor shall not be required to have an individual branch-circuit short-circuit and ground-fault protective device, provided they comply with one of the following:

(1) No conductor to the motor shall have an ampacity less than that of the branch-circuit conductors.
(2) No conductor to the motor shall have an ampacity less than one-third that of the branch-circuit conductors, with a minimum in accordance with Sections 12.5 and 12.6, the conductors to the motor overload device being not more than 7.5 m (25 ft) long and being suitably protected from physical damage in accordance with Chapter 13.
(3) Conductors from the point of the tap from the branch-circuit to a listed manual motor controller additionally marked "Suitable for Tap Conductor Protection in Group Installations" or to a branch circuit protective device shall be permitted to have an ampacity not less than 1/10 the rating or setting of the branch-circuit short-circuit and ground-fault protective device. The conductors from the

Table 7.2.10.4 Relationship Between Conductor Size and Maximum Rating or Setting of Short-Circuit Protective Device for Power Circuits Group Installations

Conductor Size (AWG)	Maximum Rating Fuse or Inverse Time* Circuit Breaker (amperes)
18	See footnote.
16	See footnote.
14	60
12	80
10	100
8	150
6	200
4	250
3	300
2	350
1	400
0	500
2/0	600
3/0	700
4/0	800

*Maximum ratings and type of branch short-circuit and ground-fault protective devices for 16 AWG and 18 AWG shall be determined in accordance with 12.6.1.

controller to the motor shall have an ampacity in accordance with Sections 12.5 and 12.6. The conductors from the point of the tap to the controller shall (1) be enclosed either by an enclosed controller or by a raceway and be not more than 3 m (10 ft) long or (2) have an ampacity not less than that of the branch-circuit conductors.

7.2.11 Resistance Heating Branch-Circuit Overcurrent Protection.

7.2.11.1 If the branch circuit supplies a single non-motor-operated load rated at 16.7 amperes or more, the overcurrent device rating shall not exceed 150 percent of the load rating.

7.2.11.2 Equipment employing resistance-type heating elements rated at more than 48 amperes shall have the heating elements subdivided. Each subdivided load shall not exceed 48 amperes and shall be protected at not more than 60 amperes.

Exception: A single sheath-type heating element requiring more than 48 amperes shall be protected at not more than 125 percent of the load where the element is integral with and enclosed within the machine housing.

7.2.11.3 The additional overcurrent protective devices shall be all of the following:

(1) Installed within or on the machinery or provided as a separate assembly
(2) Accessible (but need not be readily accessible)
(3) A branch-circuit overcurrent protective device

7.2.11.4 The main conductors supplying these additional overcurrent protective devices shall be considered branch-circuit conductors.

7.2.12 Programmable Electronic System Power Supply Input Overcurrent Protection. Programmable electronic system power supply inputs shall be protected by overcurrent protective devices either externally or internally. The overcurrent protection size or rating shall be in accordance with the manufacturer's instructions.

7.2.13 Control Devices. Pushbuttons, selector switches, sensors, and limit switches shall in no case be connected to a circuit rated larger than 10 amperes.

7.2.14 Common Overcurrent Device. The use of the same overcurrent device to provide the protection called for in 7.2.4, 7.2.6, and 7.2.7 shall be permitted.

7.3 Overload Protection of Motors. Overload devices shall be provided to protect each motor, motor controller, and branch-circuit conductor against excessive heating due to motor overloads or failure to start.

7.3.1 Motors. Motor overload protection shall be provided in accordance with Article 430, Part III, of *NFPA 70.*

7.3.2 Resetting. Resetting of the overload device shall not restart the motor.

Exception: Where the machine has only a single motor of 2 hp or less, an overload reset operator mounted on the motor shall be permitted to restart the motor provided that the distance between the overload reset operator and the machine start pushbutton operator is 300 mm (12 in.) or less, and a suitable warning label is attached on or adjacent to the overload reset operator.

7.3.3 Number of Overloads. The minimum number and location of running overload units shall be determined from Table 7.3.3.

7.3.3.1 An overload unit in each phase shall not be required where overload protection is provided by other approved means.

7.3.3.2 Short-time–rated motors or high-reversing duty motors that are unable to be protected by external overload devices shall be protected by a thermal device mounted in the motor and sensitive to the temperature of the motor, or to both motor temperature and current.

7.3.3.3 Motors that are an integral part of a refrigeration compressor of the hermetic or semihermetic type shall be protected in accordance with the compressor manufacturer's recommendations.

7.4* Abnormal Temperature Protection. Resistance heating or other circuits that are capable of attaining or causing abnormal temperatures and, therefore, cause a hazardous condition shall be provided with suitable detection to initiate an appropriate control response.

7.5 Protection Against Supply Interruption or Voltage Reduction and Subsequent Restoration.

7.5.1 General. Where a supply interruption or a voltage reduction can cause a hazardous condition or damage to the machine or to the work in progress, undervoltage protection shall be provided (e.g., to switch off the machine) at a predetermined voltage level. Where only a part of the machine or of the group of machines working together in a coordinated manner is affected by the voltage reduction or supply interruption, the undervoltage protection shall initiate appropriate control responses to ensure coordination.

7.5.2 Undervoltage Protection. Where the operation of the machine allows for an interruption or a reduction of the voltage for a short time period, delayed undervoltage protection shall be permitted to be provided. The operation of the undervoltage device shall not impair the operation of any stopping control of the machine.

7.5.3 Restarting. Upon restoration of the voltage or upon switching on the machine supply circuit, automatic or unintentional restarting of the machine shall be prevented when such a restart causes a hazardous condition.

7.6 Overspeed Protection.

7.6.1* Motor Overspeed Protection. Unless the inherent characteristics of the motor or the controller, or both, are such

as to limit the speed adequately, drive systems motors shall include protection against motor overspeed where overspeed results in a hazardous condition.

7.6.2 Equipment Overspeed Protection. Where the safe operating speed of the equipment is less than that of the drive motor, means shall be provided to limit the speed of the equipment.

7.7* Phase Sequence Protection. Where a phase loss or an incorrect phase sequence of the supply voltage causes a hazardous condition or damage to the machine, protection shall be provided.

7.8 Protection Against Overvoltages Due to Lightning and Switching Surges.

7.8.1* Surge-Protective Devices (SPDs). Industrial machinery with safety circuits not effectively protected from the effects of overvoltages due to lightning or switching surges shall have surge protection installed.

Exception: SPDs shall not be required where the risks associated with the effects of overvoltages are mitigated such that the safety performance determined by a risk assessment is met.

7.8.2 Connections. Where provided, SPDs shall be connected in accordance with product markings and installation instructions.

7.8.3 SPD Type and Location. The type of SPD provided shall be suitable for the circuit location within the electrical equipment of the industrial machinery. Type 1, Type 2, and Type 3 SPDs shall be listed devices.

7.8.3.1 Type 1 SPD. Where the SPD is located on the line side of the service disconnect overcurrent protection, a Type 1 SPD shall be provided,

7.8.3.2 Type 2 SPD. Where the SPD is located on the load side of the service disconnect overcurrent protection, feeder circuit, or separately derived system, a Type 1 or Type 2 SPD shall be provided. Where Type 2 SPDs are provided, the SPD shall be on the load side of an overcurrent protective device.

7.8.3.3 Type 3 SPD. Where the SPD is located on the load side of the branch-circuit overcurrent protective device, a Type 1, Type 2, or Type 3 SPD shall be provided. Where Type 3 SPDs are provided and where included in the manufacturer's instructions, the Type 3 SPD connection shall be a minimum of 10 m (30 ft) of conductor distance from the service or separately derived system disconnect.

Δ **Table 7.3.3 Running Overload Units**

Kind of Motor	Supply System	Number and Location of Overload Units (Such as Trip Coils, Relays, or Thermal Cutouts)
1-phase, ac or dc	2-wire, 1-phase ac or dc ungrounded	One in either conductor
1-phase, ac or dc	2-wire, 1-phase ac or dc, one conductor grounded	One in ungrounded conductor
1-phase, ac or dc	3-wire, 1-phase ac or dc, one conductor grounded	One in either ungrounded conductor
3-phase, ac	Any 3-phase	Three, one in each phase

Note: For 2-phase power supply systems, see 430.37 of *NFPA 70.*

7.8.3.4 Component Assembly and Other Type 4 SPD. Component assembly SPDs (Type 1, 2, or 3) shall be applied in accordance with 7.8.3.1 through 7.8.3.3 and any additional conditions of use specified by the device manufacturer. Where a Type 4 component assembly SPD or other component type is used, it shall be identified as suitable for the intended use. Component assembly SPDs or other component type SPDs shall only be installed by the industrial control panel manufacturer.

7.8.4 Short-Circuit Current Rating. The SPD shall be marked with a short-circuit current rating and shall not be installed at a point on the system where the available fault current is in excess of that rating.

7.9 Power Factor Correction Capacitor Overcurrent Protection. Where capacitors are installed for motor power factor correction on circuits of 1000 volts, nominal, and under, overcurrent protection for the conductors shall be provided. Each capacitor cell or capacitor bank shall be protected against rupture of the individual cells. Protection included as a part of the capacitor assembly shall be permitted.

Chapter 8 Grounding and Bonding

8.1* General.

8.1.1 Applicability. This chapter provides the requirements for grounding, bonding, and for the grounded conductor.

N **8.1.2 Separately Derived Systems.** Separately derived systems shall be installed in accordance with 250.30 of *NFPA 70.*

8.1.3 Connections. Except at either the source or first disconnecting means of a separately derived system, grounded conductors shall not be connected to the equipment grounding conductor.

8.1.4 Mounting. Mounting hardware shall not be used for terminating conductors used for grounding or bonding.

8.2 Equipment Grounding Conductors and Bonding Jumpers.

8.2.1 Equipment Parts. The equipment frame and all non-current-carrying conductive parts, material, or other equipment likely to become energized shall be bonded together and connected to an equipment grounding conductor or bonding jumper.

Exception: Small parts such as screws, rivets, and nameplates that are not likely to become energized shall not be required to be grounded.

8.2.1.1 Effective Ground-Fault Current Path. The effective ground-fault current path shall be capable of safely carrying the maximum ground-fault current likely to be imposed on it from any point where a ground fault could occur from the point of connection of the supply circuit conductors to the electrical equipment of the machine.

8.2.1.2 Equipment Grounding and Bonding.

8.2.1.2.1 The machine and all exposed, non-current-carrying conductive parts, material, and equipment likely to become energized shall be connected in a manner that provides an effective ground-fault current path.

8.2.1.2.2 Where electrical devices are mounted on metal mounting panels that are located within nonmetallic enclosures, the metal mounting panels shall be connected to an equipment grounding conductor or bonding jumper.

8.2.1.2.3 Where specified by the manufacturer, components and subassemblies shall be bonded in accordance with the manufacturer's instructions.

8.2.1.3* Equipment Grounding Conductor Terminal.

8.2.1.3.1 For each machine supply circuit, an equipment grounding conductor terminal shall be provided in the vicinity of the associated phase conductor terminals and shall be connected to the equipment grounding conductor.

8.2.1.3.2 The equipment grounding conductor terminal shall accommodate an equipment grounding conductor sized in accordance with Table 8.2.2.4.

8.2.1.3.3* The equipment grounding conductor terminal shall be identified with the word "GROUND," the letters "GND" or "GRD," the letter "G," the color GREEN, or the symbol shown in Figure 8.2.1.3.3; in addition, the letters "PE" shall also be permitted to identify this terminal.

8.2.1.3.4 Where an auxiliary grounding electrode is specified by the industrial machinery manufacturer or provider, a terminal shall accommodate this additional grounding electrode conductor.

8.2.2 Equipment Grounding Conductors and Bonding Jumpers.

8.2.2.1 Equipment grounding conductors and bonding jumpers shall be identified in accordance with 13.2.2.

8.2.2.2 Conductors used for grounding and bonding purposes shall be copper.

8.2.2.2.1 Stipulations on stranding and flexing as outlined in Chapter 12 shall apply.

8.2.2.3 Equipment grounding conductors and bonding jumpers shall be insulated, covered, or bare and shall be protected against physical damage.

8.2.2.4 Equipment grounding conductors and bonding jumpers of the wire type shall not be smaller than shown in Table 8.2.2.4, but shall not be required to be larger than the circuit conductors supplying the equipment.

8.2.3 Continuity.

8.2.3.1 Continuity of equipment grounding conductors and bonding jumpers shall be ensured by effective connections.

8.2.3.2 Equipment grounding conductors and bonding jumpers shall be installed in a manner such that removal of a wiring device, such as a receptacle or switch, does not interrupt the continuity of the equipment grounding conductor or bonding conductor.

8.2.3.3 Bonding of equipment with bolts or other identified means shall be permitted if paint and dirt are removed from the joint surfaces or the bonded members are effectively penetrated.

FIGURE 8.2.1.3.3 Grounding Symbol.

Table 8.2.2.4 Minimum Size of Equipment Grounding Conductors and Bonding Jumpers

Rating or Setting of Automatic Overcurrent Device in Circuit Ahead of the Equipment (Not Exceeding Amperes)	Copper Conductor Size (AWG or kcmil)
10	16
15	14
20	12
30	10
40	10
60	10
100	8
200	6
300	4
400	3
500	2
600	1
800	1/0
1000	2/0
1200	3/0
1600	4/0
2000	250
2500	350
3000	400
4000	500
5000	700
6000	800

8.2.3.4 Equipment containing energized conductors shall be provided with a separate wire-type equipment grounding conductor or bonding jumper.

8.2.3.5 Doors or Covers.

8.2.3.5.1 Where electrical devices are mounted on conductive doors or covers, an equipment bonding jumper shall be installed.

8.2.3.5.2 Where required, an equipment bonding jumper shall connect the conductive door or cover to the equipment enclosure or to an equipment grounding terminal within the enclosure.

8.2.3.6 Portable, pendant, and resilient-mounted equipment shall be bonded by separate conductors. Where multiconductor cable is used and an equipment grounding conductor is required to carry fault current, the equipment grounding conductor shall be used to provide the bonding.

△ **8.2.4* Exclusion of Switching Devices.**

8.2.4.1 The equipment grounding circuit shall not contain any switches or overcurrent protective devices.

8.2.4.2 Separable connections such as those provided in drawout equipment or attachment plugs and mating connectors and receptacles shall provide for first-make, last-break of the equipment grounding conductor.

8.2.4.3 First-make, last-break shall not be required where interlocked equipment, plugs, receptacles, and connectors preclude energization without grounding continuity.

8.2.5 Equipment Grounding Conductor Connecting Points.

8.2.5.1 All equipment grounding conductors shall be terminated in accordance with 13.1.1, and the equipment grounding conductor connecting points shall have no other function.

8.2.5.2* The equipment grounding conductor connecting points, other than the equipment grounding terminal, shall be identified by the color GREEN, by the bicolor combination of GREEN-AND-YELLOW, or by use of the symbol shown in Figure 8.2.1.3.3.

8.3 Control Circuits. Control circuits shall be permitted to be grounded or ungrounded.

Exception: Exposed control circuits as permitted by Section 6.4 shall be grounded.

△ **8.3.1** If the control system is grounded, the output shall be grounded as near as practicable to the control power source and before the first control device. Switching devices shall not be permitted in a grounded conductor(s) unless the control circuit conductor(s) is opened simultaneously.

Exception: Overload relay contacts shall be permitted in the grounded conductor(s) if the conductor(s)does not extend beyond the control enclosure.

8.3.2 Ungrounded control circuits shall be provided with an insulation-monitoring device that either indicates a ground fault or interrupts the circuit automatically after a ground fault.

Exception: Class 2 circuits as defined in Article100 and as covered in Article 725 of NFPA 70 shall not require insulation monitoring unless required by 9.4.2.1.

8.4 Lighting Circuits.

8.4.1 One conductor of all machine lighting and maintenance lighting circuits shall be grounded. The grounded conductor(s) shall be identified in accordance with Section 13.2.

8.4.2 Where the lighting circuit is supplied by a separate isolation transformer, one terminal of the secondary of the transformer shall be directly connected to the equipment grounding circuit.

8.4.3 The grounded conductor, where run to a screw-shell lampholder, shall be connected to the screw-shell.

Chapter 9 Control Circuits and Control Functions

9.1 Control Circuits.

9.1.1 Control Circuit Supply.

9.1.1.1 Where control circuits are supplied from an ac source, control transformers shall be used for supplying the control circuits. Control circuits shall not be derived from autotransformers. Control circuits supplied from windings of multiwinding power transformers shall be permitted if the output voltage of the winding supplying the control circuit does not exceed 120 volts ac and the available fault current does not exceed 1000 amperes rms.

9.1.1.2 Where dc control circuits are connected to the equipment grounding circuit, they shall be supplied from a separate winding of the ac control circuit transformer or by another control circuit transformer or a listed dc power supply.

9.1.1.3 Transformers shall not be required if the supply voltage does not exceed 120 volts ac and the available fault current does not exceed 1000 amperes rms.

9.1.1.4 The source of supply for all control circuits shall be taken from the load side of the supply disconnecting means.

Exception: Control circuits meeting the requirements of excepted circuits in 5.1.13.1(4) shall be permitted to be taken from the line side of the supply disconnecting means or other power source. The marking requirements of 16.2.4 shall apply.

• **9.1.2 Control Circuit Voltages.**

9.1.2.1 AC Control Circuit Voltages. The ac voltage for control circuits shall not exceed 120 volts, ac single phase.

Exception No. 1: Other voltages shall be permitted, where necessary, for the operation of electronic, precision, static, or similar devices used in the control circuit.

Exception No. 2: Any electromechanical magnetic device having an inrush current exceeding 20 amperes at 120 volts shall be permitted to be energized above control voltage through contactor or relay contacts. The contactor or relay contacts shall break both sides of the circuit powering the magnetic device. The relay coil shall be connected to the control circuit.

9.1.2.2 DC Control Circuit Voltages. DC control voltage shall be 250 volts or less.

9.1.3 Protection. Control circuits shall be provided with overcurrent protection in accordance with Chapter 7.

9.1.4 Connection of Control Circuit Devices.

9.1.4.1 All operating coils of electromechanical magnetic devices and indicator lamps (or transformer primary windings for indicator lamps) shall be directly connected to the same side of the control circuit. All control circuit contacts shall be connected between the coil and the other side of the control circuit.

Exception No. 1: Overload relay contacts where the wiring to these contacts does not extend beyond the control enclosure.

Exception No. 2: Contacts of multipole control circuit switching devices that simultaneously open both sides of the control circuit.

Exception No. 3: Ground test switching device contacts in ungrounded control circuits.

Exception No. 4: Solenoid test switching device contacts in ungrounded circuits.

Exception No. 5: Coils or contacts used in electronic control circuits where the wiring to these coils or contacts does not extend beyond the control enclosure.

Exception No. 6: "Run" pushbuttons for two-hand operation, such as for presses having ground detection circuits and overcurrent protection in each conductor.

9.1.4.2 Contacts shall not be connected in parallel where the purpose is to increase ampacity.

9.2* Control Functions. Safety circuits shall meet the safety performance requirements determined by the risk assessment of the machine and the applicable functional safety standards.

9.2.1 Start Functions. Start functions shall operate by energizing the relevant circuit.

9.2.2* Stop Functions. Stop functions shall override related start functions. The reset of the stop functions shall not initiate any hazardous conditions. The three categories of stop functions shall be as follows:

(1) Category 0 is an uncontrolled stop by immediately removing power to the machine actuators.

(2) Category 1 is a controlled stop with power to the machine actuators available to achieve the stop then power is removed when the stop is achieved.

(3) Category 2 is a controlled stop with power left available to the machine actuators.

9.2.3 Operating Modes.

9.2.3.1 Each machine shall be permitted to have one or more operating modes (e.g., automatic, manual, normal, and bypass) determined by the type of machine and its application.

9.2.3.2 Where a hazardous condition results from mode selection, inadvertent selection shall be prevented from occurring (e.g., key-operated switch, access code). Mode selection by itself shall not initiate machine operation. A separate action by the operator shall be required.

9.2.3.3* Safeguarding means shall remain effective for all operating modes.

9.2.3.4 Indication of the selected operating mode shall be provided (e.g., position of mode selector, provision of indicating light, visual display indication).

9.2.4 Overriding Safeguards. Where it is necessary to temporarily override one or more safeguards, a mode selection device or means capable of being secured (e.g., locked) in the desired mode shall be provided to prevent automatic operation. The control circuit for the suspension of a safeguard shall have the same safety requirements as the suspended safeguard itself. In addition, one or more of the following measures shall be provided:

(1) Initiation of motion by a hold-to-run or other control device.

(2) A portable control station (e.g., pendant) with an emergency stop device, and where used, an enabling device. Where a portable station is used, motion shall only be initiated from that station.

(3) Limiting the speed or the power of motion.

(4) Limiting the range of motion.

9.2.5 Operation.

9.2.5.1 General.

9.2.5.1.1 The necessary interlocks shall be provided for safe operation.

9.2.5.1.2 Measures shall be taken to prevent movement of the machine in an unintended manner after any stopping of the machine (e.g., locked-off condition, power supply fault, battery replacement, lost signal condition with cableless control).

9.2.5.2 Start.

9.2.5.2.1 The start of an operation shall be possible only where all of the safeguards are in place and functional except for conditions as described in 9.2.4.

9.2.5.2.2 On those machines where safeguards cannot be applied for certain operations, manual control of such operations shall be by hold-to-run controls together with enabling control, where appropriate.

9.2.5.2.3 Interlocks shall be provided to ensure correct sequential starting.

9.2.5.2.4 On machines requiring the use of more than one control station to initiate a start, the following criteria shall be met:

(1) Each control station shall have a separate manually actuated start control device.
(2) All required conditions for machine operation shall be met.
(3) All start control devices shall be in the released (off) position before a start operation is permitted.
(4) All start control devices shall be actuated concurrently.

9.2.5.3 Stop.

9.2.5.3.1* Category 0, Category 1, and/or Category 2 stops shall be provided as required with the minimum of at least one stop function. The number of stop functions and the stop function category shall be determined by the risk assessment and the functional requirements of the machine. Category 0 and Category 1 stops shall be operational regardless of operating modes, and Category 0 shall take priority.

9.2.5.3.2 Where required, provisions to connect protective devices and interlocks shall be provided. Where applicable, the stop function shall signal the logic of the control system that such a condition exists.

9.2.5.4* Emergency Operations (Emergency Stop, Emergency Switching Off). Emergency operation requirements are as follows:

(1) This section specifies the requirements for the emergency stop and the emergency switching-off functions of the emergency operations, both of which are initiated by a single human action.
(2) Once active operation of an emergency stop *(see Section 10.7)* or emergency switching off *(see Section 10.8)* actuator has ceased following a command, the effect of this command shall be sustained until it is reset. This reset shall be possible only at that location where the command has been initiated. The reset of the command shall not restart the machinery but only permit restarting.
(3) It shall not be possible to restart the machinery until all emergency stop commands have been reset. It shall not be possible to reenergize the machinery until all emergency switching off commands have been reset.

9.2.5.4.1 Emergency Stop. Emergency stop functions provided in accordance with 9.2.5.3 shall be designed to be initiated by a single human action.

9.2.5.4.1.1 In addition to the requirements for stop, the emergency stop shall have the following requirements:

(1) It shall override all other functions and operations in all modes.
(2) Power to the machine actuators, which causes a hazardous condition(s), shall be removed as quickly as possible without creating other hazards (e.g., by the provision of mechanical means of stopping requiring no external power, by reverse current braking for a Category 1 stop).
(3) The reset of the command shall not restart the machinery but only permit restarting.

9.2.5.4.1.2 Where required, provisions to connect additional emergency stop devices shall be provided in accordance with Section 10.7.

9.2.5.4.1.3 The emergency stop shall function as either a Category 0 or a Category 1 stop *(see 9.2.2)*. The choice of the category of the emergency stop shall be determined by the risk assessment of the machine.

Exception: In some cases, to avoid creating additional risks, it can be necessary to perform a controlled stop and maintain the power to machine actuators even after stopping is achieved. The stopped condition shall be monitored and upon detection of failure of the stopped condition, power shall be removed without creating a hazardous situation.

9.2.5.4.1.4* Where a Category 0 or Category 1 stop is used for the emergency stop function, it shall have a circuitry design (including sensors, logic, and actuators) according to the relevant risk as required by Section 4.1 and 9.4.1. Final removal of power to the machine actuators shall be ensured and shall be by means of electromechanical components. Where relays are used to accomplish a Category 0 emergency stop function, they shall be nonretentive relays.

Exception: Drives, or solid state output devices, designed for safety-related functions shall be allowed to be the final switching element, when designed according to relevant safety standards.

9.2.5.4.2* Emergency Switching Off. Where the emergency switching-off function is used, it shall be initiated by a single human action.

9.2.5.4.2.1 Emergency switching off shall be permitted under any of the following conditions:

(1) Where protection against direct contact (e.g., with collector wires, collector bars, slip-ring assemblies, control gear in electrical operating areas) is achieved only by placing out of reach or by obstacles
(2) Where other hazards or damage caused by electricity are possible

9.2.5.4.2.2 Emergency switching off shall be accomplished by disconnecting the machine supply circuit of the machine effecting a Category 0 stop. Where the machine cannot tolerate the Category 0 stop, it shall be necessary to provide other protection (e.g., against direct contact), so that emergency switching off is not necessary.

9.2.5.5 Hold-to-Run Controls.

9.2.5.5.1* Hold-to-run controls (e.g., jog, inch functions) shall require continuous actuation of the control device(s) to achieve operation.

9.2.5.5.2 Jog or inch functions shall operate only in the manual mode. Manual reverse shall be considered a jog function. The prevention of run or automatic operation during jog or inch shall be accomplished by an operator interface and a separate jog or inch selection method.

9.2.5.6* Two-Hand Controls. All two-hand controls shall have the following features:

(1) The provision of two control devices shall require the concurrent actuation by both hands.
(2) It shall be necessary to actuate the control devices within a certain time limit of each other, not exceeding 0.5 second.

(3) Where this time limit is exceeded, both control devices shall be released before operation is initiated.
(4) The control devices shall require continuous actuation during the hazardous conditions.
(5) Machine operation shall cease upon the release of either control device when hazardous conditions are still present.
(6) Machine operation shall require the release of both control devices before the machine operation is re-initiated.

9.2.5.7 Enabling Control.

9.2.5.7.1 An enabling control function incorporating the use of an enabling device shall, when activated, allow machine operation to be initiated by a separate start control and, when deactivated, stop the machine and prevent initiation of machine operation. An enabling device provided as a part of the enabling control function shall be designed to allow motion when actuated in one position only. In any other position, motion shall be inhibited.

9.2.5.7.2 Enabling controls shall have the following features:

(1) Connect to a Category 0 or a Category 1 stop *(see 9.2.2)*
(2) Design follows ergonomic principles
(3) For two-position types, the positions are as follows:

    (a) Position 1 is the off function of the switch (actuator is not operated).
    (b) Position 2 is the enabling function (actuator is operated).

(4) For three-position types, the positions are as follows:

    (a) Position 1 is the off function of the switch (actuator is not operated).
    (b) Position 2 is the enabling function (actuator is operated in its mid position).
    (c) Position 3 is the off function of the switch (actuator is operated past its mid position).

(5) A three-position enabling control shall require manual operation to reach Position 3. When returning from Position 3 to Position 2, the function shall not be enabled.

9.2.5.7.3 An enabling control shall automatically return to its off function when its actuator is not manually held in the enabling position.

9.2.6 Combined Start and Stop Controls. A single pushbutton and other devices that alternately start and stop motion shall only be used for secondary functions where no hazardous condition arises when they are operated.

9.2.7 Cableless Control Functions.

9.2.7.1* General. Cableless control (e.g., radio, infrared) techniques for transmitting commands and signals between a machine control system and operator control station(s) shall meet the requirements of 9.2.7.1.1 through 9.2.7.1.4.

9.2.7.1.1 Means shall be provided to verify the memory elements of the operator control station with the machine.

9.2.7.1.2 Means (e.g., key-operated switch, access code) shall be provided, as necessary, to prevent unauthorized use of the operator control station.

9.2.7.1.3 Each operator control station shall carry an unambiguous indication of which machine(s) is intended to be controlled by that operator control station.

9.2.7.1.4 Means shall be provided for visual or audible indication of active and inactive status.

9.2.7.2 Cableless Control Limitation.

9.2.7.2.1 Measures shall be taken to prevent the machine from responding to signals other than those from the intended operator control station(s).

9.2.7.2.2 Where necessary to prevent a hazardous condition, means shall be provided so that the machine can be controlled only from operator control station(s) in one or more predetermined zones or locations.

9.2.7.3 Stop Function.

9.2.7.3.1 A machine that is equipped with cableless control shall have a means of automatically initiating the stopping of the machine and preventing a potentially hazardous operation in the following situations:

(1) When a stop signal is received
(2) When a fault is detected in the cableless control system
(3)* When a valid signal has not been detected within a specified period of time
(4) When the control panel is taken outside the range of the cableless control where no hazardous situation can occur

9.2.7.3.2 Where an emergency stop device is installed on a cableless control panel it shall meet the following requirements:

(1) The device shall provide a level of integrity equivalent to that of hardware-based components installed in accordance with this standard for emergency stop functions.
(2) A continuous and distinctive visual or audible alarm shall be annunciated by the cableless operator control station in the event that the emergency stop initiating device has been actuated.

Δ **9.2.7.4* Serial Data Communication.** In a machine where the safety-circuit relies on serial data transfer, correct communications shall be ensured by using an error detection method that is able to cope with up to three error bits in any command sequence. The safety capability of the serial data communication system shall be listed to have the same degree of safety capability as hardware-based components installed in accordance with this standard.

9.2.7.5 Use of More Than One Operator Control Station. Where a machine has more than one operator control station, measures shall be taken to ensure that only one control station shall be enabled at a given time. Indication of which operator control station is in control of the machine shall be provided at locations where necessary for the safety requirements of the machine.

Exception: A stop command from any one of the control stations shall be effective where necessary for the safety requirements of the machine.

9.2.7.6 Battery-Powered Operator Control Stations. A variation in the battery voltage shall not cause a hazardous condition. If one or more potentially hazardous motions are controlled using a battery-powered operator control station, a clear indication shall be given to warn the operator when a variation in battery voltage exceeds specified limits. Under those circumstances, the operator control station shall remain functional long enough to put the machine into a nonhazardous condition.

9.3 Protective Interlocks.

9.3.1 Reclosing or Resetting of an Interlocking Safeguard. The reclosing or resetting of an interlocking safeguard shall not initiate machine motion or operation that results in a hazardous condition.

9.3.2* Exceeding Operating Limits. Movement or action of a machine or part of a machine that can result in a hazardous condition shall be monitored by providing, for example, overtravel limiters, motor overspeed detection, mechanical overload detection, or anti-collision devices. Where an operating limit (e.g., speed, pressure, position) can be exceeded, leading to a hazardous condition, means shall be provided to detect when a predetermined limit(s) is exceeded and initiate an appropriate control action.

9.3.3 Operation of Auxiliary Functions.

9.3.3.1 Appropriate devices (e.g., pressure sensors) shall check the correct operation of the auxiliary functions.

9.3.3.2 Where the nonoperation of a motor or device for an auxiliary function (e.g., lubrication, coolant, swarf removal) causes a hazardous condition or causes damage to the machine or to the work in progress, interlocking shall be provided.

9.3.4 Interlocks Between Different Operations and for Contrary Motions.

9.3.4.1 All contactors, relays, and other control devices that control elements of the machine that cause a hazardous condition when actuated at the same time (e.g., those that initiate contrary motion) shall be interlocked against incorrect operation.

9.3.4.2 Motor contactors and starters that initiate opposing motion shall be both mechanically and electrically interlocked to prevent simultaneous operation. Relays and solenoids that are mechanically interlocked shall be electrically interlocked.

9.3.4.3 Where certain functions on the machine are required to be interrelated for safeguarding or for continuous operation, their coordination shall be ensured by interlocks. For a group of machines working together in a coordinated manner and having more than one controller, provision shall be made to coordinate the operations of the controllers as necessary.

9.3.4.4 Where a failure of a mechanical brake actuator results in the brake being applied when the associated machine actuator is energized and a hazardous situation results, interlocks shall be provided to switch off the machine actuator.

9.3.5 Reverse Current Braking.

9.3.5.1 Where reverse current braking is used on a motor, effective measures shall be taken to prevent the motor starting in the opposite direction at the end of braking where this reversal will cause a hazardous condition or damage to the machine or to the work in progress. For this purpose, the use of a device operating exclusively as a function of time shall not be allowed.

9.3.5.2 Control circuits shall be arranged so that rotation of a motor shaft, manually or otherwise, shall not result in a hazardous condition.

Δ **9.3.6 Protective Interlock.** Where doors or guards have interlocked switches used in safety circuits, the interlocking devices shall be listed, either have direct opening operation or provide

similar reliability, and prevent the operation of the equipment when the doors or guards are open (difficult to defeat or bypass).

9.4 Control Functions in the Event of Failure. Where failures or disturbances in the electrical equipment cause a hazardous condition or damage to the machine or the work in progress, measures shall be taken to minimize the probability of the occurrence of such failures or disturbances. The electrical control circuits shall have an appropriate level of performance that has been determined from the risk assessment of the machine.

9.4.1* Risk Reduction Measures. Measures to reduce these risks shall include, but are not limited to, one or more of the following:

(1) Protective devices on the machine (e.g., interlock guards, trip devices)
(2) Protective interlocking of the electrical circuit
(3) Use of proven circuit techniques and components
(4) Provisions of partial or complete redundancy or diversity
(5) Provision for functional tests

9.4.2 Protection Against Unintended Operation Due to Ground Faults and Voltage Interruptions.

9.4.2.1 Ground Faults. Ground faults on any control circuit shall not cause unintentional starting or potentially hazardous motions or prevent stopping of the machine. Grounded control circuits shall be in accordance with Section 8.2 and Section 8.3. Ungrounded control circuits shall be provided with an insulation monitoring device that either indicates a ground fault or interrupts the circuit automatically after a ground fault. A restart of the machine with a detected ground fault shall be prevented.

Exception: Ungrounded Class 2 circuits as defined in Article 100 and as covered in Article 725 of NFPA 70 shall not require insulation monitoring so long as the ground fault(s) will not cause unintentional starting or potentially hazardous motions or prevent stopping of the machine.

9.4.2.2 Voltage Interruptions.

9.4.2.2.1 The requirements detailed in Section 7.5 shall apply.

9.4.2.2.2 Where a memory is used, its functioning in the event of power failure shall be ensured (e.g., by using a nonvolatile memory) where such loss of memory results in a hazardous condition.

9.4.3* Control Systems Incorporating Software- and Firmware-Based Controllers.

9.4.3.1 Software Modification. Programmable electronic systems shall be designed and constructed so that the ability to modify the application program shall be limited to authorized personnel and shall require special equipment or other means to access the program (e.g., access code, key-operated switch).

Exception: The manufacturer or supplier shall be permitted to retain the right not to allow the user to alter the program.

9.4.3.2 Memory Retention and Protection.

9.4.3.2.1 Means shall be provided to prevent memory alteration by unauthorized persons.

9.4.3.2.2 Loss of memory shall not result in a hazardous condition.

9.4.3.2.3 Power supplies for electronic equipment requiring memory retention shall have battery backup of sufficient capacity to prevent memory loss for a period of at least 72 hours.

9.4.3.3 Software Verification. Equipment using reprogrammable logic shall have means for verifying that the software is in accordance with the relevant program documentation.

9.4.3.4* Use in Safety Circuits.

Δ **9.4.3.4.1** Software- and firmware-based controllers used in safety-circuits shall be listed for such use.

Δ **9.4.3.4.2** Safety circuits incorporating software- and firmware-based controllers shall be self-monitoring and conform to all of the following:

(1) In the event of any single failure, the failure shall be as follows:

    (a) Not lead to the loss of the safety-related function(s)
    (b) Lead to the shutdown of the system in a safe state
    (c) Prevent subsequent operation until the component failure has been corrected
    (d) Prevent unintended startup of equipment upon correction of the failure

(2) The safety circuit shall provide protection equivalent to that of control systems incorporating hardwired/hardware components.

(3) The safety circuit shall be designed in conformance with an approved standard that provides requirements for such systems.

Chapter 10 Operator Interface and Control Devices

10.1 General.

10.1.1* Applicability. This chapter shall contain the requirements for devices mounted outside or partially outside control enclosures.

10.1.2 Location and Mounting.

10.1.2.1 Control Devices. As far as is practicable, control devices shall be as follows:

(1) Readily accessible for service and maintenance
(2) Mounted in such a manner as to minimize the possibility of damage from activities such as material handling

10.1.2.2 Hand-Operated Control Devices. The actuators of hand-operated control devices shall be selected and installed as follows:

(1) They are not less than 0.6 m (2 ft) above the servicing level and are accessible from the normal working position of the operator.
(2) The operator is not placed in a hazardous situation when operating them.
(3) The possibility of inadvertent operation is minimized.

10.1.2.3 Machine-Mounted Control Equipment.

10.1.2.3.1 Control equipment (e.g., limit switches, brakes, solenoids, position sensors) shall be mounted rigidly in a reasonably dry and clean location, unless designed for a specific environment, shall be protected from physical damage, and shall be free from the possibility of accidental operation by normal machine movements or by the operator.

Exception No. 1: A solenoid sealed in an individual oil-filled container shall be permitted.

Exception No. 2: Prewired devices (e.g., limit switches, proximity switches) provided with an identified cable need not be equipped with provisions for termination of conduit.

10.1.2.3.2 All limit switches or position sensors shall be installed so that accidental overtravel by the machine will not damage the limit switch or sensor.

10.1.2.3.3 Solenoids for operating devices shall be mounted so that liquids drain away from the electrical component enclosure.

10.1.3* Protection. Operator interface, control devices, and enclosures shall be suitable for the environment and shall withstand the stresses of expected use.

10.1.4 Position Sensors.

10.1.4.1 Position sensors (e.g., limit switches, position switches, proximity switches) shall be arranged so that they will not be damaged in the event of overtravel.

Δ **10.1.4.2*** Position sensors used in safety circuits shall either have direct opening operation or provide similar reliability.

10.1.5 Portable and Pendant Control Stations.

10.1.5.1 Portable and pendant operator control stations and their control devices shall be selected and arranged to minimize the possibility of inadvertent machine operations.

10.1.5.2 Pendant control stations that are vertically suspended from overhead shall comply with 13.4.2.4 or 13.5.10.

10.1.6 Operator Interface Devices.

10.1.6.1 Location of Operator Interface Devices.

10.1.6.1.1 Operator interface devices shall be mounted in locations that will minimize exposure to oil, coolant, and other contaminants.

10.1.6.1.2 Operator interface devices shall be within normal reach of the machine operator and shall be placed so that the operator is not exposed to hazards.

10.1.6.1.3 Operator interface devices shall be located so that unintentional operation by normal movement of the machine, operator, or work will be unlikely.

10.1.6.2 Arrangement of Operator Interface Devices. All start pushbuttons shall be mounted above or to the left of their associated stop pushbuttons.

Exception No. 1: This requirement shall not apply to start pushbuttons in series, such as operating pushbuttons on punch presses.

Exception No. 2: This requirement shall not apply to emergency stop devices.

10.1.7 Foot-Operated Switches. Foot-operated switches used for applications where accidental actuation could create a hazardous situation shall be protected to prevent accidental actuation by falling or moving objects and from unintended operation by accidental stepping onto the switch.

Exception: Foot-operated switches used for emergency stop in accordance with 10.7.2.1 shall not be of the covered or hooded type.

N **Table 10.3.3 Machine Indicator Lights and Icons**

Color	Meaning	Explanation	Action by Operator
RED	Emergency	Hazardous condition	Immediate action to deal with hazardous condition (for example, switching off the machine supply, being alert to the hazardous condition, and staying clear of the machine)
YELLOW	Abnormal	Abnormal condition Impending critical condition	Monitoring and/or intervention (for example, by re-establishing the intended function)
BLUE	Mandatory	Indication of a condition that requires action by the operator	Mandatory action
GREEN	Normal	Normal condition	Optional
WHITE	Neutral	Other conditions; can be used whenever doubt exists about the application of RED, YELLOW, GREEN, BLUE	Monitoring

10.2 Pushbutton Actuators and Color Graphic Interface Devices.

10.2.1 Pushbutton Actuators. Pushbutton actuators used to initiate a stop function shall be of the extended operator or mushroom-head type.

10.2.2 Colors. Pushbutton actuators and action initiating icons of color graphic interface devices shall be color-coded in accordance with 10.2.2.1 through 10.2.2.6.

10.2.2.1 Start or On. The preferred color of start or on shall be GREEN, except that BLACK, WHITE, or GRAY shall be permitted. RED shall not be used for start or on.

10.2.2.2 Stop or Off. The preferred color of stop or off shall be RED, except that BLACK, WHITE, or GRAY shall be permitted. GREEN shall not be used for stop or off.

Exception: Stop function operators of the wobble-stick or rod-operated types in the bottom of a pendant station need not be colored RED.

10.2.2.3 Emergency Stop. RED shall be used for emergency stop actuators in accordance with 10.7.3.

10.2.2.4 Alternate Action. Pushbuttons that, when pressed, act alternately as start and stop or on and off shall be BLACK, WHITE, or GRAY. RED, YELLOW, or GREEN shall not be used.

10.2.2.5 Abnormal Conditions. The color YELLOW shall be used for actuators used to respond to abnormal conditions.

10.2.2.6 Hold to Operate. Pushbuttons that cause movement when pressed and stop movement when they are released (e.g., jogging) shall be BLACK, WHITE, GRAY, or BLUE, with a preference for BLACK.

10.2.2.7 Reset. Reset pushbuttons shall be BLUE, BLACK, WHITE, or GRAY except when they also act as a stop or off button, in which case they shall be RED.

10.2.3 Legends.

10.2.3.1 A legend or symbol shall be provided for each operator interface device to identify its function and shall be located so that it can be easily read by the machine operator from the normal operator position. Legends and symbols shall be marked in accordance with Section 16.3.

Exception: Emergency stop devices require no legend or symbol if they meet the requirements of 10.7.3.

10.2.3.2 For illuminated pushbuttons, the function(s) of the light is separated from the function(s) of the button by a virgule (/).

10.3 Indicator Lights and Icons of Color Graphic Interface Devices.

10.3.1 Modes of Use. Indicator lights and icons of color graphic interface devices shall provide the following information:

(1) Indication to attract the operator's attention or to indicate that a certain task should be performed. The colors RED, YELLOW (AMBER), GREEN, and BLUE are normally used in this mode.

(2) Confirmation of a command or a condition, or the termination of a change or transition period. The colors BLUE and WHITE are normally used in this mode. GREEN shall be permitted to be used in some cases.

10.3.2 Indicator Light Circuits for Warning or Danger. Indicator light circuits used for warning or danger lights shall be fitted with facilities to check the operability of these lights.

10.3.3* Colors. Indicator lights and icons of color graphic interface devices shall be color-coded with respect to the condition (status) of the machine in accordance with Table 10.3.3. Alternative purposes shall be permitted to indicate machine or process status.

Shaded text = Revisions.   Δ = Text deletions and figure/table revisions.   • = Section deletions.   *N* = New material.

2021 Edition

10.3.4* Flashing Lights. Flashing lights shall be permitted to be used for any of the following purposes:

(1) Attract attention
(2) Request immediate action
(3) Indicate a discrepancy between the command and actual states
(4) Indicate a change in process (flashing during transition)

10.4 Illuminated Pushbuttons. Illuminated pushbutton actuators shall be color-coded in accordance with Section 10.2. The color RED for the emergency stop actuator shall not depend on the illumination source.

10.5 Rotary Control Devices. Devices having a rotational member, such as potentiometers and selector switches, shall be mounted in such a way as to prevent rotation of the stationary member. Friction alone shall not be relied upon to prevent rotation.

10.6 Start Devices. Actuators used to initiate a start function or the movement of machine elements (e.g., slides, spindles, carriers) shall be constructed and mounted to minimize inadvertent operation. Mushroom-head type actuators for two-hand control initiation shall conform to 9.2.5.6.

10.7 Devices for Stop and Emergency Stop.

10.7.1 Location and Operation.

10.7.1.1 Stop and emergency stop pushbuttons shall be continuously operable and readily accessible.

10.7.1.2 Stop or emergency stop pushbuttons shall be located at each operator control station. Emergency stop pushbuttons shall also be located at other locations where emergency stop is required.

10.7.2 Types.

10.7.2.1 The types of devices for emergency stop shall include, but are not limited to, the following:

(1) Pushbutton-operated switches in accordance with 10.7.2.2 and 10.7.3
(2) Pull-cord–operated switches
(3) Foot-operated switches without a mechanical guard
(4) Push-bar–operated switches
(5) Rod-operated switches

10.7.2.2* Pushbutton-type devices for emergency stop shall be of the self-latching type and shall have direct opening operation.

N **10.7.2.3** The devices for emergency stop described in 10.7.2.1shall be listed as emergency stop devices.

10.7.2.4 Emergency stop switches shall not be flat switches or graphic representations based on software applications.

10.7.3 Emergency Stop Actuators. Actuators of emergency stop devices shall be colored RED. The background immediately around pushbuttons and disconnect switch actuators used as emergency stop devices shall be colored YELLOW. The actuator of a pushbutton-operated device shall be of the palm or mushroom-head type and shall effect an emergency stop when depressed. The RED/YELLOW color combination shall be reserved exclusively for emergency stop applications.

Exception: The RED/YELLOW color combination shall be permitted for emergency stop actuators in accordance with 10.8.4.

10.7.4 Local Operation of the Supply Disconnecting Means to Effect Emergency Stop.

10.7.4.1 The supply disconnecting means shall be permitted to be locally operated to serve the function of emergency stop as follows:

(1) Where it is readily accessible to the operator
(2) Where it is of the type described in 5.1.10(1) through 5.1.10(5)

10.7.4.2 Where used as an emergency stop, the supply disconnecting means shall meet the color requirements of 10.7.3.

10.7.4.3 Disconnecting (isolating) electrical devices as described in 5.2.2, where accessible to the operator, shall also be permitted to serve the function of emergency stop.

10.8 Devices for Emergency Switching Off.

10.8.1 Location. Emergency switching off devices as described in 9.2.5.4.2 shall be located as necessary for the given application.

10.8.2 Types.

10.8.2.1* The types of devices that initiate an emergency switching off operation shall be permitted to include, but are not limited to, the following:

(1) Pushbutton-operated switches
(2) Pull-cord–operated switches

10.8.2.2 The pushbutton-operated switch shall be permitted in a break-glass enclosure.

10.8.2.3 Emergency switching off devices shall not be flat switches or graphic representations based on software applications.

10.8.3 Restoration of Normal Function After Emergency Switching Off. It shall not be possible to restore an emergency switching off circuit until the emergency switching off circuit has been manually reset.

10.8.4 Actuators.

10.8.4.1 Actuators of emergency switching off devices shall be colored RED. The background immediately around the device actuator shall be permitted to be colored YELLOW.

10.8.4.2* Where the emergency switching off initiating device is separate from the emergency stop device, the emergency switching off initiating device shall be functionally identified.

10.8.5 Local Operation of the Supply Disconnecting Means to Effect Emergency Switching Off. Where the supply disconnecting means is to be locally operated for emergency switching off, it shall be readily accessible and shall meet the color requirements of 10.8.4.1.

10.9* Displays. Displays (e.g., visual display units, alarm annunciators, indicator lights, and the action-initiating icons of graphic interface devices) shall be selected and installed in such a manner as to be visible from the normal position of the operator.

Chapter 11 Control Equipment: Location, Mounting, and Enclosures

11.1 General Requirements.

11.1.1 All control equipment shall be located and mounted so as to facilitate the following:

(1) Accessibility and maintenance of the equipment
(2) Protection against the external influences or conditions under which the equipment is intended to operate
(3) Operation and maintenance of the machine and its associated equipment

11.1.2 Minimum control enclosure construction shall comply with UL 508, UL 508A, UL 50, or NEMA 250 for metallic and nonmetallic enclosures.

11.1.3 The depth of the enclosure or compartment, including doors or covers, shall not be less than the maximum depth of the enclosed equipment plus the required electrical clearances.

11.1.4 Any door(s) that permits access to live parts operating at 50 volts ac (rms value) or 60 volts dc or more shall comply with 6.2.3.2 or 6.2.3.1.

11.2 Location and Mounting.

11.2.1 Accessibility and Maintenance.

11.2.1.1 All items of control equipment shall be placed and oriented so that they can be identified without moving them or the wiring.

11.2.1.1.1 Where practicable, with items that require checking or adjustment for correct operation or that are liable to need replacement, those actions shall be possible without dismantling other equipment or parts of the machine (except opening doors or removing covers).

11.2.1.1.2 Terminals not associated with control equipment shall also conform to these requirements.

11.2.1.1.3 The requirements in 11.2.1.1, 11.2.1.1.1, and 11.2.1.1.2 shall not apply to modules or subassemblies that are disposable, permanently sealed, or unable to be opened.

11.2.1.2 Terminal blocks shall be mounted to provide unobstructed access to the terminals and their conductors.

11.2.1.3 Exposed, nonarcing, bare, live parts operating at 50 volts ac (rms value) or 60 volts dc or more within an enclosure or compartment shall have an air space of not less than 13 mm (½ in.) between them and the uninsulated walls of the enclosure or compartment, including conduit fittings. The air space for uninsulated doors of the enclosure shall be not less than 25 mm (1 in.). Where barriers between metal enclosures or compartments and arcing parts are required, they shall be of flame-retardant, noncarbonizing insulating materials.

11.2.1.4* All control equipment shall be mounted so as to facilitate its operation and maintenance. Where a special tool is necessary to remove a device, the tool shall be supplied.

11.2.1.5 Threaded fasteners with machine threads shall be used to attach components to a subplate and shall provide sufficient thread engagement to maintain secure mounting.

11.2.1.5.1 Steel subplate thickness shall provide engagement of at least 2 full threads.

Exception: A screw with 32 threads per 25.4 mm (32 threads per in.) shall be permitted into a 1.35 mm (0.053 in.) thick steel subplate.

11.2.1.5.2 Aluminum subplate thickness shall provide engagement of at least 3 full threads.

11.2.1.5.3 Thread cutting or thread forming screws shall be permitted if the thread engagement requirements of 11.2.1.5.1 and 11.2.1.5.2 are met.

11.2.1.5.4 Sheet metal screws, rivets, welds, solders, or bonding materials shall not be used to mount components to a subplate.

Exception: Rivets shall be permitted to be used for attaching mounting rails and wiring channels, provided the exposed surface is smooth and free from any portion of a protruding stud.

11.2.1.6 Swing frames or swing-out panels shall be permitted, provided the swing is more than 110 degrees. Wiring shall not inhibit swing. Panel-mounted components behind swing frames shall be accessible when open.

11.2.1.7* Where control devices are connected through plug-in arrangements, their association shall be made clear by type (shape), marking, or reference designation, singly or in combination.

11.2.1.8 Attachment plugs and receptacles that are handled during normal operation shall be located and mounted so as to provide unobstructed access.

11.2.1.9 Test points, where provided, shall be mounted to provide unobstructed access, plainly marked to correspond with markings on the drawings, adequately insulated, and sufficiently spaced for connection of test leads.

11.2.1.10 Busbars shall be securely fastened in place. The minimum spacing between uninsulated parts of busbars, busbar terminals, and other bare metal parts for busbars in feeder circuits shall not be less than specified in Table 430.97(D) of *NFPA 70*.

11.2.2 Physical Separation or Grouping.

11.2.2.1 Machine compartments containing control equipment shall be completely isolated from coolant and oil reservoirs.

11.2.2.1.1 Compartments containing equipment required to be readily accessible, such as branch circuit overcurrent devices, shall be readily accessible and completely enclosed.

11.2.2.1.2 The compartment shall not be considered enclosed where it is open to the floor, to the foundation upon which the machine rests, or to other compartments of the machine that are not clean and dry.

11.2.2.2 Pipelines, tubing, or devices (e.g., solenoid valves) for handling air, gases, or liquids shall not be located in enclosures or compartments containing electrical control equipment.

Exception No. 1: Equipment for cooling electronic devices

Exception No. 2: Pipelines, tubings, or devices that are an integral part of listed equipment and are separated by suitable barriers

11.2.2.3 Control devices mounted within the control enclosure and connected to the supply voltage, or to both supply and control voltages, shall be grouped separately from those connected only to the control voltages.

11.2.2.4 Terminals shall be separated into groups for power circuits, associated control circuits, and other control circuits, fed from external sources (e.g., for interlocking).

11.2.2.5 Terminal groups for power circuits, associated control circuits, and other control circuits shall be permitted to be mounted adjacently, provided that each group is readily identified (e.g., by markings, by use of different sizes, by use of barriers, by colors).

11.2.3 Heating Effects. Heat-generating components (e.g., heat sinks, power resistors) shall be located so that the temperature of each component in the vicinity remains within the component manufacturer's specified limits.

11.3 Degrees of Protection.

11.3.1* The protection of control equipment against ingress of solid foreign objects and of liquids shall be adequate, taking into account the external influences under which the machine is intended to operate (i.e., the location and the physical environmental conditions, including dust, coolants, and swarf).

11.3.2 Enclosures of control equipment shall provide the degree of protection required for the environment. A minimum degree of protection of at least Type 1 is required.

Exception: Where removable collectors on collector wire or collector bar systems are used and Type 1 enclosures are not practicable, suitable protection shall be provided (e.g., elevation, guarding).

11.4 Enclosures, Doors, and Openings.

11.4.1 Enclosures shall be constructed and finished using materials capable of withstanding the mechanical, electrical, and thermal stresses, as well as the effects of humidity and corrosion, that are likely to be encountered in normal service.

11.4.2 Where corrosion protection beyond normal requirements is needed, nonmetallic enclosures identified for the purposes shall be permitted if they meet the requirements of UL 50 and UL 50E.

11.4.3 Subplates having a surface area of more than 1.5484 m^2 (2400 in.^2) shall have supports provided in addition to the panel mounting means to aid in subplate installation.

11.4.4 Enclosures and subplates shall be free of burrs and sharp edges.

11.4.5 Inherently corrosion-resistant surfaces of the enclosure interior, exterior, and subplates shall not be painted unless the paint process is suitable for the adhesion of the paint to the surface material.

11.4.6 Fasteners used to secure doors shall be of the captive type.

11.4.7 Door fasteners on enclosures and compartments with door openings shall comply with UL 50, UL 508, UL 508A, or NEMA 250.

11.4.8 A print pocket sized to accommodate physical electrical diagrams or software media shall be attached to the inside or outside of the door of the control enclosure or compartment.

11.4.8.1 It shall be permissible to place a pocket that is suitable for the environment outside the door of the control enclosure or compartment in a well-identified location.

11.4.8.2 Single-door and multi-door enclosures shall have at least one print pocket.

11.4.9 The joints or gaskets of doors, lids, covers, externally mounted accessories, interconnect panels, and enclosures shall withstand the deleterious effects of liquids, vapors, or gases used on the machine. The means used to maintain the enclosure's degree of protection on doors, lids, and covers that require opening or removal for operation or maintenance shall be securely attached to either the door/cover or the enclosure and not deteriorate due to removal or replacement of the door or the cover, which would impair the degree of protection.

11.4.10 All openings in the enclosure, including those toward the floor or foundation or to other parts of the machine, shall be closed by the supplier(s) in a manner ensuring the protection specified for the equipment. Openings for cable entries shall be easily reopened on site. A suitable opening shall be permitted in the base of enclosures within the machine so that moisture due to condensation is allowed to drain.

11.4.11 Openings shall not be permitted between enclosures containing electrical equipment and compartments containing coolant, lubricating fluids, or hydraulic fluids, or compartments into which oil, other liquids, or dust can penetrate. This requirement shall not apply to electrical devices specifically designed to operate in oil (e.g., electromagnetic clutches) or to electrical equipment in which coolants are used.

11.4.12 Where there are holes in an enclosure for mounting purposes, after mounting, the holes shall not impair the required protection.

11.4.13 Equipment that, in normal or abnormal operation, attains a surface temperature sufficient to cause a risk of fire or harmful effect to an enclosure material shall be one of the following:

(1) Located within an enclosure that will withstand, without risk of fire or harmful effect, such temperatures as can be generated

(2) Mounted and located at a sufficient distance from adjacent equipment so as to allow dissipation of heat without creating a hazard *(see also 11.2.3)*

(3) Otherwise screened by material that can withstand, without risk of fire or harmful effect, the heat emitted by the equipment

11.5* Spaces Around Control Cabinets and Compartments. Access and working space for control cabinets and compartments operating at 1000 volts, nominal, or less to ground and likely to require examination, adjustment, servicing, or maintenance while energized shall comply with the provisions of Chapter 11. Sufficient access and working space shall be provided and maintained around all control cabinets and compartments to permit ready and safe operation and maintenance of such control cabinets and compartments. Working space for cabinets and compartments that contain supply conductors to industrial machinery that are covered by Article 670 of *NFPA 70* shall be in accordance with the *NEC.*

11.5.1 Working Space.

11.5.1.1 The depth of the working space in the direction of access to live parts shall not be less than indicated in Table

11.5.1.1. Distances shall be measured from the control cabinet or compartment front or opening.

Exception No. 1: Working space shall not be required in back or sides of control cabinets or compartments, where there are no renewable or adjustable parts on the back or sides and where all connections are accessible from locations other than the back or sides. Where rear access is required to work on de-energized parts on the back of enclosed control cabinet and compartment, a minimum working space of 762 mm (2½ ft) horizontally shall be provided.

Exception No. 2: By special permission, working space clearance depth of 762 mm (2½ ft) or less shall be permitted where all uninsulated parts are at a voltage no greater than 50 volts rms ac or 60 volts dc.

Exception No. 3: Condition 2 working clearance depth shall be permitted between control cabinets or compartments located across the aisle from each other or across from non-machinery-associated switchgear, panelboards, or motor control centers where conditions of maintenance and supervision ensure that written procedures have been adopted to prohibit the affected equipment doors on both sides of the aisle from being open at the same time and qualified persons who are authorized will service the installation.

Exception No. 4: Condition 1 working clearance depth shall be permitted between control cabinets or compartments located across the aisle from each other, or across from a grounded surface, where all associated control cabinet or compartment devices and equipment operating at greater than 50 volts rms ac or 60 volts dc are separately enclosed, guarded, or constructed so that openings to live parts of the devices and equipment will not permit the entry of a 12.5 mm (0.5 in.) diameter rod.

Exception No. 5: By special permission, the minimum working space clearance depth of 762 mm (2½ ft) shall be permitted where all of the following conditions are met:

(1) The control cabinet or compartment is operating at not over 150 volts line-to-line or line-to-ground.
(2) The conditions of maintenance and supervision ensure that only qualified persons will service the installation.
(3) The control cabinet and compartment require a tool to open.
(4) Where only diagnostic troubleshooting and testing on live parts are involved.
(5) The door(s) of the control cabinet and compartment open at least 90 degrees or are removable.

11.5.1.2 The width of the working space in front of control cabinets and compartments shall be the width of the opening or 762 mm (30 in.), whichever is greater. Where control equipment or devices are mounted on or through the fixed area around the opening into the control cabinet or compartment, the width of the working space in front of the control cabinet or compartment shall include the width of the fixed area containing the control equipment and devices.

11.5.1.3 The working space height shall be clear and extend from the grade, floor, or platform to a height of 2.0 m (6½ ft). Within the height requirements of Section 11.5, other equipment associated with the machine located above or below the control cabinet or compartment shall be permitted to extend not more than 150 mm (6 in.) beyond the front of the electrical control cabinet or compartment.

11.5.1.4 The working space shall permit at least 90-degree opening of control cabinet and compartment doors or hinged panels.

Table 11.5.1.1 Working Space Depth

Nominal Voltage to Ground	Minimum Clear Distance		
	Condition 1	**Condition 2**	**Condition 3**
0–150	900 mm (3 ft)	900 mm (3 ft)	900 mm (3 ft)
151–600	900 mm (3 ft)	1.0 m (3½ ft)	1.2 m (4 ft)
601–1000	900 mm (3 ft)	1.2 m (4 ft)	1.5 m (5 ft)

Note: Where the conditions are as follows:
Condition 1 — Exposed live parts on one side and no live or grounded parts on the other side of the working space, or exposed live parts on both sides effectively guarded by insulating materials. Insulated wire or insulated busbars operating at not over 300 volts to ground shall not be considered live parts.
Condition 2 — Exposed live parts on one side and a grounded surface on the other side. Concrete, brick, or tile walls shall be considered as grounded.
Condition 3 — Exposed live parts on both sides of the working space (not guarded as provided in Condition 1) with the operator between.

11.5.2 Access. At least one entrance of sufficient area shall be provided to give access to the working space around control cabinets or compartments.

11.5.2.1 Working space required by Section 11.5 shall not be used for storage.

11.5.2.2 When enclosed live parts are exposed for inspection or servicing, the working space, if in a passageway or general open space, shall be suitably guarded.

11.5.3 Doors in gangways and for access to electrical operating areas shall be at least 0.7 m (2 ft 4 in.) wide and 2.0 m (6½ ft) high, open outward, and have a means (e.g., panic bolts or panic bars) to allow opening from the inside without the use of a key or tool.

Chapter 12 Conductors, Cables, and Flexible Cords

Δ **12.1 General Requirements.**

12.1.1* General. Conductors, cables, and flexible cords shall be selected for the operating conditions and external influences that can exist. Conductors, cables, and flexible cords shall be identified for their intended use.

12.1.2 Conductor Insulation. Conductors shall be insulated.

Exception No. 1: Busbars shall not be required to be insulated.

Exception No. 2: Bare conductors, such as capacitor or resistor leads and jumpers between terminals, shall be permitted where the method of securing provides electrical clearance.

Exception No. 3: Equipment grounding conductors and bonding jumpers shall be permitted to be covered or bare.

12.1.3 Type MI Cable. Mineral-insulated, metal-sheathed cable, Type MI, shall be permitted. Temperature range shall be 85°C (185°F) for dry and wet locations.

Δ **Table 12.2.2 Single Conductor Characteristics**

Conductor Size (AWG or kcmil)	Cross-Sectional Area, Nominal (cm/mm²)	DC Resistance at 25°C (77°F) (ohms/1000 ft)	Minimum Number of Strands		
			Nonflexing (ASTM Class)	Flexing (ASTM Class)	Constant Flex (ASTM Class/AWG Size)
22 AWG	640/0.324	17.2	7(')	7(')	19(M/34)
20	1020/0.519	10.7	10(K)	10(K)	26(M/34)
18	1620/0.823	6.77	16(K)	16(K)	41(M/34)
16	2580/1.31	4.26	19(C)	26(K)	65(M/34)
14	4110/2.08	2.68	19(C)	41(K)	41(K/30)
12	6530/3.31	1.68	19(C)	65(K)	65(K/30)
10	10380/5.261	1.060	19(C)	104(K)	104(K/30)
8	16510/8.367	0.6663	19(C)	(\)	(−)
6	26240/13.30	0.4192	19(C)	(\)	(−)
4	41740/21.15	0.2636	19(C)	(\)	(−)
3	52620/26.67	0.2091	19(C)	(\)	(−)
2	66360/33.62	0.1659	19(C)	(\)	(−)
1	83690/42.41	0.1315	19(B)	(\)	(−)
1/0	105600/53.49	0.1042	19(B)	(\)	(−)
2/0	133100/67.43	0.08267	19(B)	(\)	(−)
3/0	167800/85.01	0.06658	19(B)	(\)	(−)
4/0	211600/107.2	0.05200	19(B)	(\)	(−)
250 kcmil	−/127	0.04401	37(B)	(\)	(−)
300	−/152	0.03667	37(B)	(\)	(−)
350	−/177	0.03144	37(B)	(\)	(−)
400	−/203	0.02751	37(B)	(\)	(−)
450	−/228	0.02445	37(B)	(\)	(−)
500	−/253	0.02200	37(B)	(\)	(−)
550	−/279	0.02000	61(B)	(\)	(−)
600	−/304	0.01834	61(B)	(\)	(−)
650	−/329	0.01692	61(B)	(\)	(−)
700	−/355	0.01572	61(B)	(\)	(−)
750	−/380	0.01467	61(B)	(\)	(−)
800	−/405	0.01375	61(B)	(\)	(−)
900	−/456	0.01222	61(B)	(\)	(−)
1000	−/507	0.01101	61(B)	(\)	(−)

Notes:
(B), (C), (K): ASTM Class designation B and C per ASTM B8; Class designation K per ASTM B174.
('): A class designation has not been assigned to this conductor, but it is designated as 22-7 AWG in ASTM B286 and is composed of strands 10 mils in diameter (30 AWG).
(\): Nonflexing construction shall be permitted for flexing service per the ASTM Class designation B174, Table 3.
(−): Constant flexing cables are not constructed in these sizes.

12.1.4 Conductor/Terminal Compatibility. The conductor(s) shall be compatible with the device terminal(s), and the conductor size(s) shall not exceed the range recommended by the device manufacturer.

12.2 Conductors.

12.2.1 Conductor Material. Conductors shall be copper.

Exception: Aluminum alloy busbars, located internal to the enclosure, shall be permitted where suitable for the application.

12.2.2* Stranded Conductors. Conductors 22 through 4/0 AWG and 250 through 1000 kcmil shall be only of stranded soft-annealed copper. Requirements for conductor cross-sectional area, dc resistance, and stranding shall be in accordance with Table 12.2.2.

Exception: Conductors with stranding other than that specified in Table 12.2.2 shall be permitted on individual devices that are purchased completely wired (e.g., motor starters).

12.2.3 Constant Flexing. Where constant flexing service is required, conductor stranding shall conform to Table 12.2.2.

12.2.4 Solid Conductors. Solid conductors 24 to 30 AWG of soft-annealed copper shall be permitted for use within control enclosures where not subject to flexing.

12.2.5 Printed Wire Assemblies. Printed wire assemblies of flame-retardant material shall be permitted in place of conductor assemblies, provided they are within control enclosures and are mounted in such a way as to minimize flexing or stress.

12.2.6 Shielded Conductors. Where shielding is used around conductors in single or multiconductor cables, a foil shield shall be permitted for nonflexing applications. A continuous drain wire shall be provided for foil shield types. A braided shield shall be used where subject to longitudinal flexing. Torsional flexing applications (e.g., a robot arm) shall require shields designed specifically for their use. The shields and drain wire shall be covered with an outer jacket that is suitable for the environment. In all cases the shield shall provide a continuous conduction surface in the presence of bending and flexing.

12.3 Insulation.

12.3.1 The insulation and the finished conductors and cables shall have flame-retardant properties and temperature limits and characteristics as follows:

(1) MTW — Moisture-, Heat-, and Oil-Resistant Thermoplastic 60°C (140°F) Wet Locations 90°C (194°F) Dry Locations
(2) THHN — Heat-Resistant Thermoplastic 90°C (194°F) Dry Locations
(3) THW — Moisture- and Heat-Resistant Thermoplastic 75°C (167°F) Dry and Wet Locations
(4) THWN — Moisture- and Heat-Resistant Thermoplastic 75°C (167°F) Dry and Wet Locations
(5) RHH — Thermoset 90°C (194°F) Dry Locations
(6) RHW — Moisture-Resistant Thermoset 75°C (167°F) Dry and Wet Locations
(7) RHW-2 — Moisture-Resistant Thermoset 90°C (194°F) Dry and Wet Locations
(8) XHHW — Moisture-Resistant Thermoset 75°C (167°F) Wet Locations 90°C (194°F) Dry Locations
(9) XHHW-2 — Moisture-Resistant Thermoset 90°C (194°F) Dry and Wet Locations

12.3.2 The average and the minimum thickness of the insulation in constructions A and B shall be in accordance with Table 12.3.2.

Δ **Table 12.3.2 Thickness of Single Conductor Insulation (mils)**

Conductor Size (AWG or kcmil)	Construction A* Average/ Minimum	Construction B† Average/ Minimum (Jacket)
22 AWG	30/27	15/13(4)
20	30/27	15/13(4)
18	30/27	15/13(4)
16	30/27	15/13(4)
14	30/27	15/13(4)
12	30/27	15/13(4)
10	30/27	20/18(4)
8	45/40	30/27(5)
6	60/54	30/27(5)
4–2	60/54	40/36(6)
1–4/0	80/72	50/45(7)
250–500 kcmil	95/86	60/54(8)
550–1000	110/99	70/63(9)

*A: No outer covering.
†B: Nylon covering.
Source: UL 1063, Table 1.1, *NEC* Construction.

12.3.3 Construction B shall have a nylon jacket applied directly over the insulation. The jacket shall be snug on the insulation and shall be at least as thick as indicated in Table 12.3.2.

12.4 Conductor Markings.

12.4.1 A durable legend printed on the outer surface of the insulation of construction A, on the outer surface of the nylon jacket of construction B, on the outer surface of the insulation under the jacket of construction B (only if readable through the nylon), or on the outer surface of the jacket of a multiconductor cable shall be repeated at intervals of no more than 610 mm (24 in.) throughout the length of the single-conductor or the multiconductor cable.

Exception: Sizes smaller than 16 AWG shall be permitted to be marked on the reel or on the smallest unit of the shipping carton.

12.4.2* The legend shall include the manufacturer's name or trademark, insulated conductor type, voltage rating (where permitted by *NFPA 70*), and gauge or size.

12.4.3 Where the conductor is 16 through 10 AWG and the stranding is intended for flexing service, the legend shall include "flexing" or "Class K."

12.4.4 Conductor insulation shall be identified and adequate for the voltage on that conductor.

12.5 Conductor Ampacity.

12.5.1 The ampacities of conductors shall not exceed the corresponding temperature values given in Table 12.5.1 before any correction factors for ambient temperature or adjustment factors for the number of current-carrying conductors have been applied.

12.5.2* Conductors with higher insulation temperatures than specified for the termination(s) shall be permitted to be used for ampacity adjustment, correction, or both, provided the final ampacity does not exceed the lowest value of any termination.

Exception: Ampacities of 90°C (194°F) insulated conductors or other special purpose conductors with higher temperature ratings can be determined in accordance with 310.15 of NFPA 70.

12.5.3 Motor circuit conductors supplying a single motor shall have an ampacity not less than 125 percent of the motor full-load current rating.

12.5.4 Combined load conductors shall have an ampacity not less than 125 percent of the full-load current rating of all resistance heating loads plus 125 percent of the full-load current rating of the highest rated motor plus the sum of the full-load current ratings of all other connected motors and apparatus based on their duty cycle in operation at the same time.

Δ **Table 12.5.1 Conductor Ampacity Based on Copper Conductors with 60°C (140°F), 75°C (167°F), and 90°C (194°F) Insulation in an Ambient Temperature of 30°C (86°F)**

Conductor Size (AWG)	Ampacity		
	60°C (140°F)	75°C (167°F)	90°C (194°F)
30	—	0.5	0.5
28	—	0.8	0.8
26	—	1	1
24	2	2	2
22	3	3	3
20	5	5	5
18	7	7	14
16	10	10	18
14	15	20	25
12	20	25	30
10	30	35	40
8	40	50	55
6	55	65	75
4	70	85	95
3	85	100	115
2	95	115	130
1	110	130	145
1/0	125	150	170
2/0	145	175	195
3/0	165	200	225
4/0	195	230	260
250	215	255	290
300	240	285	320
350	260	310	350
400	280	335	380
500	320	380	430
600	355	420	475
700	385	460	520
750	400	475	535
800	410	490	555
900	435	520	585
1000	455	545	615

Notes:
(1) Conductor types listed in 12.3.1 shall be permitted to be used at the ampacities listed in this table.
(2) The source for the ampacities in this table is Table 310.15(B)(16) of *NFPA 70*.

12.5.5 Where ampacity correction for ambient temperature correction for other than 30°C (86°F) or adjustment for more than three current-carrying conductors in a raceway or cable is required, the factor(s) shall be taken from Table 12.5.5(a) and Table 12.5.5(b). Sizing of conductors within control enclosures in wiring harnesses or wiring channels shall be based on the ampacity in cable or raceway. These factors shall apply to Class 1 control conductors, Article 725 of *NFPA 70* only if their continuous load exceeds 10 percent of the conductor ampacity.

Exception: The provisions of 376.22 of NFPA 70 shall be permitted to be applied for conductors in metallic wireways.

12.5.6 The maximum size of a conductor selected from Table 12.5.1 and connected to a motor controller shall not exceed the values given in Table 12.5.6.

Exception: Where other motor controllers are used, the maximum conductor size shall not exceed that specified by the manufacturer.

Table 12.5.5(a) Ambient Temperature Correction Factors

For ambient temperatures other than 30°C (86°F), multiply the allowable ampacity by the appropriate factor shown below.

Ambient Temperature (°C)	Correction Factor 60°C	Correction Factor 75°C	Correction Factor 90°C
21–25	1.08	1.05	1.04
26–30	1.00	1.00	1.00
31–35	0.91	0.94	0.96
36–40	0.82	0.88	0.91
41–45	0.71	0.82	0.87
46–50	0.58	0.75	0.82
51–55	0.41	0.67	0.76
56–60	—	0.58	0.71
61–70	—	0.33	0.58
71–80	—	—	0.41

Table 12.5.5(b) Adjustment Factors for More Than Three Current-Carrying Conductors in a Raceway or Cable

Number of Current-Carrying Conductors	Percent of Values in Table 12.5.5(a) as Adjusted for Ambient Temperature if Necessary
4–6	80
7–9	70
10–20	50
21–30	45
31–40	40
41 and above	35

Table 12.5.6 Maximum Conductor Size for Given Motor Controller Size

Motor Controller Size	Maximum Conductor Size (AWG or kcmil)
00	14 AWG
0	10
1	8
2	4
3	1/0
4	3/0
5	500 kcmil

Note: See NEMA ICS 2, Table 2, 110-1.

12.6 Conductor Sizing.

12.6.1 Conductors shall not be smaller than 14 AWG for power circuits unless otherwise permitted in 12.6.1.1, 12.6.1.2, or 12.6.1.3.

12.6.1.1 16 AWG shall be permitted if part of a jacketed multiconductor cable assembly or flexible cord, or individual conductors used in a cabinet or enclosure, under the following conditions:

(1) Non-motor power circuits of 8 amperes or less, provided all the following conditions are met:

 (a) Circuit is protected in accordance with Chapter 7.
 (b) Overcurrent protection does not exceed 10 amperes.
 (c) Overcurrent protection is provided by one of the following:
   i. A listed molded-case circuit breaker marked for use with 16 AWG wire
   ii. Listed fuses marked for use with 16 AWG wire
   iii. Class CC, Class J, Class CF, or Class T fuses

(2) Motor power circuits supplying a motor having a full-load current rating of 8 amperes or less, provided all the following conditions are met:

 (a) Circuit is protected in accordance with Chapter 7.
 (b) Circuit is provided with Class 10 overload protection.
 (c) Overcurrent protection is provided by one of the following:
   i. A listed molded-case circuit breaker marked for use with 16 AWG wire
   ii. Listed fuses marked for use with 16 AWG wire
   iii. Class CC, Class J, or Class CF fuses

(3) Motor power circuits supplying a motor having a full-load current rating of 5.5 amperes or less, provided all the following are met:

 (a) Circuit is protected in accordance with Chapter 7.
 (b) Circuit is provided with Class 20 overload protection.
 (c) Overcurrent protection is provided by one of the following:
   i. A listed molded-case circuit breaker marked for use with 16 AWG wire
   ii. Listed fuses marked for use with 16 AWG wire
   iii. Class CC, Class J, or Class CF fuses

12.6.1.2 18 AWG shall be permitted if part of a jacketed multiconductor cable assembly or flexible cord, or individual conductors used in a cabinet or enclosure, under the following conditions:

(1) Non-motor power circuits of 5.6 amperes or less, provided all the following conditions are met:

 (a) Circuit is protected in accordance with Chapter 7.
 (b) Overcurrent protection does not exceed 7 amperes.
 (c) Overcurrent protection is provided by one of the following:
   i. A listed molded-case circuit breaker marked for use with 18 AWG wire
   ii. Listed fuses marked for use with 18 AWG wire
   iii. Class CC, Class J, or Class CF, Class T fuses

(2) Motor power circuits supplying a motor having a full-load current rating of 5 amperes or less, provided all the following conditions are met:

 (a) Circuit is protected in accordance with Chapter 7.
 (b) Circuit is provided with Class 10 overload protection.
 (c) Overcurrent protection is provided by one of the following:
   i. A listed molded-case circuit breaker marked for use with 18 AWG wire
   ii. Listed fuses marked for use with 18 AWG wire
   iii. Class CC, Class J, or Class CF, Class T fuses

(3) Motor power circuits supplying a motor having a full-load current rating of 3.5 amperes or less, provided all the following are met:

 (a) Circuit is protected in accordance with Chapter 7.
 (b) Circuit is provided with Class 20 overload protection.
 (c) Overcurrent protection is provided by one of the following:
   i. A listed molded-case circuit breaker marked for use with 18 AWG wire
   ii. Listed fuses marked for use with 18 AWG wire
   iii. Class CC, Class J, or Class CF, Class T fuses

12.6.1.3* 16 AWG and 18 AWG shall be permitted for motor and non-motor power circuits where part of a listed power cable assembly identified as suitable for the intended use and provided with overcurrent protection in accordance with its ratings.

12.6.2 Conductors shall not be smaller than 16 AWG for lighting and control circuits conductors on the machine and in raceways or 18 AWG where part of a jacketed, multiconductor cable assembly.

12.6.3 Conductors shall not be smaller than 18 AWG for control circuits within control enclosures or operator stations.

12.6.4* Conductors for electronic control input/output and control devices shall not be smaller than permitted in 12.6.4.1 through 12.6.4.3.

12.6.4.1 Conductors installed in raceways shall not be smaller than 24 AWG.

Exception: 30 AWG or larger shall be permitted if part of a jacketed, multiconductor cable assembly or cord.

12.6.4.2 Conductors installed within control enclosures shall not be smaller than 26 AWG.

Exception: Conductors 30 AWG or larger shall be permitted for jumpers and special wiring applications.

12.6.4.3 Conductors that are part of a jacketed, multiconductor cable identified as suitable for the application and installed in accordance with Chapter 13 shall not be smaller than 30 AWG.

12.6.5 Shielded conductors shall consist of stranded, annealed copper of 25 AWG or larger for single conductors used in subassemblies and 22 AWG or larger for all other uses.

12.7 Conductors and Cables Used for Flexing Applications.

12.7.1 General.

12.7.1.1 Conductors and cables used for flexing applications shall be selected from Table 12.2.2.

Exception: Special cables and conductors identified as suitable for flexing applications shall be permitted.

12.7.1.2* Cables that are subjected to severe duties shall be constructed to protect against the following:

(1) Abrasion due to mechanical handling and dragging across rough surfaces
(2) Kinking due to operation without guides
(3) Stress resulting from guide rollers and forced guiding and being wound and rewound on cable drums

12.7.2 Mechanical Rating. The cable handling system of the machine shall be so designed to keep the tensile stress of the conductors as low as practicable during machine operations. The tensile stress shall not exceed manufacturer's specifications.

12.7.3* Current-Carrying Capacity of Cables Wound on Drums. Cables to be wound on drums *(see Table 12.7.3)* shall be selected with conductors of a cross-sectional area such that, when fully wound on and carrying the normal service load, the maximum allowable operating temperature is not exceeded.

12.8 Cords.

12.8.1 Cords shall be suitable for the intended use and be of the type listed in Table 12.8.2. Other cords of the types identified in *NFPA 70*, Table 400.4 that are part of a listed assembly and are suitable for the intended use shall be permitted.

Exception: Other cord types shall be permitted where part of a listed assembly or otherwise identified as suitable for the intended application.

12.8.2* Ampacity of Cords. The continuous current by cords shall not exceed the values given in Table 12.8.2.

12.8.3 Where ampacity adjustment is required for more than three current-carrying conductors, the factor(s) shall be taken from Table 12.5.5(b).

Table 12.8.2 Allowable Ampacity for Cords [Based on Ambient Temperature of 30°C (86°F)]

| Size (AWG) | Thermoset Types S, SJ, SJO, SJOW, SJOO, SJOOW, SO, SOW, SOO, SOOW | |
| | Thermoplastic Types SE, SEW, SEO, SEOW, SEOOW, SJE, SJEW, SJEO, SJEOW, SJEOOW, SJT, SJTW, SJTO, SJTOW, SJTOO, SJTOOW, STO, STW, STOW, STOO, STOOW | |
	A*	B†
18	7	10
17	—	12
16	10	13
14	15	18
12	20	25
10	25	30
8	35	40
6	45	55
4	60	70
2	80	95

*The allowable currents apply to 3-conductor cords and other multiconductor cords connected to utilization equipment so that only 3 conductors are current carrying.
†The allowable currents apply to 2-conductor cords and other multiconductor cords connected to utilization equipment so that only 2 conductors are current carrying.

Table 12.7.3 Derating Factors for Cables Wound on Drums

| Drum Type | Number of Layers of Cable | | | | |
	Any Number	1	2	3	4
Cylindrical ventilated	—	0.85	0.65	0.45	0.35
Radial ventilated	0.85	—	—	—	—
Radial nonventilated	0.75	—	—	—	—

Notes:
(1) A radial-type drum is one where spiral layers of cable are accommodated between closely spaced flanges; if fitted with solid flanges, the drum is described as nonventilated, and if the flanges have suitable apertures, as ventilated.
(2) A ventilated cylinder drum is one where the layers of cable are accommodated between widely spaced flanges and the drum and end flanges have suitable ventilating apertures.
(3) It is recommended that the use of derating factors be discussed with the cable and the cable drum manufacturers. This can result in other factors being used.

Shaded text = Revisions.   Δ = Text deletions and figure/table revisions.   • = Section deletions.   *N* = New material.

12.9* Special Cables and Conductors.

12.9.1 Other listed cables and conductors shall be permitted where identified as suitable for the intended use.

12.9.2 Appliance wiring material (AWM) shall be permitted under any of the following conditions:

(1) Where part of an assembly that has been identified for the intended use
(2) Where the AWM has been identified for use with approved equipment and is used in accordance with the equipment manufacturer's instructions
(3) Where its construction meets all applicable requirements of Section 12.2 through Section 12.6 with modifications as follows:

    (a) Stranded conductors with wire sizes smaller than those listed in 12.2.2 shall have a minimum of seven strands.
    (b) Conductor insulation and cable jacket materials not specified in 12.3.1 shall have flame-resistant properties in compliance with applicable standards for intended use such as FT2 (horizontal wire) flame test or VW-1 (vertical wire) flame test in accordance with UL 1581.
    (c) Minimum insulation thicknesses for single-conductor AWM shall be as specified in 12.3.2. Minimum insulation thickness for conductors that are part of a multiconductor jacketed AWM cable shall be as specified by the AWM style number and by the marked voltage rating of the cable.
    (d) AWM shall be marked in accordance with 12.4.1, 12.4.3, and 12.4.4. The legend shall include manufacturer's name or trademark, AWM style number, voltage rating (unless marking is prohibited by 12.4.2), wire gauge(s), temperature rating, and flame resistance. Additional markings for properties such as oil, water, UV, and chemical resistance identifiers shall be permitted where in compliance with applicable standards for intended use. Where markings alone are insufficient to identify for the intended application, suitable information shall be included with the machine technical documentation.

Chapter 13 Wiring Practices

13.1 Connections and Routing.

13.1.1 General Requirements.

13.1.1.1 All connections shall be secured against accidental loosening and shall ensure a thoroughly good connection. Thread-locking sealants, epoxies, glues, or other similar compounds shall not be used.

13.1.1.2 The means of connection shall be identified for the cross-sectional areas and the type of conductors being terminated.

13.1.1.3 Terminals for more than one conductor shall be so identified.

13.1.1.4 A power distribution block designed for multiple tap conductors (e.g., single or multiple conductors "in" and multiple conductors "out") shall be permitted for additional tap connections and circuit branching.

13.1.1.5 Soldered connections shall only be permitted where terminals are provided that are identified for soldering.

13.1.1.6 Terminals on terminal blocks shall be plainly identified to correspond with markings on the diagrams.

13.1.1.7 The installation of flexible conduits and cables shall be such that liquids drain away from the fittings. Where practicable, raceway connections shall enter the sides or bottom of an enclosure or box.

13.1.1.8 Means of retaining conductor strands shall be provided when terminating conductors at devices or terminals that are not equipped with this facility. Solder shall not be used for that purpose.

13.1.1.9 Shielded conductors shall be terminated so as to prevent fraying of strands and to permit easy disconnection.

13.1.1.10* Identification tags shall be readable, permanent, and identified for use in the physical environment.

13.1.1.11* Terminal blocks shall be mounted and wired so that the internal and external wiring does not cross over the terminals.

13.1.1.12 Where AWM cables or conductors permitted in accordance with Section 12.9 will be field installed, installation information shall be provided in the machine technical documentation.

13.1.2 Conductor and Cable Runs.

13.1.2.1* Conductors and cables shall be run from terminal to terminal without splices or joints. Connections using plug and receptacle combinations with protection against accidental disconnection shall not be considered to be joints for this requirement.

Exception No. 1: Splices shall be permitted to leads attached to electrical equipment, such as motors and solenoids. Such splices shall be insulated with oil-resistant electrical tape or insulation equivalent to that of the conductors and installed in a suitable enclosure.

Exception No. 2: Where it is impracticable to provide terminals in a junction box (e.g., on mobile machines, on machines having long flexible cables), the use of splices or joints shall be permitted.

13.1.2.2 Mating insulated connectors using crimped terminations shall not be considered a splice or a joint when used or contained in an enclosure, machine compartment, or conduit body.

13.1.2.3* Factory-applied connectors molded onto cables shall be permitted. Such connectors shall not be considered as splices or joints.

13.1.2.4* Cable assemblies with factory-applied connectors and their associated wiring devices shall be permitted, and such connectors shall not be considered as splices or joints.

13.1.2.5 Where it is necessary to connect and disconnect cables and cable assemblies, an additional length shall be provided for that purpose.

13.1.2.6 The terminations of cables shall be supported to prevent mechanical stresses at the termination of the conductors.

13.1.2.7 The equipment grounding conductor shall be placed as close as practicable to the associated live (insulated) conductors to decrease the impedance of the loop in the event of a fault.

13.1.3 Conductors of Different Circuits. Conductors of different circuits shall be permitted to be laid side by side and occupy the same raceway or be in the same multiconductor cable assembly, provided that the arrangement does not impair the functioning of the respective circuit. Functionally associated circuit conductors, including power, control, remote input/output, signaling, and communication cables shall be permitted in the same raceway or cable assembly regardless of voltage, provided all are insulated for the maximum voltage of any circuit within the raceway or cable assembly. Where those circuits operate at different voltages, the conductors shall be separated by barriers or shall be insulated for the highest voltage to which any conductor within the same raceway or cable assembly is subjected.

Exception: Different voltage insulation levels or conductor properties shall be permitted in the same cable assembly, provided the cable assembly has been designed and tested to the identified application.

13.1.4 Equipment Supplied from Separate Supply Circuit Disconnects or Two or More Sources of Power. Where equipment is supplied from two or more sources of power or from two or more independent supply circuit disconnecting means, the power wiring from each supply source or from each supply circuit disconnecting means shall be run in separate raceways and shall not terminate in or pass through common junction boxes.

13.1.5* Connection Between Pick-Up and Pick-Up Converter of an Inductive Power Supply System. The cable between the pick-up and the pick-up converter as specified by the manufacturer of the inductive power supply shall have the following characteristics:

(1) Be as short as practicable
(2) Be adequately protected against mechanical damage

13.1.6 Cables.

13.1.6.1 Exposed cables installed along the structure of the equipment or system or in the chases of the machinery shall be permitted and shall be installed to closely follow the surface and structural members of the machinery.

13.1.6.2 Cables shall be supported by the equipment or system structure as follows:

(1) In such a manner that the cable will not be damaged by normal equipment use
(2) Every 305 mm (12 in.) in a nonvertical run

Exception: The supporting distance shall be permitted to be increased up to 914 mm (36 in.) where the structure of the machine or system makes support impractical every 305 mm (12 in.).

(3) Every 914 mm (36 in.) in a vertical run

Exception: Supporting distance shall be permitted to be increased to 2.44 m (96 in.), where the structure of the machine or system makes support impractical every 914 mm (36 in.).

(4) When suspended in air spanning a distance up to 457 mm (18 in.)

Exception: Span distance shall be permitted to be increased up to 914 mm (36 in.), where the structure of the machine or system makes support impractical every 457 mm (18 in.).

13.1.6.3 Cables shall not be supported by machinery guards that are likely to be removed for maintenance access.

Exception: Wiring for components that are an integral part of the guard and designed to remain on the guard when the guard is removed for maintenance access shall be permitted to be supported by the guard.

13.1.6.4 Multiple cables shall be permitted to be supported and fastened together in a bundle, provided the method of support and fastening is sufficient to support the mechanical weight and strain of the bundle.

13.1.6.5 Cables shall be fastened where supported.

Exception No. 1: Where horizontal runs are inherently supported by the machine or system structure or by a floor or deck, fastening is not required.

Exception No. 2: Where run at not more than a 45-degree angle from horizontal, fastening is not required.

13.1.6.6 Cables shall be fastened with cable mounting clamps or with cable ties supported by any of the following methods:

(1) Screw-on cable tie mounts
(2) Hammer-on cable tie mounting clips
(3) Around the machine or system structural members
(4) Through holes in the machine or system structural members
(5) Other methods identified as acceptable for the purpose

13.1.6.7 The free ends of cable ties shall be cut flush after final adjustment and fastening. Cable ties of the reusable or releasable type shall not be permitted for use as a permanent fastening method.

13.1.6.8 Cables subjected to physical damage shall be protected as follows:

(1) By alternative routing
(2) With additional guarding or railings
(3) When supported by flooring or decking, with walk over or drive over cable protective devices
(4) By installation in a wire way
(5) By installation in a floor or deck covering trapezoidal walk over raceway specifically designed for cable protection

13.1.6.9 Bends in cables shall be made so as not to cause undue stress. The radius of the curve (measured from the inside edge of the bend) shall not be less than five times the diameter of the cable.

13.1.6.10 Where a cable is used in a length longer than optimally required, the excess cable shall be coiled in loops. The coil shall be fastened to itself and to the machinery structure.

Exception: When an excess cable is associated with a horizontal cable run that is inherently and fully supported, the coil is not required to be fastened to the equipment or system structure.

13.1.7 Cord.

13.1.7.1* Manufactured assemblies with factory-applied molded connectors applied to cord shall be permitted.

13.1.7.2 The use of cord shall be limited to individual exposed lengths of 15 m (50 ft) or less.

13.1.7.3 Cord shall be installed in accordance with the provision of 13.1.6.

13.1.7.4 Cord shall be permitted for use with flexible connections to pendant pushbutton stations. Chains or wire rope external to the cord shall support the weight of pendant stations.

Exception: Cords listed for the purpose shall be permitted to be used without an external chain or wire rope.

13.1.7.5 Cord shall be permitted for use with connections involving small or infrequent movements. Cord shall also be permitted to complete the connection to normally stationary motors, limit switches, and other externally mounted devices.

13.1.7.6 Connections to frequently moving parts shall be made with conductors for flexing service in accordance with Section 12.7. Cord with conductors for flexing service shall have vertical connections and shall be installed to avoid excessive flexing and straining.

Exception: Horizontal connections shall be permitted where the cord is adequately supported.

13.2 Identification of Conductors.

13.2.1 General Requirements.

13.2.1.1 Conductors shall be identified at each termination by number, letter, color (either solid or with one or more stripes), or a combination thereof and shall correspond with the technical documentation as defined in Chapter 17. Internal wiring on individual devices purchased completely wired shall not require additional identification.

13.2.1.2 Where numbers are used to identify conductors, they shall be Arabic; letters shall be roman (either uppercase or lowercase).

13.2.2 Identification of the Equipment Grounding Conductor.

13.2.2.1* The color GREEN with or without one or more YELLOW stripes shall be used to identify the equipment grounding conductor where insulated or covered. This color identification shall be strictly reserved for the equipment grounding conductor. GREEN shall be the predominant color when used in combination with one or more YELLOW stripes.

Exception No. 1: Conductors with green insulation or insulation that is green with one or more yellow stripes shall be permitted to be used for other than equipment grounding purposes where all of the following conditions are met:

(1) The conductor is part of a multiconductor cable.
(2) The multiconductor cable containing the conductor contains only circuits supplied from a source limited to less than 50 volts.
(3) The multiconductor cable containing the conductor contains only circuits supplied from a source limited to no more than a power-limited Class 2 energy level.
(4) The conductor is reidentified at all accessible locations, or the multiconductor cable is part of a listed assembly.

Exception No. 2: It shall be permitted to use conductors of any color, provided the insulation or cover is appropriately identified at all points of access.

Exception No. 3: For grounded control circuits, use of a GREEN insulated conductor with or without one or more YELLOW stripes or a bare conductor from the transformer terminal to a grounding terminal on the control panel shall be permitted.

13.2.2.2 Where the equipment grounding conductor is identified by its shape, position, or construction (e.g., a braided conductor) or where the insulated conductor is not readily accessible, color coding throughout its length shall not be required. The ends or accessible portion shall be clearly identified by the symbol in Figure 8.2.1.3.3, the color GREEN with or without one or more YELLOW stripes, or the bicolor combination GREEN-AND-YELLOW.

13.2.3 Identification of the Grounded Circuit Conductor.

13.2.3.1* Where an ac circuit includes a grounded conductor, this conductor shall be WHITE, GRAY, or three continuous WHITE stripes on other than GREEN, BLUE, or ORANGE insulation along its entire length.

Exception: Grounded conductors in multiconductor cables shall be permitted to be permanently identified at their terminations at the time of installation by a distinctive white marking or other equally effective means.

Δ **13.2.3.2** The use of other colors for the following applications shall be as follows:

(1) WHITE with BLUE stripe for grounded (current-carrying) dc circuit conductor
(2) WHITE with ORANGE stripe for grounded (current-carrying) conductor, which remains energized when the main supply circuit disconnecting means is in the off position
(3) Whichever color stripe is selected, that color stripe shall be consistent with the ungrounded conductor of the excepted circuit described in 5.1.13.

Exception No. 1: Multiconductor cables shall be permitted to be permanently reidentified at the time of installation.

Exception No. 2: Where the identification of machine power and control wiring is such that compliance with the mandatory color codes is too restrictive for specific applications, it shall be permitted to use additional identification at selected locations as an alternative. This means of identification shall be permitted to be by separate color coding, marking tape, tagging, or other approved means and shall be permanently posted on the inside of the main electrical control panel enclosure in a visible location.

13.2.3.3 Where identification by color is used, busbars used as grounded conductors shall be either colored by a stripe, 15 mm to 100 mm (0.6 in. to 3.9 in.) wide in each compartment or unit or at each accessible position, or colored throughout their length.

13.2.4 Identification by Color for Other Conductors.

13.2.4.1* The color ORANGE shall be used to identify ungrounded conductors that remain energized when the main supply circuit disconnecting means is in the off position. This color identification shall be strictly reserved for this application only.

Exception No. 1: Internal wiring on individual devices purchased completely wired

Exception No. 2: Where the insulation used is not available in the colors required (e.g., high temperature insulation, chemically resistant insulation)

13.2.4.2 Where color is used for identification, the color shall be used throughout the length of the conductor either by the color of the insulation or by color markers.

Exception: Multiconductor cables shall be permitted to be permanently reidentified at the time of installation.

13.2.4.3 Where color-coding is used for identification of conductors, the following color codes shall be permitted to be used:

(1) BLACK for ungrounded ac and dc power conductors
(2) RED for ungrounded ac control conductors
(3) BLUE for ungrounded dc control conductors

13.2.4.4 Where the identification is other than as permitted in 13.2.4.3, the means of identification shall be permanently posted on the inside of the main electrical control panel enclosure in a visible location.

Exception: Internal wiring on individual devices purchased completely wired

13.3 Wiring Inside Enclosures.

13.3.1* Nonmetallic wiring channels shall be permitted only when they are made with a flame-retardant insulating material.

13.3.2 Electrical equipment mounted inside enclosures shall be installed in such a way as to permit access to the wiring.

13.3.3 Conductors and cables used to connect devices mounted on doors or to other movable parts shall comply with flexing requirements of Section 12.7. Conductors and cables used for flexing applications shall be of sufficient length to permit full movement of the door or the movable part. The conductors shall be anchored to the fixed part and to the movable part independently of the electrical connection.

13.3.4 Conductors inside enclosures shall be supported where necessary to keep them in place, and those that are not in wiring channels shall be supported.

13.3.5 Multiple-device control panels shall be equipped with terminal blocks or with attachment plugs and receptacles for all outgoing control conductors. Wiring directly to the terminal connection points on input or output modules of programmable electronic systems shall be permitted.

13.3.6 The direct connection of power cables and cables of measuring circuits to the terminals of the devices for which the connections were intended shall be permitted.

13.3.7 Flexible cords, ac receptacles, ac plugs, appliance couplers, and power cord sets shall be permitted inside enclosures for internal wiring and connections between assemblies with ac power where used in accordance with their listing.

13.4 Wiring Outside Enclosures.

13.4.1 General Requirements. The means of entry of cables, cords, or wireways with their individual glands, bushings, and so forth into an enclosure shall ensure that the degree of protection of the enclosure is not reduced.

13.4.2 External Raceways.

13.4.2.1 All conductors of the same ac circuit routed to the same location shall be contained in the same raceway.

13.4.2.2 Conductors external to the electrical equipment enclosure(s) shall be enclosed in raceways described in Section 13.5.

Exception: Cables and cable connectors shall not be required to be enclosed in a raceway where they are protected and supported in accordance with 13.1.6.

13.4.2.3 Fittings used with raceways or multiconductor cable shall be identified for use in the physical environment.

13.4.2.4 Flexible conduit or multiconductor cable with flexible properties shall be used where it is necessary to employ flexible connections to pendant pushbutton stations. The weight of the pendant stations shall be supported by means other than the flexible conduit or the multiconductor cable with flexible properties, except where the conduit or cable is specifically designed for that purpose.

13.4.2.5 Flexible conduit or multiconductor cable with flexible properties shall be used for connections involving small or infrequent movements. They shall also be permitted to complete the connection to stationary motors, position switches, and other externally mounted devices. Where prewired devices (e.g., position switches, proximity switches) are supplied, the integral cable shall not be required to be enclosed in a raceway.

13.4.3 Connection to Moving Elements of the Machine.

13.4.3.1 Connections to moving parts shall be made using conductors in accordance with Section 12.7. Flexible cable and conduit shall have vertical connections and shall be installed to avoid excessive flexing and straining. Horizontal connections shall be permitted where the flexible cable or conduit is adequately supported. Cable with flexible properties and flexible conduit shall be so installed as to prevent excessive flexing and straining, particularly at the fittings.

13.4.3.1.1 Cables with flexible properties subject to movement shall be supported in such a way that there is neither mechanical strain on the connection points nor any sharp flexing. When this is achieved by the use of a loop, it shall provide for the cable with a bending radius of at least 10 times the diameter of cable.

13.4.3.1.2 Cable with flexible properties of machines shall be installed or protected so as to minimize the possibility of external damage due to factors that include the following cable use or potential abuse:

(1) Being run over by the machine itself
(2) Being run over by vehicles or other machines
(3) Coming into contact with the machine structure during movements
(4) Running in and out on cable baskets or on or off cable drums
(5) Acceleration forces and wind forces on festoon systems or suspended cables
(6) Excessive rubbing by cable collector
(7) Exposure to an excessive radiated heat source

13.4.3.1.3 The cable sheath shall be resistant to the wear from movement and the effects of atmospheric contaminants (e.g., oil, water, coolants, dust).

13.4.3.1.4 Where cables subject to movement are close to moving parts, precautions shall be taken to maintain a space of at least 25.4 mm (1 in.) between the moving parts and the cables. Where that distance is not practicable, fixed barriers or cable tracks shall be provided between the cables and the moving parts.

13.4.3.1.5 Where flexible conduit is adjacent to moving parts, the construction and supporting means shall prevent damage to the flexible conduit under all conditions of operation. Flexible conduit shall not be used for rapid movements except when specifically designed for that purpose.

13.4.3.2 Cable Handling System.

13.4.3.2.1 The cable handling system shall be so designed that lateral cable angles do not exceed 5 degrees, avoiding torsion in the cable when being wound on and off cable drums and approaching and leaving cable guidance devices.

13.4.3.2.2 Measures shall be taken to ensure that at least two turns of flexible cables always remain on a drum.

13.4.3.2.3 Devices serving to guide and carry a cable with flexible properties shall be designed so that the inner bending radius is not less than the values given in Table 13.4.3.2.3.

Exception: A smaller bending radius shall be permitted if the cable is identified for the purpose.

13.4.3.2.4 The straight section between two bends shall be at least 20 times the diameter of the cable.

13.4.4 Interconnection of Devices on the Machine. Where practicable, for machine-mounted switching devices (e.g., position sensors, pushbuttons) that are connected in series or in parallel, such connections, between those devices, shall be made through terminals forming intermediate test points. Such terminals shall be conveniently placed, protected from the environment, and shown on the relevant diagrams.

13.4.5 Attachment Plug and Receptacle Combinations.

13.4.5.1 Where equipment is removable, connections to it through a polarized attachment plug and receptacle combination shall be permitted. With power on the system, there shall be no shock hazard present on the exposed male pins of either part of an unplugged attachment plug and receptacle combination.

13.4.5.2 Attachment plug and receptacle combinations shall be listed for the intended use and shall be of the locking type where rated greater than 20 amperes. Where used on circuits of more than 300 volts to ground or 300 volts phase-to-phase, they shall be skirted and constructed to contain any arc generated when a connection is made or broken.

13.4.5.3 Attachment plug and receptacle combinations shall be designed so that both of the following occur:

(1) The equipment grounding circuit connection is made before any current-carrying connections are made.

(2) The equipment grounding circuit connection is not disconnected until all current-carrying connections in the plug are disconnected.

Exception: Connections used in PELV circuits or the connectors used only to facilitate assembling and disassembling (multipole connectors) shall not be required to meet these requirements.

13.4.5.4 Attachment plug and receptacle combinations used for carrying motor loads shall meet the conditions of 5.1.11.2 if the circuit is likely to be opened under load.

13.4.5.5 Where more than one attachment plug and receptacle combination is used at the same location, they shall be mechanically coded or be clearly identified to prevent incorrect insertion.

13.4.5.6 Attachment plug and receptacle combinations that are used for industrial power purposes or of a type used for domestic applications shall not be used for control circuits.

13.4.5.7 Means shall be provided to cover externally mounted receptacles when the plugs are removed.

13.4.6 Dismantling for Shipment. Where it is necessary that wiring be disconnected for shipment and where practicable, terminals or attachment plug and receptacle combinations shall be provided at the sectional points. Such terminals shall be suitably enclosed and attachment plug and receptacle combinations shall be protected from the physical environment during transportation and storage. Raceway and enclosure openings shall be sealed prior to shipment. With power on the system, there shall be no shock hazard present on the exposed male pins of either part of an unplugged attachment plug and receptacle combination.

13.5 Raceways, Support Systems (Cable Supports), Connection Boxes, and Other Boxes.

13.5.1 General Requirements.

13.5.1.1 Raceways, factory elbows and couplings, and associated fittings shall be listed and shall be identified for the environment.

Exception: Raceways fabricated as part of the machine that comply with the requirements of 13.5.6 shall not be required to be listed.

13.5.1.2 All sharp edges, burrs, rough surfaces, or threads that the insulation of the conductors can come in contact with shall be removed from raceways and fittings. Where necessary, additional protection consisting of a flame-retardant, oil-resistant insulating material shall be provided to protect conductor insulation.

Table 13.4.3.2.3 Minimum Permitted Bending Radii for the Forced Guiding of Flexible Cables

Application	Cable Diameter or Thickness of Flat Cable (d)					
	mm	in.	mm	in.	mm	in.
	$d \leq 8$	$d \leq 0.315$	$8 < d \leq 20$	$0.315 < d \leq 0.787$	$d > 20$	$d > 0.787$
Cable drums	6 d		6 d		8 d	
Guide rollers	6 d		8 d		8 d	
Festoon systems	6 d		6 d		8 d	
All others	6 d		6 d		8 d	

13.5.1.3 Drain holes shall not be permitted in raceways, junction boxes, and pull boxes where the holes would compromise the intended enclosure integrity. Drain holes of 6.4 mm (¼ in.) diameter shall be permitted in wireways, connection boxes, and other boxes used for wiring purposes that are subject to accumulations of oil or moisture.

13.5.1.4 Raceways shall be securely fastened in place and supported.

Exception: Flexible raceways shall not be required to be secured or supported where elsewhere permitted in this chapter.

13.5.2* Percentage Fills of Raceways. The combined cross-sectional area of all conductors and cables shall not exceed 50 percent of the interior cross-sectional area of the raceway. The fill provisions shall be based on the actual dimensions of the conductors or cables used.

13.5.3 Rigid Conduit and Fittings.

13.5.3.1 General Requirements.

13.5.3.1.1 The minimum electrical trade size shall be metric designator 16 (trade size ½).

13.5.3.1.2* The maximum electrical trade size shall be metric designator 155 (trade size 6).

13.5.3.1.3 Where conduit enters a box or enclosure, a bushing or fitting providing a smoothly rounded insulating surface shall be installed to protect the conductors from abrasion, unless the design of the box or enclosure is such that it provides the same protection. Where conduit bushings are constructed entirely of insulating material, a locknut shall be provided both inside and outside the enclosure to which the conduit is attached.

Exception: Where threaded hubs or bosses that are an integral part of an enclosure provide a smoothly rounded or flared entry for conductors.

13.5.3.1.4 Conduit bends shall be made in such a manner that the conduit shall not be damaged and the internal diameter of the conduit shall not be effectively reduced. The radius of the curve of any field bend to the center line of the conduit shall be not less than shown in Table 13.5.3.1.4.

13.5.3.1.5 A run of conduit shall contain not more than four quarter bends or a combination of bends totaling 360 degrees between pull points.

13.5.3.2 Metal-Type Nonflexible Conduit.

13.5.3.2.1 General Requirements.

13.5.3.2.1.1 Conduits shall be securely held in place and supported at each end.

13.5.3.2.1.2 Fittings shall be compatible with the conduit and identified for the application. Fittings shall meet the following requirements:

(1) Fittings and conduits shall be threaded using an electrical conduit die unless structural difficulties prevent assembly.
(2) Running threads shall not be used on conduit for connection at couplings.
(3) Metallic tubing shall not be threaded.
(4) Where threadless fittings are used, the conduit shall be securely fastened to the equipment.

13.5.3.2.2* Rigid Metal Conduit (RMC). Rigid metal conduit and fittings shall be of galvanized steel or of a corrosion-resistant material identified for the conditions of service.

13.5.3.2.3* Intermediate Metal Conduit (IMC). Intermediate metal conduit shall be a steel raceway of circular cross-section with integral or associated couplings, approved for the installation of electrical conductors and used with approved fittings to provide electrical continuity.

13.5.3.2.4* Electrical Metallic Tubing (EMT). Electrical metallic (steel) tubing shall be a metallic tubing of circular cross-section approved for the installation of electrical conductors when joined together with approved fittings. The maximum size of tubing shall be metric designator 103 (trade size 4).

13.5.3.3 Rigid Nonmetallic Conduit (RNC) (PVC Schedule 80).

13.5.3.3.1* Rigid nonmetallic conduit (RNC) (PVC Schedule 80) shall be of nonmetallic material approved for the installation of electrical conductors and identified for use where subject to physical damage.

Table 13.5.3.1.4 Minimum Radii of Conduit Bends

Metric Designator	Trade Size	One-Shot and Full-Shoe Benders mm	in.	Other Bends mm	in.
16	½	101.6	4	101.6	4
21	¾	114.3	4½	127	5
27	1	146.05	5¾	152.4	6
35	1¼	184.15	7¼	203.2	8
41	1½	209.55	8¼	254	10
53	2	241.3	9½	304.8	12
63	2½	266.7	10½	381	15
78	3	330.2	13	457.2	18
91	3½	381	15	533.4	21
103	4	406.4	16	609.6	24
129	5	609.6	24	762	30
155	6	762	30	914.4	36

13.5.3.3.2 Conduit shall be securely held in place and supported as specified in Table 13.5.3.3.2. In addition, conduit shall be securely fastened within 900 mm (3 ft) of each box, enclosure, or other conduit termination.

13.5.3.3.3* Expansion fittings shall be installed to compensate for thermal expansion and contraction.

13.5.3.3.4 All joints between lengths of conduit and between conduit and couplings, fittings, and boxes shall be made with fittings approved for the purpose.

13.5.4 Flexible Metal Conduit (FMC) and Fittings.

13.5.4.1 General Requirements.

13.5.4.1.1 Flexible metal conduit (FMC) and liquidtight flexible metal conduit (LFMC) minimum electrical trade size shall be metric designator 12 (trade size ⅜).

Exception: Thermocouples and other sensors

13.5.4.1.2* The maximum size of FMC and LFMC shall be metric designator 103 (trade size 4).

13.5.4.1.3 FMC and LFMC shall be installed in such a manner that liquids will tend to run off the surface instead of draining toward the fittings.

13.5.4.1.4 Fittings shall be compatible with the conduit and identified for the application. Connectors shall be the "union" types.

13.5.4.2 Flexible Metal Conduit (FMC). Flexible metal conduit shall be identified for use in the expected physical environment.

13.5.4.3 Liquidtight Flexible Metal Conduit (LFMC). Liquidtight flexible metal conduit shall be identified for use in the expected physical environment.

13.5.5 Liquidtight Flexible Nonmetallic Conduit (LFNC) and Fittings.

13.5.5.1 LFNC shall be resistant to kinking and shall have physical characteristics of the sheath of multiconductor cables.

13.5.5.2 The conduit shall be identified for use in the expected physical environment.

13.5.5.3 LFNC minimum electrical trade size shall be metric designator 12 (trade size ⅜ in.).

13.5.5.4* The maximum electrical trade size of LFNC shall be metric designator 103 (trade size 4 in.).

Table 13.5.3.3.2 Support of Rigid Nonmetallic Conduit (RNC)

Conduit Size		Maximum Spacing Between Supports	
Metric Designator	Trade Size	mm or m	ft
16–27	½–1	900 mm	3
35–53	1¼–2	1.5 m	5
63–78	2½–3	1.8 m	6
91–129	3½–5	2.1 m	7
155	6	2.5 m	8

13.5.5.5 Fittings shall be compatible with the conduit and identified for the application.

13.5.5.6 Flexible conduit shall be installed in such a manner that liquids will tend to run off the surface instead of draining toward the fittings.

13.5.6 Wireways.

13.5.6.1 Wireways external to enclosures shall be rigidly supported and clear of all moving or contaminating portions of the machine.

13.5.6.2 Covers shall be shaped to overlap the sides; gaskets shall be permitted.

13.5.6.2.1 Covers shall be attached to wireways by hinges or chains and held closed by means of captive screws or other suitable fasteners.

13.5.6.2.2 On horizontal wireways, the cover shall not be on the bottom.

13.5.6.2.3 Hinged covers shall be capable of opening at least 90 degrees.

13.5.6.3 Where the wireway is furnished in sections, the joints between sections shall fit tightly, but shall not be required to be gasketed.

13.5.6.4 The only openings permitted shall be those required for wiring or for drainage.

13.5.6.5 Wireways shall not have opened but unused knockouts.

13.5.6.6 Metal thickness and construction of wireways shall comply with UL 870.

13.5.7* Machine Compartments and Wireways. The use of compartments or wireways within the column or base of a machine to enclose conductors shall be permitted, provided the compartments or wireways are isolated from coolant or oil reservoirs and are entirely enclosed. Conductors run in enclosed compartments or wireways shall be secured and arranged so that they are not subject to damage.

13.5.8 Connection Boxes and Other Boxes.

13.5.8.1 Connection boxes and other boxes used for wiring purposes shall be readily accessible for maintenance. Those boxes shall provide protection against the ingress of solid bodies and liquids, taking into account the external influences under which the machine is intended to operate.

13.5.8.2 Those boxes shall not have opened but unused knockouts or any other openings and shall be constructed so as to exclude materials such as dust, flyings, oil, and coolant.

13.5.9 Motor Connection Boxes.

13.5.9.1 Motor connection boxes shall enclose only connections to the motor and motor-mounted devices (e.g., brakes, temperature sensors, plugging switches, tachometer generators).

13.5.9.2 Electrical connections at motor terminal boxes shall be made with an identified method of connection. Twist-on wire connectors shall not be used for this purpose.

13.5.9.3 Connectors shall be insulated with a material that will not support combustion.

13.5.9.4 Soldered or insulation-piercing–type connectors (lugs) shall not be used.

13.5.10 Cable Trays. Cable trays to be used for cable or raceway support on industrial machines shall be permitted. Cable trays shall be permitted to support the following:

(1) Single conductors 1/0 or larger that are otherwise permitted on industrial machines
(2) Multiconductor flexible cables and cables with flexible properties that are otherwise permitted on industrial machines
(3) Raceways functionally associated with industrial manufacturing systems
(4) Special conductors and cables that are otherwise permitted on industrial machines (*See Section 12.9.*)

13.5.11 Cords in Cable Trays. Cords shall not be installed in cable trays.

Chapter 14   Electric Motors and Associated Equipment

14.1* General Requirements. Motors shall be suitable for the environment in which they are installed.

14.2 Conductors Supplied from Separate Disconnects. Where the equipment has two or more sources of power or two or more independent disconnecting means, power wiring from each disconnecting means shall be run in separate raceways and shall not terminate in or pass through common junction boxes.

14.3 Reserved.

14.4* Motor Dimensions. As far as is practicable, the dimensions of the motors shall comply with those given in NEMA MG-1, IEC 60072-1, or IEC 60072-2.

14.5 Motor Mounting and Compartments.

14.5.1 Each motor and its associated couplings, belts and pulleys, or chains and sprockets shall be mounted so that they are adequately protected from physical damage and are easily accessible for inspection, maintenance, adjustment and alignment, lubrication, and replacement. The motor mounting arrangement shall be so that all motor hold-down means are removable and all terminal boxes are accessible. An adjustable base or other means of adjustment shall be provided when belt or chain drives are used.

14.5.2 Motors shall be mounted so that proper cooling is ensured and the temperature rise remains within the limits of the insulation class.

14.5.3 Motor compartments shall be clean and dry, and, when required, shall be ventilated directly to the exterior of the machine. The vents shall be so that ingress of swarf, dust, or water spray is at an acceptable level.

14.5.4 All openings between the motor compartment and any other compartment shall meet the motor compartment requirements. Where a raceway is run into the motor compartment from another compartment not meeting the motor compartment requirements, any clearance around the raceway shall be sealed.

14.6 Criteria for Selection. The characteristics of motors and associated equipment shall be selected in accordance with the anticipated service and physical environment conditions. The points that shall be considered include the following:

(1) Type of motor
(2) Type of duty cycle
(3) Fixed speed or variable speed operation (and consequent variable influence of the ventilation)
(4) Mechanical vibration
(5) Type of converter for motor speed control
(6) Influence of the harmonic spectrum of the voltage and/or current feeding the motor (when it is supplied from a converter) on the temperature rise
(7) Method of starting and possible influence of the inrush current on the operation of other users, taking into account possible special considerations stipulated by the supply authority
(8) Variation of counter torque load with time and speed
(9) Influence of loads with large inertia
(10) Influence of constant torque or constant power operations
(11) Possible need of inductive reactors between motor and converter

14.7* Protective Devices for Mechanical Brakes. Operation of the overload and overcurrent protective devices for mechanical brake actuators shall initiate the simultaneous de-energization (release) of the associated machine actuators.

14.8 Direction Arrow. Where reverse rotation produces an unsafe condition or causes damage to connected equipment, a direction arrow shall be installed. The arrow shall be adjacent to the motor and visible.

14.9 Marking on Motors. Motors shall be marked in accordance with 430.7 of *NFPA 70*.

Δ **14.10 Motor Controllers.** Motor controllers shall be provided in accordance with Article 430, Part VII, of *NFPA 70*.

Chapter 15   Accessories and Lighting

15.1 Accessories.

15.1.1 Receptacles for Accessory Equipment. Where the machine or its associated equipment is provided with receptacle outlets to be used for accessory equipment (e.g., handheld power tools, test equipment), the following conditions shall apply:

(1) Receptacles mounted externally or internally to the enclosure shall be ground-fault circuit-interrupter (GFCI)–protected.
(2) Receptacles shall be supplied from a grounded 120-volt ac source.
(3) Receptacles shall be of the parallel blade grounding type, 125-volt, single-phase, 15- or 20-ampere configuration and listed for the applied voltage.
(4) Receptacles with their associated attachment plugs (plug/sockets) shall be in accordance with 13.4.5.3.
(5) The continuity of the equipment grounding circuit to the receptacle outlet shall be verified by Section 18.2.

Exception: Verification is not required for PELV circuits in accordance with Section 18.2.

(6) All ungrounded (unearthed) conductors connected to the receptacle outlet shall be protected against overcurrent in accordance with the provisions of 7.2.5, and these circuits shall not be connected to other machine circuits.

(7) Where the power supply to the receptacle outlet is not disconnected by the supply disconnecting device for the machine or section of the machine, the safety sign requirements of 5.1.13.4 shall apply.

(8) Receptacles shall be suitable for the environment, and those mounted external to the enclosure and subject to dirt, dust, oil, or other contaminants shall be provided with a means to cover the receptacle when the plug is removed.

15.1.2 Receptacles for Maintenance Personnel. Receptacles that are part of the industrial machine, either internal or external to the control cabinet and intended for use by maintenance personnel, shall have ground-fault circuit-interrupter (GFCI) protection for personnel.

15.2 Local Lighting of the Machine and Equipment.

15.2.1 General.

15.2.1.1 Lighting circuits shall comply with the provisions of Section 8.4.

15.2.1.2 Luminaires used for machine work lighting shall not contain switches or receptacles where exposed to liquids or condensing mists unless identified for the purpose. Lampholders shall not incorporate a switch or receptacle. Luminaires used for machine work lighting used in wet locations shall be provided with ground-fault circuit-interrupter (GFCI) protection for personnel.

15.2.1.3 Conductors within stationary luminaires used as an integral part of the machine shall not be smaller than 18 AWG.

15.2.1.4 Flexible cords shall be Type SO, STO, or STOW or Type SJO, SJOW, or SJTO and shall not incorporate in-line switches.

15.2.1.5 Stroboscopic effects from lights shall be avoided.

15.2.2 Supply.

15.2.2.1 The lighting circuit voltage shall not exceed 150 volts between conductors.

Exception: Lighting systems designed for use and operating at voltage(s) greater than 150 volts shall be permitted where listed and installed according to the manufacturer's instructions.

15.2.2.2 Lighting circuits shall have overcurrent protection in accordance with 7.2.6 and shall be supplied from one of the following sources:

(1) A separate isolating transformer connected to the load side of the supply disconnecting means. Overcurrent protection shall be provided in the secondary circuit.

(2) A separate isolating transformer connected to the line side of the supply disconnecting means shall be permitted for the supply of a maintenance lighting circuit in control enclosures only. Overcurrent protection shall be provided in the secondary circuit.

(3) A grounded machine circuit that has separate overcurrent protection and does not exceed 150 volts to ground shall be permitted.

(4) An isolating transformer connected to the line side of the supply disconnecting device where a separate primary disconnecting means and secondary overcurrent protection are provided and mounted either externally immediately adjacent to the control enclosure or within the control enclosure adjacent to the supply disconnecting device.

(5) An externally supplied lighting circuit (e.g., factory lighting supply). This shall be permitted in control enclosures and for the machine work light(s) where the total power rating does not exceed 3 kW.

15.2.3 Protection. Local lighting circuits shall be separately protected with overcurrent protection and shall not exceed 15 amperes.

15.2.4 Luminaires.

15.2.4.1 Adjustable luminaires shall be suitable for the physical environment.

15.2.4.2 The lampholders shall be as follows:

(1) Rated for the voltage and wattage of the lamp
(2) Constructed with an insulating material protecting the lamp so as to prevent unintentional contact

15.2.4.3 Reflectors and protectors shall be supported by a bracket and not the lampholder.

Chapter 16   Marking and Safety Signs

16.1 General.

16.1.1 The electrical equipment shall be marked with the supplier's name, trademark, or other identifying symbol.

16.1.2 Safety signs, nameplates, markings, and identification plates shall be of sufficient durability to withstand the physical environment involved.

16.2 Safety Signs for Electrical Enclosures.

16.2.1* Enclosures that do not clearly show that they contain electrical devices shall be marked with a safety sign in accordance with ANSI Z535 series, which deals with product safety signs.

16.2.2 Safety signs shall be visible on the enclosure door or cover.

Δ **16.2.3*** Electrical equipment for industrial machines, such as industrial control panels and the enclosures of disconnecting devices, shall be marked with a safety sign in accordance with ANSI Z535.4 to warn qualified persons of potential electric shock and arc flash hazards.

16.2.3.1 The marking shall be located so as to be visible to qualified persons before examination, adjustment, servicing, or maintenance of the equipment.

16.2.3.2 It shall be permitted to omit safety signs where the size of the enclosure precludes placement of the label on the enclosure (e.g., operator–machine interfaces, control stations, position sensors).

16.2.4 A safety sign shall be provided adjacent to the disconnecting operating handle(s) where the disconnect(s) that is interlocked with the enclosure door or cover does not de-energize all exposed live parts when the disconnect(s) is in the open (off) position.

16.2.5 Where an attachment plug is used as the disconnecting means, a safety sign shall be attached to the control enclosure door or cover indicating that power shall be disconnected from the equipment before the enclosure is opened.

16.2.6 Where the disconnecting means is remote from the control enclosure, a safety sign shall be attached to the enclosure door or cover indicating that the power shall be disconnected from the equipment before the enclosure is opened and that the enclosure shall be closed before the power is restored.

16.3* Function Identification. Control devices, visual indicators, and displays used in the operator–machine interface shall be clearly and durably marked with regard to their functions either on or adjacent to the unit.

16.4 Machine Nameplate Data.

16.4.1 Control equipment shall be legibly and durably marked in a way that is visible after the equipment is installed. A nameplate giving the following information shall be attached to the outside of the enclosure, or on the machine immediately adjacent to the enclosure:

(1) Name or trademark of supplier
(2) Model, serial number, or other designation
(3)* Rated voltage, number of phases and frequency (if ac), and full-load current for each supply
(4) Ampere rating of the largest motor or load
(5) Maximum ampere rating of the short-circuit and ground-fault protective device, where provided
(6) Short-circuit current rating of the industrial control panel
(7) Electrical diagram number(s) or the number of the index to the electrical drawings

16.4.2 The full-load current shown on the nameplate shall not be less than the full-load currents for all motors and other equipment that can be in operation at the same time under normal conditions of use, design load, and duty cycle. Where unusual loads or duty cycles require oversized conductors, the required capacity shall be included in the full-load current specified on the nameplate.

16.4.3 Where more than one machine supply circuit is to be provided, the nameplate shall state the information in 16.4.1 for each circuit.

16.4.4 Where only a single motor or motor controller is used, the motor nameplate shall be permitted to serve as the electrical equipment nameplate where it is visible.

16.4.5 Where supply conductor and machine overcurrent protection is furnished as part of the machine, the machine shall be marked "Supply conductor and machine overcurrent protection provided at machine supply terminals." A separate nameplate shall be permitted to be used for this purpose.

16.5 Equipment Marking and Identification.

16.5.1 Where equipment is removed from its original enclosure or is placed so that the manufacturer's identification plate is not easily read, an additional identification plate shall be attached to the machine or enclosure.

16.5.2 Where a motor nameplate or connection diagram plate is not visible, additional identification shall be provided where it can be easily read.

16.5.3 Nameplates, identification plates, or safety signs shall not be removed from the equipment.

16.5.4 All control panel devices and components shall be plainly identified with the same designation as shown on the machine drawings or diagram(s). This identification shall be adjacent to (not on) the device or component.

Exception No. 1: Where the size or location of the devices makes individual identification impractical, group identification shall be used.

Exception No. 2: This requirement shall not apply to machines on which the equipment consists only of a single motor, motor controller, pushbutton station(s), and work light(s).

16.5.5 All devices external to the control panel(s) shall be identified by a nameplate with the same designation as shown on the machine drawings or diagram(s) and mounted adjacent to (not on) the device.

Exception: Devices covered by Section 16.3.

16.5.6 Terminations on multiconductor plugs and receptacles shall be plainly marked. The markings on the plug and receptacles and on drawings shall correspond.

16.5.7 Where group protection as provided for in 7.2.10 is used, information specifying the short-circuit protective device for each group protected motor branch circuit shall be included with the equipment.

Chapter 17 Technical Documentation

17.1 General.

17.1.1 The information necessary for installation, operation, and maintenance of the electrical equipment of a machine shall be supplied in the form of drawings, diagrams, charts, tables, and instructions as appropriate. The information provided shall be permitted to vary with the complexity of the electrical equipment. For very simple equipment, the relevant information shall be permitted to be contained in one document provided this document shows all the devices of the electrical equipment and enables the connections to the supply network to be made.

17.1.2 The machinery supplier shall ensure that the technical documentation specified in this chapter is provided with each machine.

17.1.3 Technical documentation shall be supplied in a medium agreed upon by the machinery supplier and the user of the machinery.

17.2 Information to Be Provided. The following information shall be provided with the electrical equipment:

(1) Clear, comprehensive description of the equipment, the installation and mounting, and the connection to the electrical supply(ies)
(2) Electrical supply circuit(s) requirements
(3) Overview (block) diagram(s) where appropriate
(4) Schematic diagram(s)
(5) Information (where appropriate) on the following:
   (a) Programming
   (b) Sequence of operation(s)
   (c) Frequency of inspection
   (d) Frequency and method of functional testing
   (e) Adjustment, maintenance, and repair
   (f) Interconnection diagram
   (g) Panel layouts
   (h) Instruction and service manuals

(i) Physical environment (e.g., lighting, vibration, noise levels, atmospheric contaminants)
(6) A description (including interconnection diagrams) of the safeguards, interacting functions, and interlocking of guards with potentially hazardous motions
(7) A description of the safeguarding means and methods provided where the primary safeguards are overridden (e.g., manual programming, program verification)
(8) Means provided for the control of hazardous energies
(9) Explanation of unique terms
(10) Parts list and recommended spare parts list
(11) Maintenance instructions and adjustment procedures
(12) Reference information (where appropriate) on the following:
    (a) Lubrication diagram
    (b) Pneumatic diagram
    (c) Hydraulic diagram
    (d) Miscellaneous system diagrams (e.g., coolant, refrigerant)

17.3 Requirements Applicable to All Documentation.

17.3.1 The documents shall be prepared in accordance with the requirements of Section 17.4 through Section 17.10.

17.3.2 For referencing of the different documents, the supplier shall select one of the following methods:

(1) Each of the documents shall carry as a cross-reference the document numbers of all other documents belonging to the electrical equipment. This method shall be used only where the documentation consists of four or fewer documents.
(2) All documents shall be listed with document numbers and titles in a drawing or document list.

17.3.3 Where appropriate, a table of contents shall appear prominently on the first sheet and shall refer to all major sections of the electrical drawings.

17.4* Basic Information. The technical documentation shall be permitted to be presented as a separate document or as part of the installation or operation documentation. The technical documentation shall contain, as a minimum, information on the following:

(1) Normal operating conditions of the electrical equipment, including the expected conditions of the electrical supply and, where appropriate, the physical environment
(2) Handling, transportation, and storage
(3) Inappropriate use(s) of the equipment

17.5 Installation Diagram.

17.5.1* The installation diagram shall provide all information necessary for the preliminary work of setting up the machine.

17.5.2 The specified position of the electrical supply to be installed on site shall be clearly indicated.

17.5.3* The data necessary for choosing the type, characteristics, rated currents, and setting of the overcurrent protective device(s) for the supply circuit conductors to the electrical equipment of the machine shall be stated.

17.5.4* Where necessary, the size, purpose, and location of any raceways in the foundation that are to be provided by the user shall be detailed.

17.5.5* The size, type, and purpose of raceways, cable trays, or cable supports between the machine and the associated equipment that are to be provided by the user shall be detailed.

17.5.6* Where necessary, the diagram shall indicate where space is required for the removal or servicing of the electrical equipment.

17.5.7* Where it is appropriate, an interconnection diagram or table shall be provided. That diagram or table shall give full information about all external connections. Where the electrical equipment is intended to be operated from more than one source of electrical supply, the interconnection diagram or table shall indicate the modifications or interconnections required for the use of each supply.

17.6* Block (System) Diagrams and Function Diagrams. Where it is necessary to facilitate the understanding of the principles of operation, a system diagram shall be provided. For the purposes of this chapter, a block diagram shall symbolically represent the electrical equipment together with its functional interrelationships without necessarily showing all of the interconnections.

17.7 Circuit Diagrams.

17.7.1* Diagrams, including machine schematics, of the electrical system shall be provided and shall show the electrical circuits on the machine and its associated electrical equipment. Electrical symbols shall be in accordance with IEEE 315 where included therein. Any electrical symbols not included in IEEE 315 shall be separately shown and described on the diagrams. The symbols and identification of components and devices shall be consistent throughout all documents and on the machine.

Exception: Wiring schematics shall not be required for commercially available or field replaceable components.

17.7.2* Pertinent information such as motor horsepower, frame size, and speed shall be listed adjacent to its symbol.

17.7.3* Where appropriate, a diagram showing the terminals for interface connections shall be provided. Switch symbols shall be shown on the electromechanical diagrams with all supplies turned off (e.g., electricity, air, water, lubricant) and with the machine and its electrical equipment in the normal starting condition and at 20°C (68°F) ambient temperature. Control settings shall be shown on the diagram.

17.7.4 Conductors shall be identified in logical order in accordance with Section 13.2.

17.7.5* Circuit Characteristics.

17.7.5.1 Circuits shall be shown in such a way as to facilitate the understanding of their function as well as maintenance and fault location.

17.7.5.2 A cross-referencing scheme shall be used in conjunction with each relay, output device, limit switch, and pressure switch so that any contact associated with the device can be readily located on the diagrams.

17.7.6 Control circuit devices shall be shown between vertical lines that represent control power wiring. The left vertical line shall be the control circuit's common and the right line shall be the operating coil's common, except where permitted by Chapter 9 design requirements. Control devices shall be shown on horizontal lines (rungs) between the vertical lines. Parallel circuits shall be shown on separate horizontal lines directly adjacent to (above or below) the original circuit.

Exception: Upon agreement between the machine manufacturer and the user, an alternative convention shall be permitted (e.g., one of the IEC standard presentation methods).

17.7.7 An interconnection diagram shall be provided on large systems having a number of separate enclosures or control stations. It shall provide full information about the external connections of all of the electrical equipment on the machine.

17.7.8 Interlock wiring diagrams shall include devices, functions, and conductors in the circuit where used.

17.7.9 Plug/receptacle pin identification shall be shown on the diagram(s).

17.8 Operating Manual.

17.8.1* The technical documentation shall contain an operating manual detailing proper procedures for setup and equipment use.

17.8.2 Where the operation of the equipment is programmable, detailed information on methods of programming, equipment required, program verification, and additional safety procedures (where required) shall be provided.

17.9 Maintenance Manual.

17.9.1* The technical documentation shall contain a maintenance manual detailing proper procedures for adjustment, servicing and preventive inspection, and repair.

17.9.2 Where methods for the verification of proper operation are provided (e.g., software testing programs), the use of those methods shall be detailed.

17.9.3 Where service procedures requiring electrical work while equipment is energized, the technical documentation shall make reference to appropriate safe work practices, such as the requirements of *NFPA 70E* or OSHA regulations in 29 CFR 1910.331–335.

17.10* Parts List.

17.10.1 The parts list shall comprise, as a minimum, information necessary for ordering spare or replacement parts (e.g., components, devices, software, test equipment, technical documentation) required for preventive or corrective maintenance, including those that are recommended to be carried in stock by the equipment user.

17.10.2 The parts list shall show the following for each item:

(1) Reference designation used in the documentation
(2) Its type designation
(3) Supplier (and supplier's part number)
(4) Its general characteristics where appropriate
(5) Quantity of items with the same reference designation

Chapter 18   Testing and Verification

18.1* General. The verification of the continuity of the effective ground-fault current path shall be conducted and documented. When the electrical equipment is modified, the requirements in Section 18.7 shall apply. Applicable tests shall be performed where deemed necessary in accordance with the references in the following list:

(1) Verification that the electrical equipment is in compliance with the technical documentation *(see Chapter 17)*
(2) Insulation resistance test *(see Section 18.3)*
(3) Voltage test *(see Section 18.4)*
(4) Protection against residual voltages test *(see Section 18.5)*
(5) Functional test *(see Section 18.6)*

18.2* Continuity of the Effective Ground-Fault Current Path. One of the following methods shall be used to verify the continuity of the effective ground-fault current path:

(1) Using an impedance measuring device, take into account any impedance in the measuring circuit. The measured impedance shall be 0.1 ohm or less.
(2) Apply a current of at least 10 amperes, 50 Hz or 60 Hz, derived from an SELV source. The tests are to be made between the equipment grounding terminal and relevant points that are part of the effective ground-fault current path; the measured voltage between the equipment grounding terminal and the points of test is not to exceed the values given in Table 18.2.

18.3 Insulation Resistance Tests. The insulation resistance measured at 500 volts dc between the power circuit conductors and the effective ground-fault current path shall not be less than 1 megohm. The test shall be permitted to be made on individual sections of the machine.

18.4* Voltage Tests. The machine shall withstand without breakdown a test voltage gradually applied from 0 volts to 1500 volts ac or 2121 volts dc and held at the maximum value for a period of at least 1 second between the conductors of all primary circuits and the effective ground-fault current path. The test voltage shall be supplied from an isolated power supply with a minimum rating of 500 volt amperes. Components that are not rated to withstand the test voltage shall be disconnected during testing.

18.5 Protection Against Residual Voltages. Residual voltage tests shall be performed to ensure compliance with Section 6.5.

18.6 Functional Tests. The functions of electrical equipment, particularly those related to safety and safeguarding, shall be tested and documented.

18.7 Retesting. Where a portion of the machine and its associated equipment is changed or modified, that portion shall be reverified and retested as appropriate.

Table 18.2 Verification of Continuity of the Effective Ground-Fault Current Path

Minimum Equipment Grounding Conductor Cross-Sectional Area of the Branch Under Test (AWG)	Maximum Measured Voltage Drop* (V)
18	3.3
16	2.6
14	1.9
12	1.7
10	1.4
>8	1.0

*Values are given for a test current of 10 amperes.

Chapter 19 Servo Drives and Motors

△ **19.1 Overcurrent Protection for Drives and Servo Motors.**

19.1.1 Branch-Circuit Overcurrent Protection. Branch-circuit overcurrent protection shall be provided for servo drives and motors in accordance with manufacturer's markings and instructions.

19.1.2 Overload Protection. Overload protection shall be provided for each motor.

19.1.3 Motor Amplifier/Drive. Where the amplifier/drive is marked to indicate that motor overload protection is included, additional overload protection shall not be required.

19.1.4 Multiple Motor Applications. For multiple motor applications, individual motor overload protection shall be provided.

19.2* Motor Overtemperature Protection.

19.2.1 General. Servo drive systems shall provide protection against motor overtemperature conditions. Protection shall be provided by one of the following means:

(1) Integral motor thermal protector(s)
(2) Servo drive controller(s) with load- and speed-sensitive overload protection and thermal memory detection upon shutdown or power loss
(3) Overtemperature protection relay(s) utilizing thermal sensors embedded in the motor
(4) Motors with cooling systems

19.2.2 Additional Conductor Protection. Overtemperature protection shall be in addition to any conductor protection.

19.2.3 Failure of Cooling System. Systems that utilize motor cooling such as forced air or water shall provide protection against a failed or inoperable cooling system.

19.2.4 Multiple Motor Applications. For multiple motor application, individual motor overtemperature protection shall be provided.

19.2.5 Other Sections. The provisions of 430.43 and 430.44 of *NFPA 70* shall apply to the motor overtemperature protection means.

19.3 Servo Drive System Conductors.

19.3.1 Servo Drive System Supply Conductors. Circuit conductors supplying servo drive systems shall be sized to have an ampacity not less than 115 percent of the rated input of the equipment.

19.3.2 Motor Circuit Conductors. Motor circuit conductors shall have an ampacity of at least 115 percent of the motor full-load current when operated in a continuous mode of operation or as specified by the servo drive system manufacturer. Motor circuit conductors for motors operating in other than continuous mode shall be permitted to have reduced ampacity based upon the design load and duty cycle.

19.3.3 Unshielded servo motor power conductors shall be run in a separate ferrous raceway from other control and instrumentation conductors, from the servo drive enclosure to the servo motor.

Exception: Where either the servo motor power, or control/instrumentation conductors, or both, are installed in raceway system(s) or by separa-

tion that shall provide the equivalent level of EMI protection as ferrous raceway utilizing Table 19.3.3

Table 19.3.3 Minimum Conductor Separation (Center to Center)

	Separation	
Ampacity	mm	in.
20 A or less	100	4
Over 20 A and not greater than 40 A	150	6
Over 40 A and not greater than 80 A	200	8
Over 80 A	*	

*Each doubling of current adds 50 mm (2 in.) more to the separation distance.

19.3.4 Where unshielded servo motor power conductors and unshielded control/instrumentation conductors are not contained in ferrous raceways and cross each other, they shall be installed perpendicular to each other.

19.3.5 Where unshielded servo motor power conductors and unshielded control/instrumentation conductors are not isolated by ferrous raceways, separation by distance shall be used per Table 19.3.3 unless otherwise specified by the manufacturer.

19.4 Contactor. Where a contactor is installed ahead of the supply conductors to the servo drive, the contactor current rating shall not be less than 115 percent of the maximum servo drive nameplate rating or shall be sized in accordance with the manufacturer's specifications.

19.5 Cable Shield. Use of a grounded servo motor conductor/cable shield shall not be permitted to satisfy the equipment grounding conductor requirements.

Annex A Explanatory Material

Annex A is not a part of the requirements of this NFPA document but is included for informational purposes only. This annex contains explanatory material, numbered to correspond with the applicable text paragraphs.

A.1.1 In this standard, the term *electrical* includes both electrical and electronic equipment. Requirements that apply only to electronic equipment are so identified.

The general terms *machine* and *machinery* as used throughout this standard mean industrial machinery. See Annex C for examples of industrial machines covered by this standard.

The publications referenced throughout Annex A are listed in Annex K with their appropriate dates of issue.

A.1.1.2 For additional requirements for machines intended to be used in hazardous (classified) areas, see Article 500 of *NFPA 70.*

A.1.5 Motor design letter designations are found in NEMA MG-1 and IEEE 100.

A.3.2.1 Approved. The National Fire Protection Association does not approve, inspect, or certify any installations, procedures, equipment, or materials; nor does it approve or evaluate testing laboratories. In determining the acceptability of installations, procedures, equipment, or materials, the authority having jurisdiction may base acceptance on compliance with NFPA or other appropriate standards. In the absence of such standards, said authority may require evidence of proper installation, procedure, or use. The authority having jurisdiction may also refer to the listings or labeling practices of an organization that is concerned with product evaluations and is thus in a position to determine compliance with appropriate standards for the current production of listed items.

A.3.2.2 Authority Having Jurisdiction (AHJ). The phrase "authority having jurisdiction," or its acronym AHJ, is used in NFPA documents in a broad manner, since jurisdictions and approval agencies vary, as do their responsibilities. Where public safety is primary, the authority having jurisdiction may be a federal, state, local, or other regional department or individual such as a fire chief; fire marshal; chief of a fire prevention bureau, labor department, or health department; building official; electrical inspector; or others having statutory authority. For insurance purposes, an insurance inspection department, rating bureau, or other insurance company representative may be the authority having jurisdiction. In many circumstances, the property owner or his or her designated agent assumes the role of the authority having jurisdiction; at government installations, the commanding officer or departmental official may be the authority having jurisdiction.

A.3.2.4 Listed. The means for identifying listed equipment may vary for each organization concerned with product evaluation; some organizations do not recognize equipment as listed unless it is also labeled. The authority having jurisdiction should utilize the system employed by the listing organization to identify a listed product.

A.3.3.3 Actuator. The actuator can take the form of a handle, knob, pushbutton, roller, plunger, touchscreen, and so forth. There are some actuating means that do not require an external actuating force but only an action. See also 3.3.4, Actuator, Machine.

N **A.3.3.4 Actuator, Machine.** Some examples of a machine actuator are a motor, solenoid, and pneumatic or hydraulic cylinder.

A.3.3.5 Adjustable Speed Drive. This term includes ac and dc voltage modes and frequency mode controls. Belt, chain, or roller shifting controllers are not included.

A variable frequency drive is one type of electronic adjustable speed drive that controls the rotational speed of an ac electric motor by controlling the frequency and voltage of the electrical power supplied to the motor. [**70:**100]

A.3.3.7 Ambient Temperature. Ambient air temperature as applied to an enclosure or housing is the average temperature of the surrounding air that comes in contact with the enclosure or housing. Ambient air temperature as applied to a component or device within the enclosure is the average temperature of the surrounding air that comes in contact with the component.

A.3.3.11 Basic Protection (Protection From Direct Contact). In previous editions of this standard, the term "protection against direct contact" was used in place of "basic protection."

A.3.3.14 Cable. For additional information on types of cable, refer to Chapter 3 of *NFPA 70.*

A.3.3.14.1 Cable with Flexible Properties. See 12.2.2.

A.3.3.14.2 Flexible Cable. See 12.2.2.

A.3.3.14.3 Special Cable. For additional information on types of special cables, see Section 12.9 or refer to Chapters 4, 6, 7, and 8 of *NFPA 70.*

A.3.3.17 Cableless Operator Control Station. These stations are not physically connected to the machine by either communications or power conductors. While all cableless devices utilize wireless technology, not all wireless devices are cableless. Examples of cableless devices include cableless teach pendants, cableless crane pendants, and cableless jog pendants.

A.3.3.18 Circuit Breaker. The automatic opening means can be integral, direct acting with the circuit breaker, or remote from the circuit breaker.

A.3.3.19 Color Graphic Interface Device. This does not include monochrome or black and white displays.

A.3.3.21.4 Liquidtight Flexible Nonmetallic Conduit (LFNC). FNMC is an alternative designation for LFNC. [**70:**356.2 Informational Note]

A.3.3.23 Control Circuit (of a machine). Power circuit protection can be provided by control shunt-tripping.

A.3.3.44 Failure (of equipment). After failure, the item has a fault. "Failure" is an event, as distinguished from "fault," which is a state. This concept as defined does not apply to items consisting of software only.

A.3.3.45 Fault. A fault is often the result of a failure of the item itself, but can exist without prior failure.

N **A.3.3.47 Fault Current, Available (Available Fault Current).** A short circuit can occur during abnormal conditions such as a fault between circuit conductors or a ground fault.

A.3.3.48 Fault Protection (Protection from Indirect Contact). In previous editions of this standard, the term "protection against indirect contact" was used in place of "fault protection."

A.3.3.56 Guard. Depending on its construction, a guard can be called a casing, a cover, a screen, a door, or an enclosing guard.

A.3.3.59 Identified (as applied to equipment). Some examples of ways to determine suitability of equipment for a specific purpose, environment, or application include investigations by a qualified testing laboratory (listing and labeling), an inspection agency, or other organizations concerned with product evaluation. [**70:**100 Informational Note]

A.3.3.68 Interrupting Rating. Equipment intended to interrupt current at other than fault levels may have its interrupting rating implied in other ratings, such as horsepower or locked rotor current. [**70:**100 Informational Note]

A.3.3.77 Overcurrent. A current in excess of rating may be accommodated by certain equipment and conductors for a given set of conditions. Therefore, the rules for overcurrent protection are specific for particular situations. [**70:**100 Informational Note]

A.3.3.79 Overcurrent Protective Device, Supplementary. Supplementary overcurrent protective devices are not general use devices, as are branch circuit devices, and must be evaluated for appropriate application in every instance where they are used. Supplementary overcurrent protective devices are extremely application oriented, and prior to applying the devices, the differences and limitations for these devices must be investigated. Such a device is allowed to be incomplete in construction or restricted in performance. Such a device is not suitable for branch circuit protection and is not used where branch circuit protection is required.

One example of differences and limitations is that a supplementary overcurrent protective device could have spacing, creepage, and clearance that are considerably less than those of a branch circuit overcurrent protective device.

Example: A supplemental protector, listed to UL 1077, has spacings that are 9.5 mm (0.375 in.) through air and 12.7 mm (0.5 in.) over surface. A branch circuit–rated UL 489 molded-case circuit breaker has spacings that are 19.1 mm (0.75 in.) through air and 31.8 mm (1.25 in.) over surface.

Another example of differences and limitations is that branch circuit overcurrent protective devices have standard overload characteristics to protect branch circuits and feeder conductors. Supplementary overcurrent protective devices do not have standard overload characteristics and could differ from the standard branch circuit overload characteristics. Also, supplementary overcurrent protective devices have interrupting ratings that can range from 32 amperes to 100,000 amperes. When supplementary overcurrent protective devices are considered for proper use, it is important to be sure that the device's interrupting rating equals or exceeds the available fault current and that the device has the proper voltage rating for the installation (including compliance with slash voltage rating requirements, if applicable).

Examples of supplemental overcurrent protective devices include, but are not limited to, those listed to the following:

(1) UL 248-14
(2) UL 1077

A.3.3.80 Overload. Overload should not be used as a synonym for overcurrent.

A.3.3.83 Programmable Electronic System (PES). This term includes all elements in the system extending from sensors to other input devices via field bus or other communication paths to the machine actuators or other output devices.

A.3.3.84 Qualified Person. Refer to *NFPA 70E* for electrical safety training requirements. [**70:**100 Informational Note]

A.3.3.90 Risk. Examples of references to risk assessment include ANSI B11.0 and ISO 12100.

N **A.3.3.95 Safety Circuit.** "Safety-related control system" and "safety interlock circuit" are common terms used to refer to the safety circuit in other standards. The safety circuit can include hardwired, communication, and software-related components.

A.3.3.98 Servo Drive System. See Figure A.3.3.98, Servo System.

A.3.3.99 Short-Circuit Current Rating (SCCR). The short-circuit current rating of an apparatus or system can be determined either by testing or by evaluation using an approved method such as Supplement SB of UL 508A.

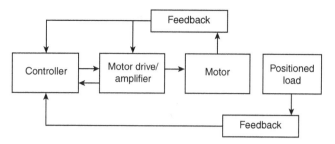

FIGURE A.3.3.98   Servo System.

A.3.3.103 Supplier. The user can also act in the capacity of a supplier to him- or herself.

A.3.3.110 Undervoltage Protection. The principal objective of this device is to prevent automatic restarting of the equipment. Standard undervoltage or low-voltage protection devices are not designed to become effective at any specific degree of voltage reduction.

A.4.1 A sample inquiry form is provided in Annex B for use in facilitating an agreement between the supplier and the user.

Hazardous situations can result from, but are not limited to, the following causes:

(1) Failures or faults in the electrical equipment resulting in the possibility of electrical shock, flash hazard, or electrical fire
(2) Failures or faults in control circuits (or components and devices associated with these circuits) resulting in malfunctioning of the machine
(3) Disturbances or disruptions in power sources as well as failures or faults in the power circuits, resulting in the malfunctioning of the machine
(4) Loss of continuity of circuits that depend upon sliding or rolling contacts, resulting in a failure of a safety-related function
(5) Electrical disturbances (e.g., electromagnetic, electrostatic, or radio interference) either from outside the electrical equipment or internally generated, resulting in the malfunctioning of the machine
(6) Release of electrical or mechanical stored energy, resulting in, for example, electric shock or unexpected movement that can cause injury
(7) Audible noise at levels that cause health problems to persons
(8) Surface temperatures that can cause injury

Safety measures are a combination of the measures incorporated at the design stage and those measures required to be implemented by the user.

Design and development should be the first consideration in the reduction of risks. Where this is not possible, safeguarding should be considered. Safeguarding includes the use of safeguards, awareness means, and safe working procedures.

Examples of references to risk assessment include ANSI B11.0 and ISO 12100.

Flash hazard analysis, calculation methods, and ways to address the hazard are found in *NFPA 70E.*

One reference to recommended practices on static electricity is NFPA 77.

Δ **A.4.2** Semiconductor manufacturing equipment for use in semiconductor fabrication facilities could be accepted by one of the following judged under the requirements of a testing laboratory to an international (e.g., IEC 60204-1 or IEC 61010-1), regional (e.g., EN 60204-1 or EN 61010-1), national (e.g., UL 508, UL 508A, UL 61010-1, this document), or industry standard [e.g., SEMI S2 or SEMI S22 electrical standard(s)] deemed appropriate by the testing laboratory, field evaluation to this document, or another approach, such as "acceptable to the local authority having jurisdiction."

A.4.4.1 Annex B provides an inquiry form to ensure all parties have reviewed supplier-specific requirements concerning equipment operation.

A.4.4.2 The short-time value for the frequency can be specified by the user *(see Annex B)*.

N **A.4.4.2.8** Electrical equipment connected to the output of power conversion equipment can exhibit different behavior due to the characteristics of the output waveform. Manufacturers of such equipment provide guidance on suitability and proper use. See Chapter 12 and A.12.1.1 for information on conductor selection.

A.4.5.1 Annex B provides an inquiry form to ensure all parties have reviewed supplier-specific requirements concerning the physical environment or operating conditions that are outside those specified in this document.

A.4.5.2 The electrical interferences generated by the equipment itself should not exceed levels specified in the relevant equipment standards and others dealing with electromagnetic compatibility (EMC) levels. The levels allowed should be determined for the specific application.

Generated interference signals can be kept to a minimum by the following:

(1) Suppression at the source by using capacitors, inductors, diodes, Zener diodes, varistors, or active devices, or a combination of these

(2) Equipment screening in a bonded electrically conductive enclosure to provide segregation from other equipment

Undesirable effects of electrostatic discharge, radiated electromagnetic energy, and supply conductor (mains borne) interference should be avoided (e.g., use of appropriate filters and time delays, choice of certain power levels, suitable wiring types and practices).

The effects of interference on equipment can be reduced by the following:

(1) *Use of surge protective devices and filters.* The installation of surge protection devices and/or filters for equipment sensitive to electromagnetic influences is recommended to improve electromagnetic compatibility with regard to conducted electromagnetic phenomena.

(2) *Reference potential circuit or common connections.* Each common connection treated as a single circuit and connected to one of several central reference points that are connected to ground (wired to earth) by insulated conductors of large cross-sectional area.

(3) *Frame connections.* In each piece of equipment all frame connections are to be taken to a common point with a conductor of large cross-sectional area (e.g., braided conductors, foil strips having a width much greater than the thickness) used between slides and enclosures. The connections to the frame are to be as short as possible.

(4) *Transmission of signals.* Electrostatic screens, electromagnetic shields, twisted conductors, and orientation (i.e., crossing cable runs at as near to 90 degrees as practicable) as necessary to ensure that the low level signal wiring is not affected by interference from control or power cables, or running the connections parallel to the ground plane as necessary.

(5) *Separation of equipment.* Separating and/or shielding sensitive equipment (e.g., units working with pulses and/or at low signal levels) from switching equipment (e.g., electromagnetic relays, thyristors); separation of low level signal wiring from control and power cables.

(6) *Electromagnetic disturbances.* Measures to limit the generation of electromagnetic disturbances — that is, conducted and radiated emissions — include the following:

(a) Power supply filtering
(b) Cable shielding
(c) Enclosures designed to minimize RF radiation
(d) RF suppression techniques.

(7) *Enhance immunity.* Measures to enhance the immunity of the equipment against conducted and radiated RF disturbance using the designs of a functional bonding system include the following:

(a) Connection of sensitive electrical circuits to the chassis. Such terminations should be marked or labeled with the IEC Symbol 5020 from IEC 60417-1. *[See Figure A.4.5.2(a).]*

(b) Connection of the chassis to earth (PE) using a conductor with low RF impedance and as short as practicable.

(c) Connection of sensitive electrical equipment or circuits directly to the PE circuit or to a functional earthing conductor (FE), to minimize common mode disturbance. This latter terminal should be marked or labeled with the IEC Symbol 5018 from IEC 60417. *[See Figure A.4.5.2(b).]*

(d) Separation of sensitive circuits from disturbance sources.

(e) Enclosures designed to minimize RF transmission.

(f) EMC wiring practices as follows:

i. Using twisted conductors to reduce the effect of differential mode disturbances

ii. Keeping distance between conductors emitting disturbances and sensitive conductors

iii. Using cable orientation as close to 90° as possible when cables cross

iv. Running the conductors as close as possible to the ground plane

v. Using electrostatic screens and/or electromagnetic shields with a low RF impedance termination

A.4.5.3 For very hot environments (e.g., hot climates, steel mills, paper mills) and for cold environments, extra requirements could be necessary. *(See Annex B.)*

A.4.5.4 For extremely dry or moist environments, extra requirements might be necessary to prevent static discharge.

A.4.5.5 Annex B provides an inquiry form to ensure all parties have reviewed requirements for electrical equipment operating at altitudes 1000 m (3300 ft) or more above sea level.

A.4.5.6 Annex B provides an inquiry form to ensure all parties have reviewed requirements for electrical equipment operating where contaminants are of a special concern.

A.4.5.7 Where equipment is subject to radiation (e.g., microwave, ultraviolet, lasers, x-rays), additional measures should be taken to avoid malfunctioning and accelerated deterioration of the insulation.

A.5.1.1 For large complex machinery comprising a number of widely spaced machines working together in a coordinated manner, more than one machine supply circuit might be needed, depending upon the site supply circuit arrangements *(see 5.1.9.7).*

A.5.1.7 See Question 14 in Annex B, Figure B.1.

A.5.1.8 For additional information on the equipment grounding conductor terminal, see 8.2.1.3.

A.5.1.9.2 When a single disconnecting means is provided, a marking such as "main machine disconnect" is sufficient to convey the purpose. Where multiple supplies are present, a descriptive marking is necessary to clearly indicate the controlled supply voltage or equipment that is disconnected, such as "main disconnect — 480V, 3ph," or "main disconnect — drive motors."

A.5.1.11.1 For additional information, see IEC 61310-3 or 404.7 of *NFPA 70* for direction of operation of the disconnecting actuator.

A.5.1.11.2 A suitably rated attachment plug and receptacle listed to UL 498 or UL 1682 is a method of meeting the requirements of 5.1.11.2(2) and 5.1.11.2(3).

A.5.3.3 The selection of other means is dependent on many factors, taking into account those persons for whom its use is intended. *(See ANSI B11.0 and ISO 12100.)*

A.6.1 The requirements of Chapter 6 reduce the likelihood that an arc flash event will occur. Only enclosures listed as arc resistant are evaluated for providing protection from arc flash events.

A.6.2.3.1 The use of a key or tool or enclosure interlocking is intended to restrict access to qualified persons. It is the responsibility of the employer to determine the relevant safe work

FIGURE A.4.5.2(a)   Symbol that Represents Functional Equipotential Bonding — IEC Symbol Number 5020.

FIGURE A.4.5.2(b)   Symbol that Represents Functional Earthing — IEC Symbol Number 5018.

practices and the qualifications necessary to perform a specific task(s). See *NFPA 70E* for additional information on work practices.

A.6.3.1 Ripple-free is conventionally defined for a sinusoidal ripple voltage as a ripple content of not more than 10 percent rms. For additional information on isolating transformers, refer to IEC 60742 and IEC 61558-1. In addition, the following measures need to be considered:

(1) The type of supply and grounding system
(2) The impedance values of the different elements of the equipment grounding system
(3) The characteristics of the protective devices used to detect insulation failure

A.7.2.1 Figure A.7.2.1(a) and Figure A.7.2.1(b) show typical circuits acceptable for the protection of current-carrying and current-consuming electrical machine components. Protective interlocks are not shown.

A.7.2.2 See 7.2.10 and Section 17.5. The size and overcurrent protection of the supply conductors to a machine are covered by Article 670 of *NFPA 70.*

A.7.2.9 Proper application of molded case circuit breakers on 3-phase systems, other than solidly grounded wye, particularly on corner grounded delta systems, considers the circuit breakers' individual pole interrupting capability.

A.7.2.10.1 In Note 6 of Table 1 of IEC 60947-4-1, the terms Type 1 and Type 2 coordinated protection are defined as follows:

(1) *Type 1 protection.* Under short-circuit conditions the contactor or starter might not be suitable for further use without repair or replacement.

(2) *Type 2 protection.* Under short-circuit conditions the contactor or starter shall be suitable for further use.

The maximum allowable values in Table 7.2.10.1 do not guarantee Type 2 protection. Type 2 protection is recommended for use in applications where enhanced performance and reliability are required.

A.7.4 An example could be a resistance heating circuit that is short-time–rated or that loses its cooling medium.

A.7.6.1 Overspeed protection means include, but are not necessarily limited to, the following:

(1) A mechanical overspeed device incorporated in the drive to remove armature voltage upon motor overspeed.
(2) An electrical overspeed detector that will remove armature voltage upon motor overspeed.
(3) Field loss detection to remove armature voltage upon the loss of field current.
(4) Voltage-limiting speed-regulated drives that operate with constant full field. In this case, protection is obtained individually for the loss of field or tachometer feedback; however, protection against simultaneous loss of field and tachometer is not provided.

A.7.7 Conditions of use that can lead to an incorrect phase sequence include the following:

(1) A machine transferred from one supply to another
(2) A mobile machine with a facility for connection to an external power supply

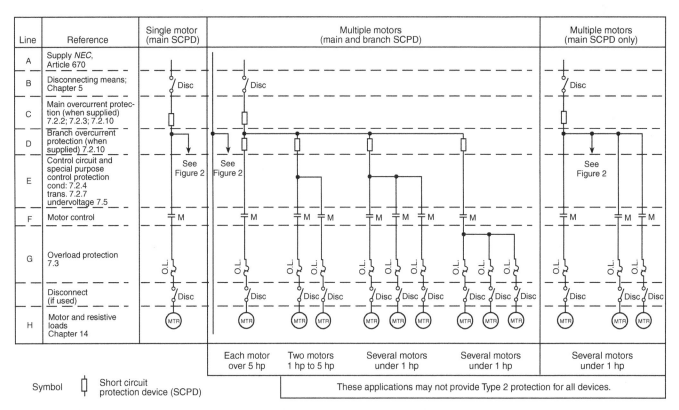

FIGURE A.7.2.1(a) One Line Representation of Electrical System Power Distribution.

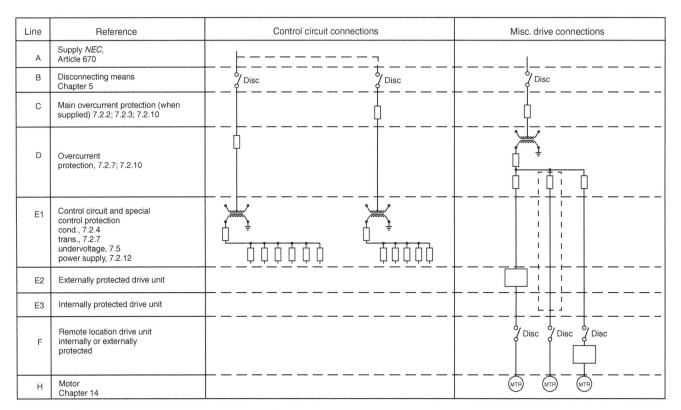

FIGURE A.7.2.1(b) One Line Representation of Electrical System Power Protection.

Shaded text = Revisions.   Δ = Text deletions and figure/table revisions.   • = Section deletions.   *N* = New material.

N **A.7.8.1** The manufacturer of the industrial machinery can determine what specific type of SPD, if any, and circuit location is to be used to provide the needed protection based on the installation and equipment design.

A risk assessment can be used to identify if the overvoltage protection for safety circuits is sufficient or if additional surge protection devices are needed.

A.8.1 See Annex J for descriptions of various grounding and bonding terminologies used in IEC and ANSI standards.

A.8.2.1.3 The minimum cross-sectional area of the external protective copper conductor can be required to be larger for IEC applications. See Table 1 in IEC 60204-1 for these requirements.

A.8.2.1.3.3 Some other standards require the letters PE for the connection to the external protective earthing system.

A.8.2.4 For additional information, see 13.4.5.3.

A.8.2.5.2 The letters PE or the bicolor combination GREEN-AND-YELLOW are used in some countries.

A.9.2 Some examples of safety-related functions are emergency stopping, interlocking, temperature or speed control, and so forth, IEC 62061, ISO 13849-1,ISO 13849-2, ANSI B11.0, ANSI B11-TR4, and ANSI B11-TR6 are examples of applicable functional safety standards. Compliance with other standards for particular applications and types of machinery can require additional or specific functional safety requirements.

A.9.2.2 For removal of power it can be sufficient to remove the power needed to generate a torque or force. This can be achieved by declutching, disconnecting, switching off, or by electronic means *(see 9.2.5.4.1.4)*. When stop functions are initiated it can be necessary to discontinue machine functions other than motion.

A.9.2.3.3 See 9.2.4 for overriding of safeguards under special conditions.

A.9.2.5.3.1 The supply circuit disconnecting means when opened achieves a Category 0 stop.

△ **A.9.2.5.4** For other safety-related stop functions, see 9.4.3.4.

Emergency stop and emergency switching off are complementary protective measures that are not primary means of risk reduction for hazards (e.g., entrapment, entanglement, electric shock, or burn) at a machine *(see ISO 12100)*.

An emergency stop function might be required based on the risk assessment and when one or more of the following criteria exist:

(1) Hazards and hazardous situations could arise rapidly as in the case of fast-moving equipment.
(2) Hazard zones for a large machine extend beyond an area immediately accessible by one person [e.g., length exceeds 10 m (30 ft)].
(3) Machine hazard zones are not completely within view from a single vantage point.
(4) There are motions accessible that are deemed low risk but still have the potential for causing harm (e.g., product moving on a roller conveyor).
(5) Multiple workstations and/or multiple personnel are involved in the normal production operation.

Principles for the design of emergency stop equipment, including functional aspects, are given in ISO 13850.

See Annex E of IEC 60204-1.

A.9.2.5.4.1.4 IEC 61508 and IEC 61800-5-2 give guidance to the manufacturer of drives on how to design a drive for safety-related functions.

A.9.2.5.4.2 The functional aspects of emergency switching off are given in 536.4 of IEC 60364-5-53.

A.9.2.5.5.1 Hold-to-run controls can be accomplished by two-hand control devices.

A.9.2.5.6 Annex B provides an inquiry form to ensure all parties have reviewed this requirement where certain conditions could be a point of concern.

A.9.2.7.1 Some of these applications and system integrity considerations can also be applicable to control functions employing serial data communication techniques where the communications link uses a cable (e.g., coaxial, twisted pair, optical).

A.9.2.7.3.1(3) A valid signal also includes the signal that confirms communication is established and maintained. *(See Annex B.)*

A.9.2.7.4 One way to determine applicable error detection methods is to refer to IEC 60870-5-1.

A.9.3.2 On some manually controlled machines, operators provide monitoring.

A.9.4.1 More information on these risk reduction techniques can be found in Annex H. In general, only single failures need to be regarded. In the event of higher levels of risk, it can be necessary to ensure that more than one failure cannot result in a hazardous condition. Where memory retention is achieved, for example, by the use of battery power, measures should be taken to prevent hazardous situations arising from failure or removal of the battery. Means should be provided to prevent unauthorized or inadvertent memory alteration by, for example, a key, an access code, or a tool.

A.9.4.3 SEMI S2 permits software- and firmware-based controllers performing safety-related functions, and SEMI S2 Related Information #14 provides additional information on how to design and implement functional safety for use in semiconductor manufacturing equipment.

A.9.4.3.4 IEC 62061, ISO 13849-1, and ISO 13849-2 provide requirements for the design of control systems incorporating the use of software- and firmware-based controllers to perform safety-related functions (i.e., safety circuits). IEC 61508 provides requirements for the design of software- and firmware-based safety controllers. IEC 61800-5-2 and IEC 61508 give guidance to the drive manufacturer on the design of drives intended to provide safety functions.

A.10.1.1 For further information on device selection, mounting, identification, and coding, see IEC 61310-1 and IEC 61310-3. Particular consideration should be taken in the selection, arrangement, programming, and use of operator input devices such as touchscreens, keypads, and keyboards, for the control of hazardous machine operations.

A.10.1.3 For further information on degrees of protection, see Annex F. Also see NEMA 250, UL 50, UL 508, and IEC 60529.

A.10.1.4.2 For further information on direct opening operation, see Annex K of IEC 60947-5-1.

A.10.3.3 Indicating towers on machines should have the applicable colors in the following order from the top down; RED, YELLOW, BLUE, GREEN, and WHITE.

A.10.3.4 For additional information, see IEC 61310-1 for recommended flashing rates and pulse/pause ratios.

A.10.7.2.2 For further information on direct opening operation, see Annex K of IEC 60947-5-1.

A.10.8.2.1 For further information on direct opening operation, see Annex K of IEC 60947-5-1.

A.10.8.4.2 Where emergency switching off devices are on operator control stations that can be disconnected, to avoid the possibility of confusion between active and inactive emergency switching off devices, it is recommended that emergency switching off devices on operator control stations that can be disconnected do not have a yellow background.

A.10.9 Displays intended to be warning devices are recommended to be of the flashing or rotary type and be provided with an audible warning device.

A.11.2.1.4 Where access is required for regular maintenance or adjustment, the location of relevant devices is recommended to be between 0.4 m (15.75 in.) and 2.0 m (6½ ft) above the servicing level to facilitate maintenance. The location of the terminals is recommended to be at least 0.2 m (7.88 in.) above the servicing level and be so placed that conductors and cables can be easily connected to them.

A.11.2.1.7 For additional information on attachment plug and receptacle combinations, see 13.4.5.

A.11.3.1 The degrees of protection against ingress of water and other liquids are covered by NEMA 250. See also Annex F.

A.11.5 Figure A.11.5 identifies the requirements for determining the working spaces for electrical equipment associated with industrial machinery.

The left side of Figure A.11.5 depicts a situation where the machine supply circuit disconnecting means, required by 5.1.9.1, is located in the industrial machine control panel or compartment.

The right side of Figure A.11.5 depicts a situation where the machine supply circuit disconnecting means, required by 5.1.9.1, is externally mounted to the industrial machine control cabinet or the compartment it supplies.

A.12.1.1 Typical operating conditions include the following:

(1) Voltage and frequency
(2) Current
(3) Protection against electric shock
(4) Grouping of cables
(5) Characteristics associated with power conversion equipment

Some insulated circuit conductors (e.g., thermoplastic) connected to the output of power conversion equipment can be susceptible to breakdown from arcing (i.e., corona discharge) occurring under certain conditions due to the characteristics of the output waveform of the drive. Factors affecting the conductors include, but are not limited to, the voltage, frequency, and current of the output; the length of the conduc-

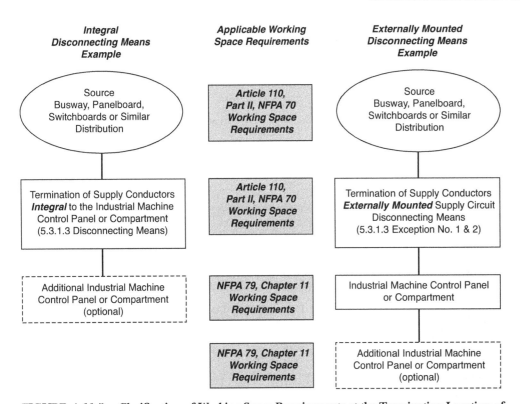

FIGURE A.11.5 Clarification of Working Space Requirements at the Termination Location of Machine Supply Circuit Conductors.

Shaded text = Revisions.   **Δ** = Text deletions and figure/table revisions.   • = Section deletions.   **N** = New material.

tors; the spacing between the conductors; and the dielectric strength of the conductor insulation. Methods to mitigate breakdown include consideration of one or more of these factors.

External influences include the following:

(1) Ambient temperature
(2) Presence of water, oil, or other fluid substances
(3) Radiation
(4) Ultraviolet light
(5) Corrosive substances
(6) Mechanical stresses due to the following:

   (a) Installation
   (b) Fire hazards

A.12.2.2 See Annex I.

A.12.4.2 Some examples of types that do not permit marking with voltage rating include Class 2 and Class 3 circuit cable, power limited tray cable, instrumentation tray cable, and communications cable, because the voltage rating is included in the cable class marking. See 12.9.2 for marking requirements for AWM.

A.12.5.2 For additional information, see 110.14(C) of *NFPA 70* for terminal temperature limitations.

A.12.6.1.3 See UL 2237 Outline.

A.12.6.4 Examples of special wiring applications include solderless wrap, wire clip–type connectors, shielded conductors, or the like.

A.12.7.1.2 Cables for such conditions are specified in relevant national standards.

The operational life of the cable will be reduced where unfavorable operating conditions such as high tensile stress, small radii, bending into another plane, and/or where frequent duty cycles coincide.

A.12.7.3 Where cables of circular cross-sectional area are installed on drums, the maximum current-carrying capacity in free air should be derated in accordance with Table 12.7.3. For additional information, also refer to Clause 44 of IEC 60621-3.

A.12.8.2 The ampacity values of Table 12.8.2 are based on Table 400.5(A) of *NFPA 70*.

A.12.9 Special cables and conductors require additional consideration of their design properties to determine suitability for intended use (e.g., chemical, flexibility, flammability resistance, shielding, conductor configuration). Those evaluated to UL 758 are often marked with multiple identifying characteristics *(see 12.3.1 and 12.8.1)* in addition to AWM.

A.13.1.1.10 A single tag bearing the complete identification is preferred.

A.13.1.1.11 For additional information on terminal blocks, refer to IEC 60947-7-1.

A.13.1.2.1 Protection against accidental disconnection includes plug and receptacle combinations having twist lock, latches, or mechanisms for this purpose.

N **A.13.1.2.3** For examples, see UL 2237 Outline and UL 2238.

Δ **A.13.1.2.4** For examples, see UL 2237 Outline and UL 2238.

A.13.1.5 The output of the pick-up can be a current source; therefore, damage to the cable can result in a high voltage hazard.

A.13.1.7.1 For additional information on flexible cords, refer to UL 62. For additional information on connectors and assemblies of connectors and cords, refer to UL 2237 Outline and UL 2238.

A.13.2.2.1 The international standards reserve the use of the bicolor combination GREEN-AND-YELLOW for this purpose. The bicolor combination is such that on any 15 mm (0.6 in.) length, one of the colors covers at least 30 percent and not more than 70 percent of the surface of the conductor, and the other color covers the remainder of the surface.

A.13.2.3.1 IEC 60204-1 reserves the use of the color BLUE for the neutral conductor and requires its use when identification is by color.

A.13.2.4.1 The 2002 edition of this standard permitted the consistent applied use of either the color orange or the color yellow in fulfillment of this requirement. For further information on excepted circuits, see 5.1.13.

A.13.3.1 For additional information on flame-retardant materials, refer to IEC 60332-1-1.

A.13.5.2 It should be recognized that, for certain conditions, a larger size raceway or a lesser raceway fill should be considered.

A.13.5.3.1.2 Metric designators and trade sizes for conduit, tubing, and associated fittings and accessories are shown in Table A.13.5.3.1.2.

A.13.5.3.2.2 The use of dissimilar metals in contact that can cause galvanic action should be avoided.

A.13.5.3.2.3 The use of dissimilar metals in contact that can cause galvanic action should be avoided.

A.13.5.3.2.4 The use of dissimilar metals in contact that can cause galvanic action should be avoided.

A.13.5.3.3.1 For additional information about rigid nonmetallic conduit, refer to UL 651.

A.13.5.3.3.3 For additional information, see Table 352.44 of *NFPA 70*.

Table A.13.5.3.1.2 Metric Designator and Trade Sizes

Metric Designator	Trade Size
12	⅜
16	½
21	¾
27	1
35	1¼
41	1½
53	2
63	2½
78	3
91	3½
103	4
129	5
155	6

Note: The metric designators and trade sizes are for identification purposes only and are not actual dimensions.

A.13.5.4.1.2 Metric trade numerical designations for flexible metal conduit and liquidtight flexible metal conduit are ⅜ = 12, ½ = 16, ¾ = 21, 1 = 27, 1¼ = 35, 1½ = 41, 2 = 53, 2½ = 63, 3 = 78, 3½ = 91, and 4 = 103.

A.13.5.5.4 Metric trade numerical designations for liquidtight flexible nonmetallic conduit are ⅜ = 12, ½ = 16, ¾ = 21, 1 = 27, 1¼ = 35, 1½ = 41, 2 = 53, 2½ = 63, 3 = 78, 3½ = 91, and 4 = 103.

A.13.5.7 See Section 16.2 for information on safety signs.

A.14.1 For additional information related to motor standards, refer to UL 1004-1, NEMA MG-1, IEEE 841, or IEC 60034-1.

The protection requirements for motors and associated equipment are given in Section 7.2 for overcurrent protection, Section 7.3 for overload protection, and Section 7.6 for overspeed protection.

A.14.4 For a comparison between kilowatt and horsepower size, see Annex G, Table G.1 and Table G.2.

A.14.7 Associated machine actuators are those associated with the same motion (e.g., cable drums and long-travel drives).

A.16.2.1 One such safety sign for consideration is the IEC symbol for risk of electric shock. See Figure A.16.2.1.

A.16.2.3 See *NFPA 70E* for assistance in determining severity of potential exposures and ANSI Z535.4 for guidelines for the design of safety signs and labels for application to products.

A.16.3 Such markings can be as agreed between the user and the supplier of the equipment. See Annex B for additional information.

For further information on symbols, see IEC 60417 and ISO 7000.

Consideration should be given to the use of IEC symbols for pushbuttons. See Figure A.16.3(a) through Figure A.16.3(d).

FIGURE A.16.2.1 Symbol that Represents Risk of Electrical Shock — IEC Symbol Number 5036.

FIGURE A.16.3(a) Symbol that Represents Start or On — IEC Symbol Number 5007.

FIGURE A.16.3(b) Symbol that Represents Stop or Off — IEC Symbol Number 5008.

FIGURE A.16.3(c) Symbol that Represents Alternatively Act as Start and Stop or On and Off — IEC Symbol Number 5010.

FIGURE A.16.3(d) Symbol that Represents Movement When Pressed and Stop Movement When Released (Jogging) — IEC Symbol Number 5011.

A.16.4.1(3) When overcurrent devices with a slash rating, such as 120/240, 480Y/277, or 600Y/347V, are connected to the supply circuit, see 7.2.1.4.

A.17.4 The technical documentation should also contain, where appropriate, information regarding load currents, peak starting currents, and permitted voltage drops. That information should be contained in either the system or circuit diagram(s).

A.17.5.1 In complex cases, it can be necessary to refer to the assembly drawings for details.

A.17.5.3 For further information regarding supply circuit conductors, see 7.2.2.

A.17.5.4 For recommendations concerning supplier agreements, see Annex B.

A.17.5.5 For recommendations concerning supplier agreements, see Annex B.

A.17.5.6 Examples of installation diagrams can be found in Annex D.

A.17.5.7 Examples of interconnection diagrams/tables can be found in Annex D.

A.17.6 Examples of block diagrams, further rules, and examples can be found in Annex D.

Function diagrams can be used as either part of, or in addition to, the block diagram. Examples of function diagrams can be found in Annex D.

A.17.7.1 See Annex D for examples of electrical diagrams.

A.17.7.2 Examples of circuit diagrams can be found in Annex D.

A.17.7.3 The diagram showing the terminals for interface connections can be used in conjunction with the circuit diagram(s) for simplification. The diagram should contain a reference to the detailed circuit diagram of each unit shown.

A.17.7.5 The class designation letters/device function designations identified in ANSI Y32.2/IEEE 315 are not intended for use on industrial control and industrial equipment as device and component designations. See Annex E for examples of device and component designations.

A.17.8.1 Particular attention should be given to the safety measures provided and to the improper methods of operation that are anticipated.

A.17.9.1 Recommendations on maintenance/service records should be part of that manual. Troubleshooting information and suggestions for locating and replacing faulty components, suggested preventative maintenance schedules, and related data should be included.

A.17.10 See Annex D, Figure D.1(o), Sample Parts list.

A.18.1 A relevant ANSI specialist standard might deem necessary tests 1 through 5 inclusively or individually. It is recommended that the sequence listed be followed. Following this order will help ensure the accuracy of the test results and the safety of personnel. Refer to SEMI S9 for additional information on performing the testing described in Section 18.1.

Δ **A.18.2** The concepts of SELV are further explained in UL 60950-1, UL 61010-1, and IEC 60364-4-41. It should be noted that there is a difference in the definitions of SELV in these standards.

A.18.4 Refer to SEMI S9 for additional information on performing this dielectric withstand (hypot) test.

A.19.2 The relationship between the motor current and motor temperature changes when the motor is operated by a servo drive. When operating at reduced speeds, overheating of motors could occur at current levels less than or equal to motor-rated full-load current. This is the result of reduced motor cooling when its shaft-mounted fan is operating less than rated nameplate rpm.

Annex B   Inquiry Form for the Electrical Equipment of Machines

This annex is not a part of the requirements of this NFPA document but is included for informational purposes only.

B.1 It is recommended that the information in Figure B.1 be provided by the intended user of the equipment. It facilitates an agreement between the user and supplier on basic conditions and additional user requirements to ensure proper design, application, and utilization of the electrical equipment of the machine *(see Section 4.1)*.

INQUIRY FORM FOR THE ELECTRICAL EQUIPMENT OF MACHINES

Name of manufacturer/supplier _____

Name of end user _____

Tender/Order No. _____ Date _____

Type of machine/serial number _____

1. Are there to be modifications as allowed for within this standard? ❑ Yes ❑ No

Operating Conditions — Special Requirements (see Chapter 4)

2. Ambient temperature range _____

3. Humidity range _____

4. Altitude _____

5. Environmental (e.g., corrosive atmospheres, particulate matter, EMC) _____

6. Non-ionizing radiation _____

7. Vibration, shock _____

8. Special installation and operation requirements (e.g., additional flame-retardant requirements for cables and conductors)
    _____

Power Supply(ies) and Related Conditions (see Chapter 4)

9. Anticipated voltage fluctuations (if more than ±10%) _____

10. Anticipated frequency fluctuations (if more than in 4.4.2.2) _____

    Specification of short-term value _____

11. Indicate possible future changes in electrical equipment that will require an increase in the electrical supply
    requirements _____

12. Indicate for each source of electrical supply required:

    Nominal Voltage (V) _____ ac _____ dc

    If ac, number of phases _____ frequency _____ Hz

    Prospective short-circuit current at the point of supply to the machine _____ kA rms *(see also question 15)*

    Fluctuations outside values given in 4.4.2.1 _____

13. Type of power supply system grounding:

    Wye phases midpoint grounded _____   Delta phases midpoint grounded _____

    Delta phases corner grounded _____   High impedance grounded _____

    Wye phases midpoint ungrounded _____   Delta phases ungrounded _____

14. Is the electrical equipment to be connected to a grounded supply conductor? *(see Section 5.1)* ❑ Yes ❑ No

15. Does the user or the supplier provide the overcurrent protection of the supply conductors? *(see 7.2.2)* ❑ Yes ❑ No

    Type and rating of overcurrent protective devices _____

16. Machine supply circuit disconnecting device means

    — Is the disconnection of the grounded conductor required? ❑ Yes ❑ No

    — Is a link for the grounded conductor permissible? ❑ Yes ❑ No

17. Type of machine supply circuit disconnecting device and associated external operating means (e.g., handle) to be
    provided
    _____

NFPA 79 (p. 1 of 2)

Δ **FIGURE B.1**   **Inquiry Form for the Electrical Equipment of Machines.**

18. Limit of power up to which three-phase AC motors can be started directly across the incoming supply lines _____ HP

19. Can the number of motor overload detection devices be reduced? *(see Section 7.3)* ❑ Yes ❑ No

20. Where the machine is equipped with local lighting:

   — Highest permissible voltage _____ V

   — If lighting circuit voltage is not obtained directly from the power supply, state preferred voltage _____ V

Other Considerations

21. Functional identification *(see Section 16.3)* _____

22. Inscriptions/special markings _____

23. Mark of certification ❑ Yes ❑ No   If YES, which one? _____

   On electrical equipment? _____   In which language? _____

24. Technical documentation *(see Section 17.1)*

   On what media? _____   In which language? _____

25. Size, location, and purpose of wireways, open cable trays, or cable supports to be provided by the user *(see Section 17.5)* (additional sheets to be provided where necessary)

   _____

   _____

   _____

26. Are locks with removable keys to be provided for fastening doors or covers? *(see 6.2.3.1)*   ❑ Yes ❑ No

27. Indicate if special limitations on the size or weight affect the transport of a particular machine or control equipment to the installation site:

   — Maximum dimensions _____

   — Maximum weight _____

28. In the case of machines with frequent repetitive cycles of operation dependent on manual control, how frequently will cycles of operation be repeated?

   _____ per hour

29. For what length of time is it expected that the machine will be operated at this rate without subsequent pause?

   _____ minutes

30. In the case of specially built machines, is a certificate of operating tests with the loaded machine to be supplied? ❑ Yes ❑ No

31. In the case of other machines, is a certificate of operating-type tests on a loaded prototype machine to be supplied? ❑ Yes ❑ No

32. For cableless control systems, specify the time delay before automatic machine shutdown is initiated in the absence of a valid signal *(see 9.2.7.3)*: _____ seconds

33. Do you need a specific method of conductor identification to be used for the conductors referred to in 13.2.4?

   ❑ Yes ❑ No   Type _____

NFPA 79 (p. 2 of 2)

Δ FIGURE B.1   *Continued*

Annex C Examples of Industrial Machines Covered by NFPA 79

This annex is not a part of the requirements of this NFPA document but is included for informational purposes only.

C.1 Machine Tools. Examples of machine tools are as follows:

(1) Metal cutting
(2) Metal forming

C.2 Plastics Machinery. Examples of plastics machinery are as follows:

(1) Injection molding machines
(2) Extrusion machinery
(3) Blow molding machines
(4) Specialized processing machines
(5) Thermoset molding machines
(6) Size reduction equipment

C.3 Wood Machinery. Examples of wood machinery are as follows:

(1) Woodworking machinery
(2) Laminating machinery
(3) Sawmill machines

C.4 Assembly Machines.

C.5 Material-Handling Machines. Examples of material-handling machines are as follows:

(1) Industrial robots

(2) Transfer machines
(3) Sortation machines
(4) Conveyors and conveying machines

C.6 Inspection/Testing Machines. Examples of inspection/testing machines are as follows:

(1) Coordinate measuring machines
(2) In-process gauging machines

C.7 Packaging Machines. Examples of packaging machines are as follows:

(1) Carton-strapping machines
(2) Drum-filling machines
(3) Palletizing machines

Annex D Technical Documentation

This annex is not a part of the requirements of this NFPA document but is included for informational purposes only.

Δ **D.1** Figure D.1(a) through Figure D.1(q) are not intended to be design guidelines. They are included only to illustrate documentation methods.

Company emblem

Designed by: Machine Supplier, Inc.
Address 1
Address 2
Address 3
Postal code(s)
E-mail address

Customer: Customer
Project: Project number, Name
Subject: Sample drawings

Utility Usage — Ratings		
Electrical		xx fla
Compressed air	psig	xx psig xx scfm
Plant water	psig	xx gpm xx °F/°C
Recirc. chill water	psig	xx gpm xx °F/°C
Steam	psig	xx lb/hr
Natural gas	psig	xx psig
Other		

Sheet #	Description of Sheet
1	Machine cover sheet & sheet index
2	System layout & installation diagram
3	Block (system) diagram
4	Inter-connection diagram
5	Elementary schematic
6	PLC input diagram
7	PLC output diagram
8	Sample enclosure layout
9	Sample enclosure layout
10	Sequence of operations — graphical
11	Sequence of operations — descriptive
12	Sample servo diagram
13	Sample PLC network — station layout
14	Sample operator station
15	Sample parts list
16	ISO (A3) drawing standard framework
17	(Selected) ANSI Y32.2 / IEEE 315 symbol table
18	
19	
20	
21	
22	
23	
24	
25	

Doc. #	References to Additional Technical Documents
1	Operating manual — manual number
2	Maintenance manual — manual number
3	PLC programming manual — manual name and number
4	Network installation manual — manual number
5	AC servo drive manual — manual number

Electrical Characteristics	
3-phase, + earth	60 Hz
Main line voltage	460 V
Control voltage	115 V ac
Total motor full load	x.xx kW
Full load current	xxx A
Disc or circuit breaker rating	
Main line rated fuse capacity	
Machine serial number	
Manufactured in year	2 xxx
Electrical diagram number	

FIGURE D.1(a)   Cover Sheet and Sheet Index.

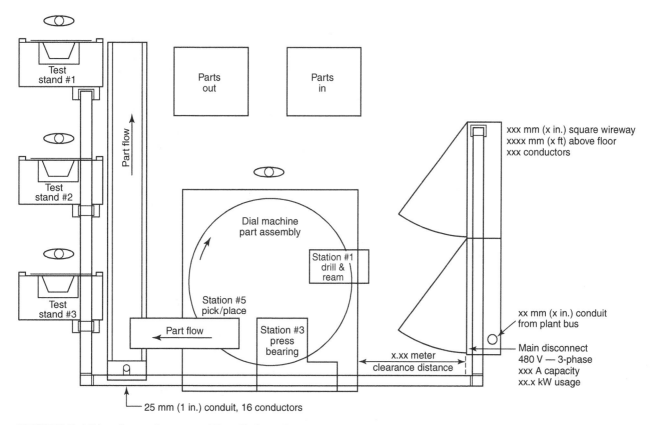

FIGURE D.1(b)   System Layout and Installation Diagram.

2021 Edition

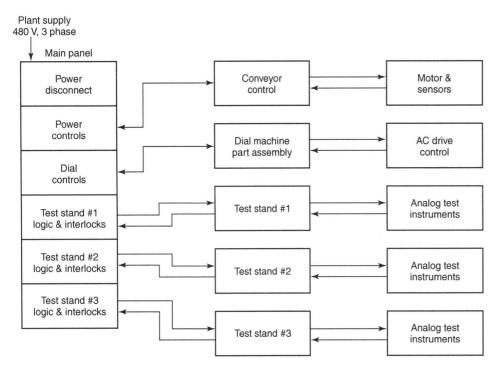

FIGURE D.1(c)   Block (System) Diagram.

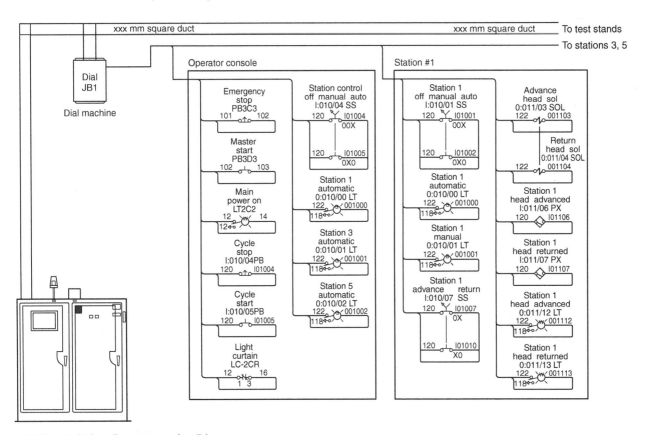

FIGURE D.1(d)   Interconnection Diagram.

Shaded text = Revisions.   Δ = Text deletions and figure/table revisions.   • = Section deletions.   *N* = New material.

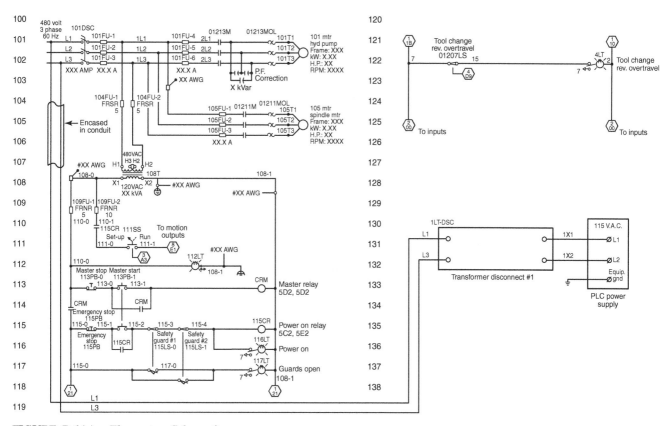

FIGURE D.1(e)   Elementary Schematic.

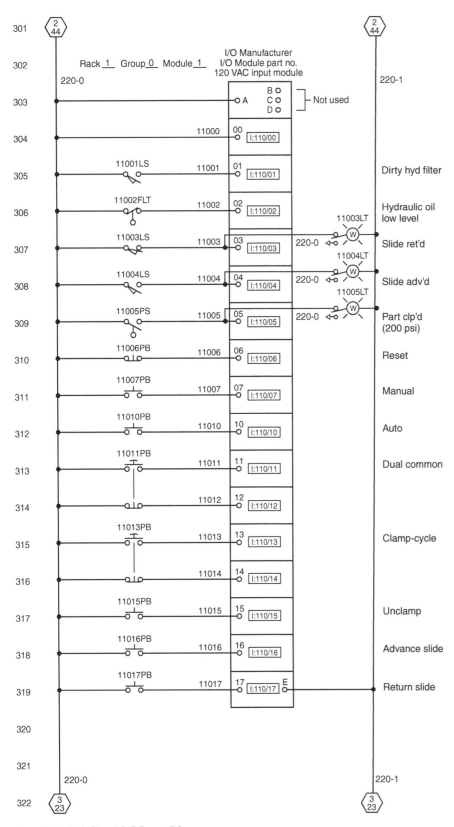

FIGURE D.1(f)   PLC Input Diagram.

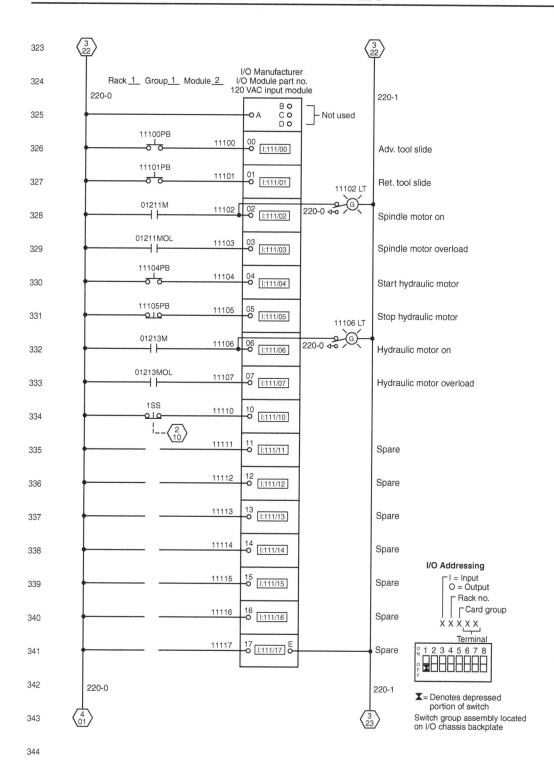

FIGURE D.1(f) *Continued*

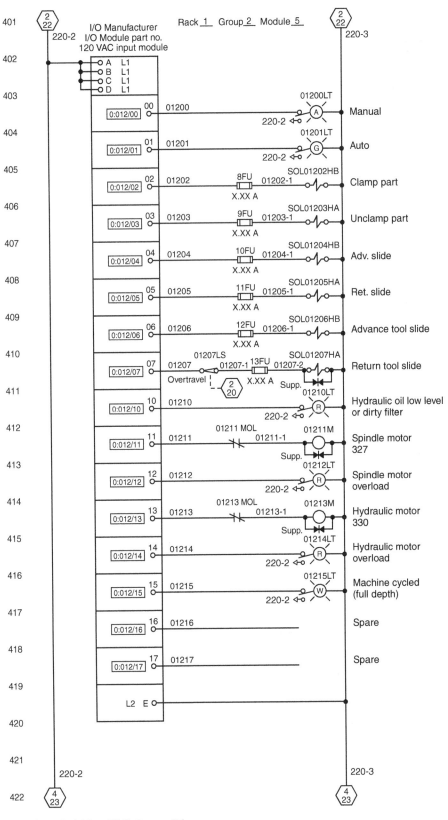

FIGURE D.1(g)   PLC Output Diagram.

423

424

425

426

427

428

429

430

431

432

433

434

435

436

437

438

439

440

441

442

443

444

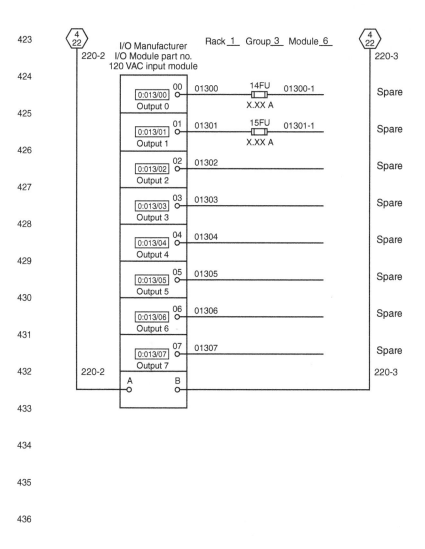

FIGURE D.1(g)   *Continued*

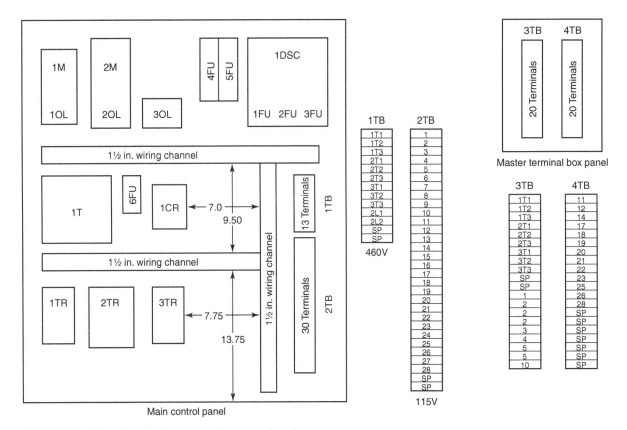

FIGURE D.1(h)   Sample Enclosure Layout — Interior.

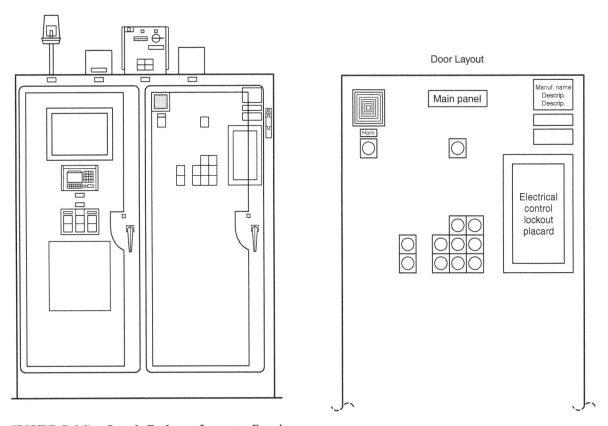

FIGURE D.1(i)   Sample Enclosure Layout — Exterior.

Shaded text = Revisions.   Δ = Text deletions and figure/table revisions.   • = Section deletions.   *N* = New material.

Solenoid No.	Air or Hyd	Action Energized Input Sensor No.	Seq. No.	Sequence Description	Cycle Time (sec)	1	2	3	4	5	6	7	8	9	10	11	12	13	14	15	16	17	18	19	20	21	22	23	24	25
—	—	I:XXX/XX PRS	1	Part present escapement delay	.5	■																								
0:XXX/XX SOL	AIR	I:XXX/XX PRS	2	Escapement opens	.75	■	■																							
—	—	—	3	Part travel to shuttle	.75		■																							
—	—	I:XXX/XX PRS	4	Part present shuttle delay	.5			■																						
0:XXX/XX SOL	AIR	I:XXX/XX PRS	5	Escapement closes	.75			■																						
0:XXX/XX SOL	AIR	I:XXX/XX PRS	6	Shuttle shifts to track #1	1.0			■	■																					
0:XXX/XX SOL	AIR	—	7	Part accel track #1 energizes	3.5				■	■	■	■																		
—	—	I:XXX/XX PRS	8	Part present loader #1 delay	.5							■																		
0:XXX/XX SOL	AIR	I:XXX/XX PRS	9	Shuttle shifts to center	1.0								■																	
0:XXX/XX SOL	AIR	I:XXX/XX PRS	10	Loader track #1 advances	1.0								■																	
—	—	—	11	Loaded track #1 advanced dwell	.5									■																
0:XXX/XX SOL	AIR	I:XXX/XX PRS	12	Loaded track #1 returns	1.0										■															
—	—	—	13	Part present escapement delay	.5									■																
0:XXX/XX SOL	AIR	I:XXX/XX PRS	14	Escapement opens	.75									■	■															
—	—	—	15	Part travel to shuttle	.75										■															
—	—	I:XXX/XX PRS	16	Part present shuttle delay	.5											■														
0:XXX/XX SOL	AIR	I:XXX/XX PRS	17	Escapement closes	.75											■														
0:XXX/XX SOL	AIR	I:XXX/XX PRS	18	Shuttle shifts to track #2	1.0												■													
0:XXX/XX SOL	AIR	—	19	Part accel track #2 energizes	3.5												■	■	■	■										
—	—	I:XXX/XX PRS	20	Part present loader #2 delay	.5															■										
0:XXX/XX SOL	AIR	I:XXX/XX PRS	21	Shuttle shifts to center	1.0																■									
0:XXX/XX SOL	AIR	I:XXX/XX PRS	22	Loader track #2 advances	1.0																■									
—	—	—	23	Loaded track #2 advanced dwell	.5																	■								
0:XXX/XX SOL	AIR	I:XXX/XX PRS	24	Loaded track #2 returns	1.0																		■							

Cycle time for one part / one track = 11.0 sec.
Cycle time for one part each track = 19.0 sec.

FIGURE D.1(j)   Sequence of Operations — Graphical.

Sequence of Operation

A. Machine operation: press "Motors Start" pushbutton 2PB. Motors start.

B. Select spindle speed by turning selector switch to 1SS to 1NC, energizing 3SOL, to increase or to DEC, energizing 4SOL, to decrease setting.

C. With correct spindle direction selected, limit switch 1LS is actuated. Press "Spindle Start" pushbutton 4PB, energizing relay 1CR, which energizes 1SOL. Spindle starts and pressure switch 1PS is actuated, 1PS energizes 1TR, and after a time delay 2SOL is energized, permitting movement of machine elements at selected feed rates.

D. Pressing "Spindle Stop" pushbutton 3PB stops spindle and feeds movements simultaneously.

E. Lubrication operation.

F. Pressure switch 2PS is closed.
   1. Timer 2TR clutch is energized when motors start.
   2. Contact 2TR1 closes and energizes timer motor MTR, starting lube timing period.
   3. Contact 2TR3 closes and energizes timer 3TR.

G. Timer 2TR times out.
   1. Contact 2TR1 opens, de-energizing timer motor MTR.
   2. Contact 2TR2 closes, energizing 5SOL.
   3. Contact 2TR3 opens, de-energizing timer 3TR.
   4. Lubrication pressure actuates pressure switch 2PS, deenergizing and resetting timer 2TR. Contacts 2TR1, 2TR2, and 2TR3 open.
   5. Contact 2TR2 opening, de-energizes 5SOL.

H. Reduced lubrication pressure deactuates pressure switch 2PS and sequence repeats.

Switch Operation

1LS (115) actuated by spindle direction lever engaged

1PS (118) operated when spindle clutch engaged

2PS (126) operated by normal lube pressure

1FS (129) operated by adequate lube supply

For panels and control station layout see _____Sheet 2_____

For hydraulic diagram see _____

For lubrication diagram see _____

Last wire number used _____28_____

Last relay number used _____1CR_____

Supplier's dwg. no. _____

Supplier's name _____

Purchase order no. _____P.O. 91011_____

Serial no. of machine _____TYP 121314_____

These diagrams used for machine no. _____

FIGURE D.1(k)   Sequence of Operations — Descriptive Graphical.

Shaded text = Revisions.   Δ = Text deletions and figure/table revisions.   • = Section deletions.   *N* = New material.

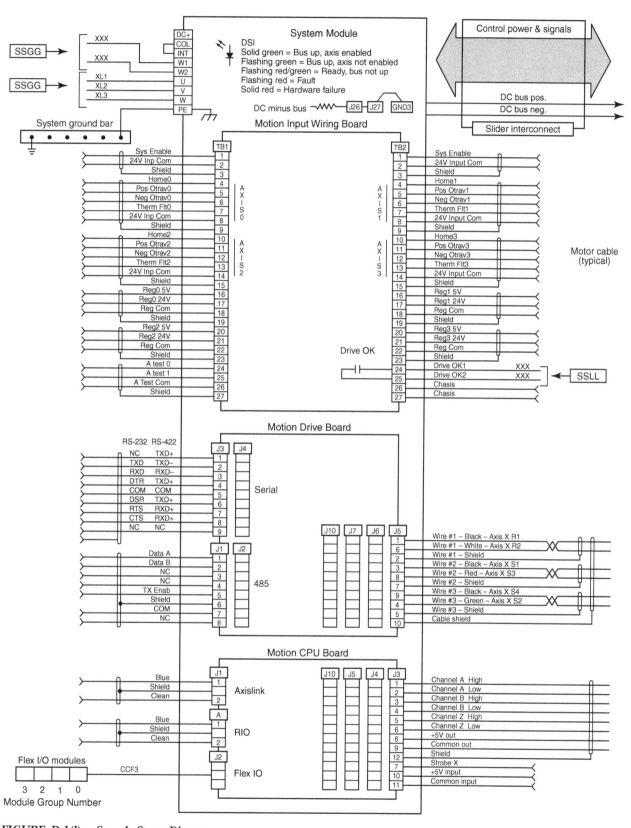

FIGURE D.1(1)   Sample Servo Diagram.

Shaded text = Revisions.   Δ = Text deletions and figure/table revisions.   • = Section deletions.   N = New material.

2021 Edition

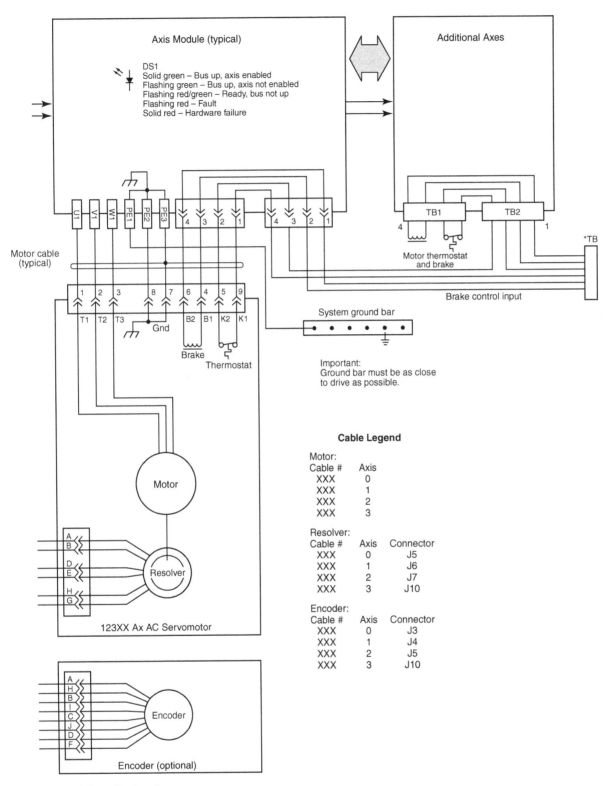

FIGURE D.1(l)   *Continued*

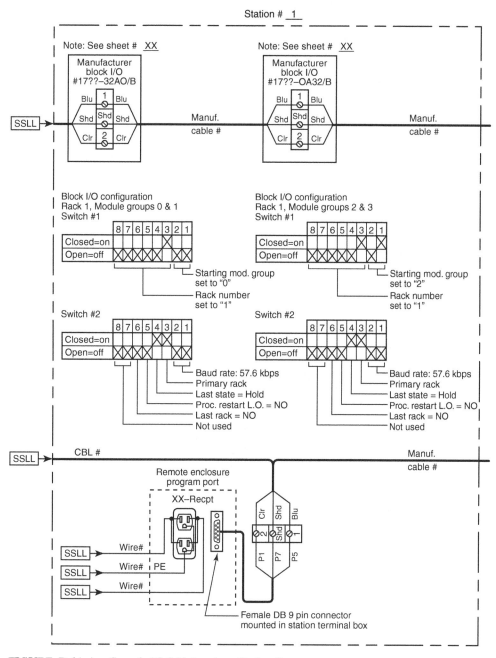

FIGURE D.1(m)   Sample PLC Network — Station Layout.

Shaded text = Revisions.   Δ = Text deletions and figure/table revisions.   • = Section deletions.   *N* = New material.

2021 Edition

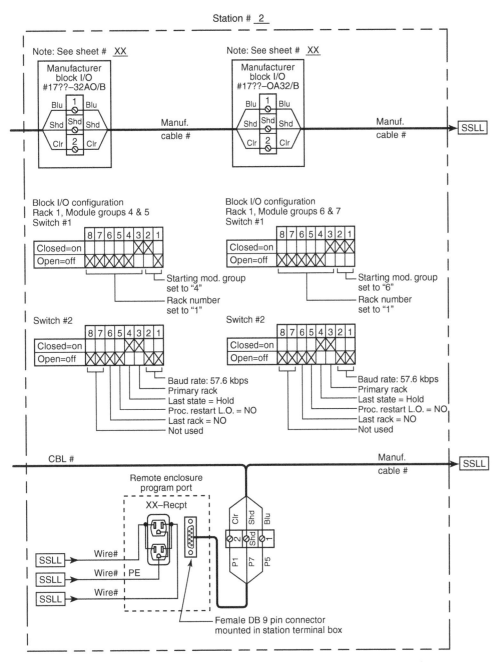

FIGURE D.1(m) *Continued*

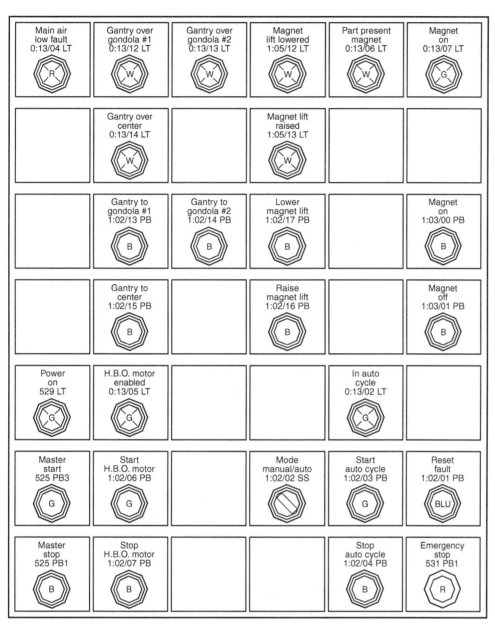

FRONT VIEW

FIGURE D.1(n)   Sample Operator Station.

Magnet on 0:13/07 LT	Part present magnet 0:13/06 LT	Magnet lift lowered 1:05/12 LT	Gantry over gondola #2 0:13/13 LT	Gantry over gondola #1 0:13/12 LT	Main air low fault 0:13/04 LT
0:13/07 (G) 5113 / 5112	0:13/06 (W) 5113 / 5112	1:05/12 (W) 5063 / 5062	0:13/13 (W) 5113 / 5112	0:13/12 (W) 5113 / 5112	0:13/04 (R) 5113 / 5112
		Raised 1:05/13 LT — 1:05/13 (W) 5063 / 5062		Center 0:13/14 LT — 0:13/14 (W) 5113	
Magnet on 1:03/00 PB — 5052 —1:03/00		Lower magnet lift 1:02/17 PB — 5052 —1:02/17	Gantry to gondola #2 1:02/14 PB — 5052 —1:02/14	Gantry to gondola #1 1:02/13 PB — 5052 —1:02/13	
Magnet off 1:03/01 PB — 5052 —1:03/01		Raise magnet lift 1:02/16 PB — 5052 —1:02/16		Gantry to center 1:02/15 PB — 5052 —1:02/15	
	In auto cycle 0:13/03 LT — 0:13/03 (G) 5113 / 5112			H.B.O. motor enabled 0:13/05 LT — 0:13/05 (G) 5113 / 5112	Power on 529 LT — 5255 (G) 5242 / 5241
Reset fault 1:02/01 PB — 5052 —1:02/01	Start auto cycle 1:02/03 PB — 5052 —1:02/03	Mode manual/auto 1:02/02 SS — 5052 —1:02/02		Start H.B.O. motor 1:02/06 PB — 5052 —1:02/06	Master start 525 PB3 — 5254 — 5255
Emergency stop 531 PB1 — 5241 — 5311	Stop auto cycle 1:02/04 PB — 5052 —1:02/04			Stop H.B.O. motor 1:02/07 PB — 5052 —1:02/07	Master stop 525 PB1 — 5241 — 5251

REAR VIEW

FIGURE D.1(n)   *Continued*

Parts List					
Detail	Qty.	Identifier	Location	Manufacturer	Part Number	Description
---	---	---	---	---	---	---
0001	1	Enclosure	—	Supplier name	A–72X7318LP	2-door enclosure, 72.12X73.12X18.12
0002	1	Panel 1	—	Supplier name	A–72P72	72X72 sub-panel
0003	1	206M	Panel	Supplier name	5KE200LBIG3522	Motor, 22KW, 1200 RPM, Fr. 200L, B3 mount
0004	1	1PWRPLG	—	Supplier name	GE–0100–60	Bus fuse — Fusible, 100A, 600V
0005	1	204CB	—	Supplier name	SELA36AT0060	3 pole/100A circuit breaker, SE100 frame
0006	1	206M	—	Supplier name	CL06A311MJ	FVNR contactor, 30HP/460V, 48.0A, 120VAC coil
0007	1	211LTDSC	—	Supplier name	TF1000–JFB	Lighting disconnect, 1000VA, 480/120V enclosed
0008	12	XXFU	—	Supplier name	Type AGT	Fuse, 600V, XX AMP
0009	2	SQ2A3, SQ2B3	Machine	Supplier name	301AEP115	Proximity switch, 115VAC, 3 pin

FIGURE D.1(o)   **Sample Parts List.**

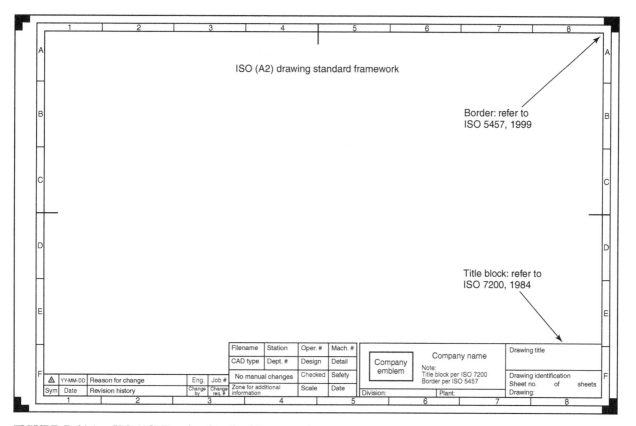

FIGURE D.1(p)   ISO (A2) Drawing Standard Framework.

ANSI Symbol	ANSI Code	IEC 61346-2 Symbol	IEC Code	Description
	CON		KM	Contactor contact open
	CON		KM	Contactor contact closed
	CR		KA	Relay contact open
	CR		KA	Relay contact closed
	TR		KT	Timed contact, N.O. – on delay (TDE)
	TR		KT	Timed contact, N.C. – on delay (TDE)
	TR		KT	Timed contact, N.C.– off delay (TDD)
	TR		KT	Timed contact, N.O. – off delay (TDD)
	SS		SA	Selector switch
	PB		SB	Pushbutton N.O.
	PB		SB	Pushbutton N.C.
	PB		SB	Pushbutton mushroom head
	FL		SL	Liquid level switch
	FLS		SF	Flow switch
	PS		SP	Pressure switch
	TS		ST	Temperature switch
	LS		SQ	Limit switch
	PRS		SQ	Proximity switch
	LT		HL	Indicating light
	CR		KA	Control relay coil
	CON		KM	Contactor coil
	M		KM	Motor starter coil
	TR		KA	Timer coil
	SOL		YV	Solenoid coil
	CTR		EC	Electromechanical counter
	CB		QF	Circuit breaker
	T1		X1 XT	Terminals (reference) Fused terminals (reference)
	FU		FU	Fuse, protective

FIGURE D.1(q)   Selections from ANSI Y32.2/IEEE 315 Symbol Table.

Shaded text = Revisions.   Δ = Text deletions and figure/table revisions.   • = Section deletions.   *N* = New material.

Annex E   Device and Component Designations

This annex is not a part of the requirements of this NFPA document but is included for informational purposes only.

E.1 Device and Compound Designations. The device and component designations given in Table E.1 are intended for use on diagrams in connection with the corresponding graphical symbols to indicate the function of the particular device. These device and component designations are based on the assignment of a standard letter or letters to the fundamental function that is performed by a component or device. Suitable numbers (1, 2, 3, etc.) and letters (A, B, C, etc.) can be added to the basic designation to differentiate between devices performing similar functions.

The assignment of a designation to a device on specific equipment is governed by the function of that device on that equipment and not by the type or nature of the device or its possible use for other functions on other equipment. The same type of device can perform different functions on different equipment or even on the same equipment and, consequently, can be identified by different designations.

Table E.1 Device and Component Designations

Designation	Device
ABE	Alarm or Annunciator Bell
ABU	Alarm or Annunciator Buzzer
AH	Alarm or Annunciator Horn
AM	Ammeter
AT	Autotransformer
CAP	Capacitor
CB	Circuit Breaker
CI	Circuit Interrupter
CNC	Computerized Numerical Controller
CON	Contactor
COs	Cable-Operated (Emergency) Switch
CPU	Central Processing Unit
CR	Control Relay
CRA	Control Relay, Automatic
CRH	Control Relay, Manual
CRL	Control Relay, Latch
CRM	Control Relay, Master
CRT	Cathode Ray Tube, Monitor or Video Display Unit
CRU	Control Relay, Unlatch
CS	Cam Switch
CT	Current Transformer
CTR	Counter
D	Diode
DISC	Disconnect Switch
DISP	Display
DR	Drive
EMO	Emergency (Machine) Off Device
END	Encoder
ESTOP	Emergency Stop
FLD	Field
FLS	Flow Switch
FS	Float Switch
FTS	Foot Switch
FU	Fuse
GEN	Generator

(continues)

Table E.1   *Continued*

Designation	Device
GRD, GND	Ground
GUI	Graphical User Interface
HM	Hour Meter
HTR	Heating Element
IC	Integrated Circuit
INST	Instrument
IOL	Instantaneous Overload
I/O	Input/Output Device
L	Inductor
LED	Light Emitting Diode
LS	Limit Switch
LT	Pilot Light
LVDT	Linear Variable Differential Transformer
M	Motor Starter
MD	Motion Detector
MF	Motor Starter – Forward
MG	Motor – Generator
MR	Motor Starter – Reverse
MTR	Motor
OIT	Operator Interface Terminal
OL	Overload Relay
PB	Pushbutton
PBL	Pushbutton, Illuminated
PC	Personal Computer
PCB	Printed Circuit Board
PEC	Photoelectric Device
PL	Plug
PLC	Programmable Logic Controller
POT	Potentiometer
PRS	Proximity Switch
PS	Pressure Switch
PWS	Power Supply
Q	Transistor
QTM	Thermistor
REC	Rectifier
RECP	Receptacle
RES	Resistor
RH	Rheostat
S	Switch
SCR	Silicon Controlled Rectifier
SOL	Solenoid
SNSR	Sensor
SS	Selector Switch
SSL	Selector Switch, Illuminated
SSR	Solid State Relay
ST	Saturable Transformer
SUP	Suppressor
SYN	Synchro or Resolver
T	Transformer
TACH	Tachometer Generator
TAS	Temperature-Actuated Switch
TB	Terminal Block
T/C	Thermocouple
TR	Timer Relay
TSDR	Transducer
TWS	Thumbwheel Switch
V	Electronic Tube
VAR	Varistor

(continues)

Shaded text = Revisions.   Δ = Text deletions and figure/table revisions.   • = Section deletions.   *N* = New material.

2021 Edition

Table E.1 *Continued*

Designation	Device
VM	Voltmeter
VR	Voltage Regulator
VS	Vacuum Switch
WLT	Worklight
WM	Wattmeter
X	Reactor
ZSS	Zero Speed Switch

Annex F   Electrical Enclosure Ratings: Type-Rating Versus IP-Rating

This annex is not a part of the requirements of this NFPA document but is included for informational purposes only.

Δ **F.1 Disclaimer.** Only IEC 60529 should be considered the source document for accurate information regarding IP-rating; UL 50, UL 508, and/or NEMA 250 should be considered the source documents regarding type-rating. The information presented in Annex F is limited and intended as introductory information. This annex is meant to give the user a sense of the IP-rating system and how it differs from the NEMA 250 type-rating system.

F.2 Rating for Electrical Enclosures.

F.2.1 Electrical enclosures are type-rated according to NEMA 250, UL 50, and UL 508 or IP-rated according to IEC 60529 based upon the degree of protection provided.

F.2.2 Type-rated and IP-rated electrical enclosures have only the following in common:

(1) A degree of protection for persons from hazardous components inside the enclosure
(2) A degree of protection for equipment inside the enclosure from ingress of solid foreign objects, including dust
(3) A degree of protection for equipment inside the enclosure from ingress of water

F.3 Type-Rating System. The type-rating system, in a single electrical enclosure document, points out additional requirements that a type-rated enclosure meets, which include the following:

(1) Mechanical impact on enclosure walls
(2) Gasket aging and oil resistance
(3) Corrosion resistance (indoor and outdoor)
(4) Door and cover latching requirements

F.4 IP-Rating System. The IEC 60529 designation consists of the letters IP followed by two numerals with optional letters.

F.4.1 The first characteristic numeral indicates the degree of protection provided by the enclosure with respect to persons and solid foreign objects entering the enclosure.

F.4.2 The second characteristic numeral indicates the degree of protection provided by the enclosure with respect to the harmful ingress of water.

F.4.3 The additional letter indicates the degree of protection for a person against access to hazardous parts. A brief description of the additional letter is in Table F.5.1.

F.5 Degree of IP Protection. This section contains general information related to degree of protection provided by an enclosure that is indicated by the IP code.

F.5.1 The arrangement of the IP code, which is the degree of protection indicated by the IP code, is shown in Table F.5.1.

F.5.2 A brief description and definitions for the degree of protection against access to hazardous parts are shown in Table F.5.2.

F.5.3 A brief description of the IP code elements is contained in Table F.5.3.

Where more than one supplementary letter is used, the following alphabetic sequence applies:

(1) *IPXXA.* Protected against access with the back of hand
(2) *IPXXB.* Protected against access with finger
(3) *IPXXC.* Protected against access with a tool
(4) *IPXXD.* Protected against access with a wire

These letter designations (A, B, C, D) can be used for referencing the protection of live parts while the enclosure is accessed. There is not a comparable NEMA 250–type rating to this application.

F.5.4 Electrical enclosures that carry only an IP-rating have not been designed to the additional NEMA 250 type–rating requirements. Therefore, a type-rating cannot be assigned to an enclosure that has only been IP-rated because of the exclusion of the additional requirements of the type-rating system. Enclosure types are shown in Table F.5.4.

F.5.5 However, because the IP requirements can be interpreted to be inclusive to the type-rating requirements, a conservative IP-rating can be assigned to a type-rated enclosure as shown in Table F.5.5.

As a practical matter, many electrical enclosures are tested to both the IP and type requirements and carry both IP-rating and type-rating designations.

Table F.5.1 Arrangement of the IP Code

Code Letters	International Protection	IP
First characteristic numeral	Numerals 0 to 6, or letter X	N (or letter X)
Second characteristic numeral	Numerals 0 to 8, or letter X	N (or letter X)
Additional letter (optional)	Letters A, B, C, D	L
Supplementary letter (optional)	Letters H, M, S, W	L
Example:	IP 23CH	TB type

Note: Where a characteristic numeral is not required to be specified, it is replaced by the letter "X" ("XX" if both numerals are omitted). Additional letters and/or supplementary letters may be omitted without replacement.

Shaded text = Revisions.   Δ = Text deletions and figure/table revisions.   • = Section deletions.   *N* = New material.

Table F.5.2 Degrees of Protection Against Access to Hazardous Parts Indicated by the First Characteristic Numeral

First Characteristic Numeral	Degree of Protection	
	Brief Description	**Definition**
0	Nonprotected	—
1	Protected against access to hazardous parts with the back of a hand	The access probe, sphere of 50 mm Ø, has to have adequate clearance from hazardous parts.
2	Protected against access to hazardous parts with a finger	The jointed test finger of 12 mm Ø, 80 mm length, has to have adequate clearance from hazardous parts.
3	Protected against access to hazardous parts with a tool	The access probe of 2.5 mm Ø is not to penetrate.
4	Protected against access to hazardous parts with a wire	The access probe of 1.0 mm Ø is not to penetrate.
5	Protected against access to hazardous parts with a wire	The access probe of 1.0 mm Ø is not to penetrate.
6	Protected against access to hazardous parts with a wire	The access probe of 1.0 mm Ø is not to penetrate.

Note: In the case of the first characteristic numeral 3, 4, 5, and 6, protection against access to hazardous parts is satisfied if adequate clearance is kept.

Shaded text = Revisions.   Δ = Text deletions and figure/table revisions.   • = Section deletions.   N = New material.

2021 Edition

Table F.5.3 IP Code Elements and Their Meaning

Element	Numerals or Letters	Meaning for the Protection of Equipment	Meaning for the Protection of Persons
Code Letters	IP		
First Characteristic Numerals		*Against ingress of solid foreign objects*	*Against access to hazardous parts with the following:*
	0	Nonprotected	Nonprotected
	1	50 mm diameter	Back of hand
	2	12.5 mm diameter	Finger
	3	2.5 mm diameter	Tool
	4	1.0 mm diameter	Wire
	5	Dust protected	Wire
	6	Dusttight	Wire
Second Characteristic Numerals		*Against ingress of water with harmful effects*	
	0	Nonprotected	
	1	Vertically dripping	
	2	Dripping (15° tilted)	
	3	Spraying	
	4	Splashing	
	5	Jetting	
	6	Powerful jetting	
	7	Temporary immersion	
	8	Continuous immersion	
Additional letter (optional)			*Against access to hazardous parts with the following:*
	A		Back of hand
	B		Finger
	C		Tool
	D		Wire
Supplementary letter (optional)		*Supplementary information specific to the following:*	
	H	High-voltage apparatus	
	M	Motion during water test	
	S	Stationary during water test	
	W	Weather conditions	

Shaded text = Revisions.   Δ = Text deletions and figure/table revisions.   • = Section deletions.   *N* = New material.

Table F.5.4 Enclosure Selection

Provides a Degree of Protection Against the Following Environmental Conditions	For Outdoor Use									
	Enclosure-Type Number									
	3	3R	3S	3X	3RX	3SX	4	4X	6	6P
Incidental contact with the enclosed equipment	X	X	X	X	X	X	X	X	X	X
Rain, snow, and sleet	X	X	X	X	X	X	X	X	X	X
Sleet*	—	—	X	—	—	X	—	—	—	—
Windblown dust	X	—	X	X	—	X	X	X	X	X
Hosedown	—	—	—	—	—	—	X	X	X	X
Corrosive agents	—	—	—	X	X	X	—	X	—	X
Temporary submersion	—	—	—	—	—	—	—	—	X	X
Prolonged submersion	—	—	—	—	—	—	—	—	—	X

Provides a Degree of Protection Against the Following Environmental Conditions	For Indoor Use									
	Enclosure-Type Number									
	1	2	4	4X	5	6	6P	12	12K	13
Incidental contact with the enclosed equipment	X	X	X	X	X	X	X	X	X	X
Falling dirt	X	X	X	X	X	X	X	X	X	X
Falling liquids and light splashing	—	X	X	X	X	X	X	X	X	X
Circulating dust, lint, fibers, and flyings	—	—	X	X	—	X	X	X	X	X
Settling airborne dust, lint, fibers, and flyings	—	—	X	X	X	X	X	X	X	X
Hosedown and splashing water	—	—	X	X	—	X	X	—	—	—
Oil and coolant seepage	—	—	—	—	—	—	—	X	X	X
Oil or coolant spraying and splashing	—	—	—	—	—	—	—	—	—	X
Corrosive agents	—	—	—	X	—	—	X	—	—	—
Temporary submersion	—	—	—	—	—	X	X	—	—	—
Prolonged submersion	—	—	—	—	—	—	X	—	—	—

*Mechanism shall be operable when ice covered.

Informational Note No. 1: The term *raintight* is typically used in conjunction with Enclosure Types 3, 3S, 3SX, 3X, 4, 4X, 6, and 6P. The term *rainproof* is typically used in conjunction with Enclosure Types 3R, and 3RX. The term *watertight* is typically used in conjunction with Enclosure Types 4, 4X, 6, 6P. The term *driptight* is typically used in conjunction with Enclosure Types 2, 5, 12, 12K, and 13. The term *dusttight* is typically used in conjunction with Enclosure Types 3, 3S, 3SX, 3X, 5, 12, 12K, and 13.

Informational Note No. 2: Ingress protection (IP) ratings may be found in IEC 60529. IP ratings are not a substitute for Enclosure Type ratings.
[**70**:Table 110.28]

Δ Table F.5.5 Assignment of IP-Ratings to Type-Rated Enclosures

A*														B†
	Enclosure Type													
IP First Character	1	2	3	3R	3S	4	4X	5	6	6P	12	12K	13	IP Second Character
IP0_	AB	AB	AB	AB	AB	AB	AB	AB	AB	AB	AB	AB	AB	IP_0
IP1_	A	AB	AB	AB	AB	AB	AB	AB	AB	AB	AB	AB	AB	IP_1
IP2_	A	AB	AB	AB	AB	AB	AB	AB	AB	AB	AB	AB	AB	IP_2
IP3_	A	—	AB	B	AB	AB	AB	AB	AB	AB	AB	AB	AB	IP_3
IP4_	—	—	AB	B	AB	AB	AB	AB	AB	AB	AB	AB	AB	IP_4
IP5_	—	—	AB	—	AB	AB	AB	A	AB	AB	A	A	A	IP_5
IP6_	—	—	A	—	A	AB	AB	—	AB	AB	—	—	—	IP_6
N/A	—	—	—	—	—	—	—	—	B	B	—	—	—	IP_7
N/A	—	—	—	—	—	—	—	—	—	B	—	—	—	IP_8

N/A: Not applicable.

*A: The first IP character designation is the protection against access to hazardous parts and solid foreign objects. The respective enclosure type meets the requirements for the IEC 60529 IP first character designation.

†B: The IP second character designation is the protection against ingress of water. The respective enclosure type meets the requirements for the IEC 60529 IP second character designation.

Notes:

(1) Type-rated enclosures for hazardous locations and potentially explosive areas have been excluded from the table. The additional and supplementary letters for IP-ratings have also been excluded from the table. *(See NEMA 250, UL 508, and IEC 60529.)*

(2) This table should be used only to assign an IP-rating to a type-rated enclosure, and not to assign a type-rating to an IP-rated enclosure. This table assists in specifying enclosure ratings and should not be used as a definitive guide. For example, if the conditions of installation require an IP 55, this table indicates that a Type 3, Type 3S, Type 4, Type 4X, Type 6, or Type 6P enclosure can be utilized. However, if the conditions of installation require a Type 4, an enclosure that is only IP-rated cannot be used as a substitute.

(3) Although the corresponding enclosure type-ratings meet or exceed the corresponding IP-ratings as indicated in the table, IEC does not currently accept these type-ratings without further IEC testing.

Annex G Kilowatt Outputs with Horsepower Equivalents

This annex is not a part of the requirements of this NFPA document but is included for informational purposes only.

G.1 Preferred Kilowatt Outputs with Horsepower Equivalents. The kilowatt and horsepower values shown in Table G.1 and Table G.2 are not exact conversion values. They give the approximate relationships between countries employing the two different systems of units.

Table G.1 Preferred kW Outputs with hp Equivalents

kW		hp (746 W)
Primary Series	Secondary Series	
0.06		$\frac{1}{12}$
0.09		$\frac{1}{8}$
0.12		$\frac{1}{6}$
0.18		$\frac{1}{4}$
0.25		$\frac{1}{3}$
0.37		$\frac{1}{2}$
0.55		$\frac{3}{4}$
0.75		1
1.1		1.5
1.5	1.8	2
2.2		3
3.7	3	5
	4	
5.5		7.5
	6.3	
7.5		10
	10	
11		15
	13	
15		20
	17	
18.5		25
	20	
22		30
	25	
30		40
	33	
37		50
	40	
45		60
	50	
55		75
	63	
75		100
	80	
90		125
	100	
110		150
	125	
132		175
150		200
160		220
185		250
200		270
220		300
250		350
280		375
300		402
315		422

(continues)

Table G.1 Continued

kW		hp (746 W)
Primary Series	Secondary Series	
335		449
355		476
375		503
400		536
425		570
450		603
475		637
500		670
530		710
560		750
600		804
630		845
670		898
710		952
750		1005
800		1072
850		1139
900		1206
950		1273
1000		1340

Note: The kW–hp conversions are approximately 1 hp = 720 W, not the stated 746 W or even the rounded-off metric units that result in 736 W.
Source: IEC 60072-1, Annex D, Tables D.5.1 and D.5.2 are provided to assist with hp and kW.

G.2 Preferred Horsepower Outputs with Kilowatt Equivalents. See Table G.2.

Table G.2 Preferred hp Outputs with kW Equivalents

hp (746 W)	kW	hp (746 W)	kW
375	280	710	530
400	298	750	560
425	317	800	597
450	336	850	634
475	354	900	671
500	373	950	709
530	395	1000	746
560	418	1060	791
600	448	1120	836
630	470	1180	880
670	500	1250	930
700*	522	1320	985

Notes:
(1) The kW–hp conversions are approximately 1 hp = 720 W, not the stated 746 W or even the rounded-off metric units that result in 736 W.
(2) Additional information is necessary in order to properly exchange motors.
*This value is introduced for use in certain countries that prefer rounded-off horsepower values.
Source: IEC 60072-1, Annex D, Table D.5.1 and Table D.5.2 are provided to assist with hp and kW.

Annex H   Minimizing the Probability of Control Function Failure

This annex is not a part of the requirements of this NFPA document but is included for informational purposes only.

H.1 Measures to Reduce Risk. The following discussion is explanatory material on Section 9.4 and 9.4.1.

H.1.1 The measures, and the extent to which they are implemented, either individually or in combination, depend on the safety requirements associated with the respective application.

H.1.2 General.

H.1.2.1 Measures to reduce these risks include, but are not limited to, the following:

(1) Protective devices on the machine (e.g., interlock guards, trip devices)
(2) Protective interlocking of the electrical circuit
(3) Use of proven circuit techniques and components *(see Section H.2)*
(4) Provisions of partial or complete redundancy *(see Section H.3)* or diversity *(see Section H.4)*
(5) Provision for functional tests *(see Section H.5)*

H.1.2.2 In general, only single failures are to be regarded. In the event of higher levels of risk, it can be necessary to ensure that more than one failure cannot result in a hazardous condition.

H.2 Measures to Minimize Risk in the Event of Failure. Use of proven circuit techniques and components measures to minimize risk in the event of failure include the use of proven circuit techniques and components. These measures include, but are not limited to, the following:

(1) Bonding of control circuits for operational purposes *(see 9.4.2.1)*
(2) One terminal of the control device (i.e., the operating coil) connected to the bonded conductor and all switching elements (e.g., contacts) connected to the non-earthed (grounded) side of the control supply *(see 9.1.4)*
(3) Stopping by de-energizing *(see 9.2.2)*
(4) Switching of all live conductors to the device being controlled
(5) Use of switching devices having direct opening operation *(see IEC 60947-5-1)*
(6) Circuit design to reduce the possibility of failures causing undesirable operations

H.3 Provisions for Redundancy.

H.3.1 By providing partial or complete redundancy it is possible to minimize the probability that one single failure in the electrical circuit can result in a hazardous condition. Redundancy can be effective in normal operation (i.e., on-line redundancy) or designed as special circuits that take over the protective function (i.e., off-line redundancy) only where the operating function fails.

H.3.2 Where off-line redundancy that is not active during normal operation is used, suitable measures should be taken to ensure that these control circuits are available when required.

H.4 Use of Diversity. The use of control circuits having different principles of operation or differing types of devices can reduce the probability of faults and failures giving rise to hazards. Examples include the following:

(1) The combination of normally open and normally closed contacts operated by interlocking guards.
(2) The use of different types of control circuit components in the circuit.
(3) The combination of electromechanical and electronic circuits in redundant configurations.
(4) The combination of electrical and nonelectrical systems (e.g., mechanical, hydraulic, pneumatic) can perform the redundant function and provide the diversity.

H.5 Functional Tests. Functional tests can be carried out automatically by the control system, or manually by inspection or tests at startup and at predetermined intervals, or a combination as appropriate. *(See also Sections 17.2 and 18.6.)*

Annex I   AWG Conductor Cross-Reference Table

This annex is not a part of the requirements of this NFPA document but is included for informational purposes only.

△ **I.1** Table I.1 provides a comparison of the conductor cross-sectional areas of the American Wire Gauge (AWG) with square millimeters, square inches, and circular mils.

The resistance for temperatures other than 20°C can be found using the formula:

[I.1]

$$R = R1\left[1 + 0.00393(t - 20)\right]$$

where:
$R1$ = resistance at 20°C
R = resistance at a temperature t (°C)

Table I.1 Comparison of Conductor Sizes

Wire Size	Gauge No.	Cross-Sectional Area		dc Resistance of Copper at 20°C (68°F)	Circular Mils
mm²	AWG	mm²	in.²	Ω/km	
0.2		0.196	0.000304	91.62	387
	24	0.205	0.000317	87.6	404
0.3		0.283	0.000438	63.46	558
	22	0.324	0.000504	55.44	640
0.5		0.5	0.000775	36.7	987
	20	0.519	0.000802	34.45	1020
0.75		0.75	0.001162	24.8	1480
	18	0.823	0.001272	20.95	1620
1		1	0.00155	18.2	1973
	16	1.31	0.002026	13.19	2580
1.5		1.5	0.002325	12.2	2960
	14	2.08	0.003228	8.442	4110
2.5		2.5	0.003875	7.56	4934
	12	3.31	0.005129	5.315	6530
4		4	0.0062	4.7	7894
	10	5.26	0.008152	3.335	10380
6		6	0.0092	3.11	11841
	8	8.37	0.012967	2.093	16510
10		10	0.0155	1.84	19735
	6	13.3	0.02061	1.32	26240
16		16	0.0248	1.16	31576
	4	21.1	0.03278	0.8295	41740
25		25	0.0388	0.734	49338
	2	33.6	0.0521	0.529	69073
	1	42.4	0.0657	0.4139	83690
50		47	0.0728	0.391	92756

Annex J   Electrical Terms Defined

This annex is not a part of the requirements of this NFPA document but is included for informational purposes only.

J.1 International Terms. This annex contains definitions from various standards to help users understand the differences between terminologies used by different standards-developing organizations.

J.2 *NFPA 70* **Terms. Bonded (Bonding).** Connected to establish electrical continuity and conductivity. [**70**:100]

Discussion. Bonding is accomplished if items are connected together regardless of whether or not there is a connection to ground (earth).

Bonding Conductor or Jumper. A reliable conductor to ensure the required electrical conductivity between metal parts required to be electrically connected. [**70**:100]

Discussion. Bonding conductor sizes are provided in the specific requirements related to what the bonding is intended to accomplish such as being suitable for fault current or minimizing voltage differences.

Bonding Jumper, Equipment. The connection between two or more portions of the equipment grounding conductor. [**70**:100]

Discussion. Equipment bonding jumpers are typically short in length and used to ensure a reliable connection such as between an enclosure and its hinged door.

Bonding Jumper, Supply-Side. A conductor installed on the supply side of a service or within a service equipment enclosure(s), or for a separately derived system, that ensures the required electrical conductivity between metal parts required to be electrically connected. [**70**:250.2]

Discussion. Conductors that are intended to carry fault current for ungrounded conductors that do not have overcurrent protection at their supply point are considered supply-side bonding jumpers. Examples are those for tap conductors and transformer secondary conductors. Conductor sizing is based on a percentage of the ungrounded conductors.

Bonding Jumper, System. The connection between the grounded circuit conductor and the supply-side bonding jumper, or the equipment grounding conductor, or both, at a separately derived system. [**70**:100]

Discussion. System bonding jumpers provide a fault current path for grounded systems. They can be conductors, busbars, or other suitable means.

Effective Ground-Fault Current Path. An intentionally constructed, low-impedance electrically conductive path designed and intended to carry current under ground-fault conditions from the point of a ground fault on a wiring system to the electrical supply source and that facilitates the operation of the overcurrent protective device or ground-fault detectors. [**70**:100]

Discussion. Equipment made of conductive materials that contains electrical conductors is commonly considered to be "likely to become energized" because an insulation failure can occur and energize the equipment. This type of equipment is generally required to be provided with an effective ground-fault current path. An equipment grounding conductor or bonding jumper is commonly used to provide an effective ground-fault current path. The earth is not permitted as the only path for this fault current.

Ground. The earth. [**70**:100]

Discussion. Systems or equipment are either connected to the earth or are considered ungrounded systems.

Ground Fault. An unintentional, electrically conductive connection between an ungrounded conductor of an electrical circuit and the normally non–current-carrying conductors, metallic enclosures, metallic raceways, metallic equipment, or earth. [**70**:100]

Discussion. An insulation failure is a common example of a condition that results in a ground fault.

Grounded (Grounding). Connected (connecting) to ground or to a conductive body that extends the ground connection. [**70**:100]

Discussion. Equipment that is connected to an equipment grounding conductor can be considered grounded, as the equipment grounding conductor extends the ground connection.

Grounded, Solidly. Connected to ground without inserting any resistor or impedance device. [**70**:100]

Discussion. Solidly grounded is a method of system grounding. Using resistors or reactors are other options for grounding some types of systems.

Grounded Conductor. A system or circuit conductor that is intentionally grounded. [**70**:100]

Discussion. The grounded conductor is commonly grounded by a grounding electrode conductor. Depending on the type of electrical system, this can be a neutral conductor, phase conductor, or line conductor. Insulated grounded conductors are generally required to be identified with white or gray coloring.

Ground-Fault Current Path. An electrically conductive path from the point of a ground fault on a wiring system through normally non–current-carrying conductors, equipment, or the earth to the electrical supply source. [**70**:100]

Informational Note: Examples of ground-fault current paths are any combination of equipment grounding conductors, metallic raceways, metallic cable sheaths, electrical equipment, and any other electrically conductive material such as metal, water, and gas piping; steel framing members; stucco mesh; metal ducting; reinforcing steel; shields of communications cables; and the earth itself. [**70**:100]

Discussion. Current will take all paths that exist when a voltage difference exists. Some of these paths can be effective ground-fault current paths and others such as the earth are not.

Grounding Conductor, Equipment (EGC). The conductive path(s) that provides a ground-fault current path and connects normally non–current-carrying metal parts of equipment together and to the system grounded conductor or to the grounding electrode conductor, or both. [**70**:100]

Informational Note No. 1: It is recognized that the equipment grounding conductor also performs bonding. [**70**:100]

Informational Note No. 2: See 250.118 for a list of acceptable equipment grounding conductors. [**70**:100]

Discussion. Equipment grounding conductors are commonly used to provide an effective ground-fault current path. Insulated equipment grounding conductors are generally required to be identified with a green coloring.

Grounding Electrode. A conducting object through which a direct connection to earth is established. [**70**:100]

Discussion. Underground metal water pipes, concrete encased steel reinforcing rods, and ground rods are typical grounding electrodes.

Grounding Electrode Conductor. A conductor used to connect the system grounded conductor or the equipment to a grounding electrode or to a point on the grounding electrode system. [**70**:100]

Discussion. Grounding electrode conductors are what actually accomplish the grounding of equipment or systems.

Metal Wireways. Sheet metal troughs with hinged or removable covers for housing and protecting electrical wires and cable and in which conductors are laid in place after the raceway has been installed as a complete system. [**70**:376.2]

Discussion. Wireways are a type of raceway used to contain electrical conductors and are commonly available in square cross sections.

Neutral Conductor. The conductor connected to the neutral point of a system that is intended to carry current under normal conditions. [**70**:100]

Discussion. Neutral conductors only exist if the system has a neutral point and are generally also grounded conductors.

Neutral Point. The common point on a wye-connection in a polyphase system or midpoint on a single-phase, 3-wire system, or midpoint of a single-phase portion of a 3-phase delta system, or a midpoint of a 3-wire, direct-current system. [**70**:100]

Informational Note: At the neutral point of the system, the vectorial sum of the nominal voltages from all other phases within the system that utilize the neutral, with respect to the neutral point, is zero potential. [**70**:100]

Discussion. A neutral point only exists on systems that have multiple "connection points" with a connection point in the middle.

Separately Derived System. An electrical source, other than a service, having no direct connection(s) to circuit conductors of any other electrical source other than those established by grounding and bonding connections. [**70**:100]

Discussion. Transformers, generators, and batteries that are not directly connected to other sources are examples of separately derived systems. System bonding jumpers, equipment grounding conductors, and grounding electrode conductors are not considered direct connections.

Service. The conductors and equipment for delivering electric energy from the serving utility to the wiring system of the premises served. [**70**:100]

Discussion. Services only exist if a utility is supplying the electricity.

Ungrounded. Not connected to ground or to a conductive body that extends the ground connection. [**70**:100]

Discussion. Systems that have no direct connection to ground (earth) are considered ungrounded, such as vehicle-supplied battery systems and transformer or generator systems that are not connected to ground. A slang term commonly used for these types of systems is "floating."

J.3 Terms and Definitions Relating to Protective and Functional Bonding Used in IEC 60204-1, 6th Edition. Cable Trunking System. A system of enclosures consisting of a base and a removable cover intended for the complete surrounding of insulated conductors, cables, and cords.

Discussion. Cable trunking is commonly used within enclosures to support and contain conductors.

Duct. An enclosed channel designed expressly for holding and protecting electrical conductors, cables, and busbars.

Equipotential Bonding. Provision of electric connections between conductive parts, intended to achieve equipotentiality.

[IEC 195-1-10]

Discussion. Connecting conductive parts together minimizes voltage differences but by itself does not provide an effective fault current path.

Exposed Conductive Part. Conductive part of electrical equipment, which can be touched and which is not live under normal operating conditions, but which can become live under fault conditions.

[IEC 826-12-10, modified]

Discussion. Often linked with "structural parts"; electrical parts that are not normally live generally do need to be bonded to the protective bonding circuit.

Extraneous Conductive Part. Conductive part not forming part of the electrical installation and liable to introduce a potential, generally the earth potential.

[IEC 826-12-11, modified]

NOTE: Examples of extraneous conductive parts can include ladders, handrails, pipes, machine parts, etc., that appear with this definition.

Discussion. Generally, the machine is considered an extraneous conductive part.

Fault Protection. Protection against electric shock under single-fault conditions.

[IEC 195-06-02]

Discussion. Overcurrent protective devices and double insulation are types of fault protection.

Functional Bonding. Equipotential bonding necessary for proper functioning of electrical equipment.

Discussion. PLCs and drives generally do not need special bonding, and there are only a few devices that need separate "functional" bonding, such as some scales.

Live Part. Conductor or conductive part intended to be energized in normal use, including a neutral conductor, but, by convention, not a PEN conductor.

NOTE: This term does not necessarily imply a risk of electric shock.

Neutral Conductor N. Conductor electrically connected to the neutral point of a system and capable of contributing to the distribution of electrical energy.

[IEC 195-02-06, modified]

Plug/Socket Combination. Component and a suitable mating component, appropriate to terminate conductors, intended for connection or disconnection of two or more conductors.

NOTE: Examples of plug/socket combinations include:

– connectors which fulfill the requirements of IEC 61984

– a plug-and-socket-outlet, a cable coupler, or an appliance coupler in accordance with IEC 60309-1

– a plug-and-socket outlet in accordance with IEC 60884-1 or an appliance coupler in accordance with IEC 608320-1

Protective Bonding. Equipotential bonding for protection against electric shock.

NOTE: Measures for protection against electric shock can also reduce the risk of burns or fire.

Discussion. The network of protective conductors, along with the necessary bonding jumpers, provide the protective bonding, including the connection to the "main earthing terminal PE."

Protective Bonding Circuit. Protective conductors and conductive parts connected together to provide protection against electric shock in the event of an insulation failure.

Protective Conductor. Conductor required for protective bonding by some measures for protection against electric shock for electrically connecting any of the following parts:

– exposed conductive parts

– extraneous conductive parts

– main earthing terminal (PE)

[IEC 826-13-22, modified]

J.4 Terms and Definitions Used in CEMA 110. Control Architecture, Centralized. A control logic architecture in which all logic solving, sensory input collection, and actuator control is executed by a single controller and control panel. An example would be a PLC control cabinet that contains a processor to solve logic, input modules for all sensor signals, and output modules for all actuator control signals. The input and output signals would be wired from the field device to the PLC control cabinet.

Control Architecture, Distributed. A control logic architecture in which all logic, sensory input, and actuator control is solved, collected, and executed by more than one controller. An example would be microcontrollers located on every conveyor motor that contain a processor to solve logic, input modules for all sensors signals, and output modules for all actuator control signals. The input and output signals would be wired from the field device to the microcontroller. Each microcontroller would solve logic and command actuators that are specific to the function of the conveyor. The coordination of all the motors (macro-commands) would be completed with intra-microcontroller communication and microcontroller communication with the machine supervisor control system.

Device Wiring Architecture, Discrete. A power and control distribution system architecture in which all sensor and actuator signals are collected and delivered by directly wiring to/from the device and the controller. An example would be a binary sensor signal that would use one wire to communicate an "on" or "off" state based on the absence or presence of voltage with respect to a voltage reference that is common to the sensor and controller.

Device Wiring Architecture, Distributed. A power and control distribution system architecture in which all sensor and actuator signals are collected and delivered by network interface modules, which then interpret the sensor signals and convert them into a message to be transmitted to the controller over a communication network. The complementary PLC sends a message to the actuator network interface, which converts the message to an output command for the actuator. An example would be a sensor wire connected to a remote input module. The remote input module and controller would be connected to an Ethernet network and would exchange data at a rate sufficient to properly control the machine.

Power Distribution Architecture, Dedicated. A power and control distribution system architecture in which each nominal voltage supply is distributed using a dedicated path and in which no overlap of function or supply function is allowed. An example would be a 480 V ac supply to motors carried on wires or busbars, a supply to 24 V dc devices carried on wires or busbars, and communication networks carried on dedicated cables.

Power Distribution Architecture, Multifunction. A system architecture in which voltage supplies share common pathways and overlap in function for power and communication distribution. Examples would include power over Ethernet (dc supply carried on Ethernet cable) or Ethernet over power (Ethernet communications carried on high power conductors).

Annex K Informational References

K.1 Referenced Publications. The documents or portions thereof listed in this annex are referenced within the informational sections of this standard and are not part of the requirements of this document unless also listed in Chapter 2 for other reasons.

K.1.1 NFPA Publications. National Fire Protection Association, 1 Batterymarch Park, Quincy, MA 02169-7471.

NFPA 70®, National Electrical Code®, 2020 edition.

NFPA 70E®, Standard for Electrical Safety in the Workplace®, 2021 edition.

NFPA 77, *Recommended Practice on Static Electricity*, 2019 edition.

K.1.2 Other Publications.

K.1.2.1 ANSI Publications. American National Standards Institute, Inc., 25 West 43rd Street, 4th Floor, New York, NY 10036.

ANSI B11.0, *Safety of Machinery*, 2015.

ANSI B11-TR4, *Selection of Programmable Electronic Systems (PES/PLC) for Machine Tools*, 2004, reaffirmed 2015.

ANSI B11-TR6, *Safety Control Systems for Machine Tools*, 2010.

ANSI Z535.4, *Product Safety Signs and Labels*, 2011, reaffirmed 2017.

N K.1.2.2 CEMA Publications. Conveyor Equipment Manufacturers Association, 5672 Strand Ct., Suite 2, Naples, FL 34110.

CEMA 110, *Electrical Terms and Definitions*, 1995.

K.1.2.3 CENELEC Publications. CENELEC, European Committee for Electrotechnical Standardization, CEN-CENELEC Management Centre, Avenue Marnix 17, 4th floor, B - 1000 Brussels.

EN 60204-1, *Safety of machinery — Electrical equipment of machines — Part 1: General requirements*, 2018.

EN 61010-1, *Safety requirements for electrical equipment for measurement, control, and laboratory use — Part 1: General requirements*, 2019.

△ K.1.2.4 IEC Publications. International Electrotechnical Commission, 3, rue de Varembé, P.O. Box 131, CH-1211 Geneva 20, Switzerland.

IEC 60034-1 Ed. 13.0, *Rotating electrical machines — Part 1: Rating and performance*, 2017.

IEC 60072-1 Ed. 6.0, *Dimensions and output series for rotating electrical machines — Part 1: Frame numbers 56 to 400 and flange numbers 55 to 1080*, 1991.

IEC 60204-1 Ed. 6.0, *Safety of machinery — Electrical equipment of machines — Part 1: General requirements*, 2016.

IEC 60332-1-1 Ed. 1.1, *Tests on electric and optical fibre cables under fire conditions — Part 1-1: Test for vertical flame propagation for a single insulated wire or cable — Apparatus*, 2004, amendment 1, 2015.

IEC 60364-4-41 Ed. 5.1, *Low voltage electrical installations — Part 4-41: Protection for safety — Protection against electric shock*, 2005, corrigendum 1, 2017.

IEC 60364-5-53 Ed. 3.2, *Electrical Installations of buildings — Part 5-53: Selection and erection of electrical equipment — Isolation, switching and control*, 2015.

IEC 60417 DB *[Database], Graphical symbols for use on equipment — Part 1: Overview and application*, 2002.

IEC 60529 Ed. 2.2, *Degrees of protection provided by enclosures (IP Code)*, 2013, corrigendum 2, 2015.

IEC 60621-3 Ed. 1.0, *Electrical installations for outdoor sites under heavy conditions (including open-cast mines and quarries) — Part 3: General requirements for equipment and ancillaries*, 1979 (withdrawn).

IEC 60742 Ed. 1.0, *Isolating transformers and safety isolating transformers*, 1983 (superseded by IEC 61558-1).

IEC 60870-5-1 Ed. 1.0, *Telecontrol equipment and systems — Part 5: Transmission protocols — Section One: Transmission frame formats*, 1990.

IEC 60947-4-1 Ed. 3.1, *Low-voltage switchgear and controlgear — Part 4-1: Contactors and motor-starters — Electromechanical contactors and motor-starters*, 2012.

IEC 60947-5-1 Ed. 4.0, *Low-voltage switchgear and controlgear — Part 5-1: Control circuit devices and switching elements — Electromechanical control circuit devices*, 2016, corrigendum 1, 2016.

IEC 60947-7-1 Ed. 3.0, *Low-voltage switchgear and controlgear — Part 7-1: Ancillary equipment — Terminal blocks for copper conductors*, 2009.

IEC 61010-1 Ed. 3.1, *Safety requirements for electrical equipment for measurement, control, and laboratory use — Part 1: General requirements*, 2016.

IEC 61310-1 Ed. 2.0, *Safety of machinery — Indication, marking and actuation — Part 1: Requirements for visual, acoustic and tactile signals*, 2007.

IEC 61310-3 Ed. 2.0, *Safety of machinery — Indication, marking and actuation — Part 3: Requirements for the location and operation of actuators*, 2007.

IEC 61508 Ed. 2.0, *[Series] Functional safety of electrical/electronic/programmable electronic safety-related systems*, 2010.

IEC 61558-1 Ed. 3.0, *Safety of transformers, reactors, power supply units and combinations thereof — Part 1: General requirements and tests*, 2017.

IEC 61800-5-2 Ed. 2.0, *Adjustable speed electrical power drive systems — Part 5-2: Safety requirements — Functional*, 2016.

IEC 62061 Ed. 1.2, *Safety of machinery — Functional safety of safety-related electrical, electronic and programmable electronic control systems*, 2005, corrigendum 1, 2015.

NOTE: The IEC publishes consolidated editions of its publications with all the amendments and corrigenda included with the base document. For example:

Edition 1.0 is a base document without any amendments.

Edition 1.1 is the base 1.0 edition consolidated with one amendment.

Edition 1.2 is the base 1.0 edition consolidated with two amendments.

Edition 2.0 is the second edition of a base document. This may include new information combined as well as amendments from edition 1.x.

Edition 2.1 is the second edition of a document consolidated with amendment 1 to that edition.

△ K.1.2.5 IEEE Publications. IEEE, 3 Park Avenue, 17th Floor, New York, NY 10016-5997.

IEEE 100 CD, *Standards Dictionary: Glossary of Terms and Definitions*, 2013.

ANSI Y32.2/IEEE 315, *IEEE Graphic Symbols for Electrical and Electronics Diagrams (Including Reference Designation Letters)*, 1993.

IEEE 841, *Petroleum and Chemical Industry — Premium-Efficiency, Severe-Duty, Totally Enclosed Fan-Cooled (TEFC) Squirrel Cage Induction Motors — Up to and Including 370 kW (500 hp)*, 2009.

△ K.1.2.6 ISO Publications. International Organization for Standardization, ISO Central Secretariat, BIBC II, Chemin de Blandonnet 8, CP 401, 1214 Vernier, Geneva, Switzerland.

ISO 5457, *Technical product documentation — Sizes and layout of drawing sheets*, 1999.

ISO 7000, *Graphical symbols for use on equipment — Registered symbols*, 2014.

ISO 7200, *Technical drawings — Title blocks*, 1984.

ISO 12100, *Safety of machinery — General principles for design — Risk assessment and risk reduction*, 2010.

ISO 13849-1, *Safety of machinery — Safety-related parts of control systems — Part 1: General principles for design*, 2015.

ISO 13849-2, *Safety of machinery — Safety-related parts of control systems — Part 2: Validation*, 2012.

ISO 13850, *Safety of machinery — Emergency stop function — Principles for design*, 2015.

K.1.2.7 NEMA Publications. National Electrical Manufacturers Association, 1300 North 17th Street, Suite 900, Arlington, VA 22209.

NEMA MG-1, *Motors and Generators*, 2014.

NEMA 250, *Enclosures for Electrical Equipment (1000 Volts Maximum)*, 2014.

K.1.2.8 SEMI Publications. Semiconductor Equipment and Materials International, 3081 Zanker Road, San Jose, CA 95134.

SEMI S2, *Environmental, Health, and Safety Guideline for Semiconductor Manufacturing Equipment*, 2010.

SEMI S9, *Safety Guideline for Electrical Design Verification Tests for Semiconductor Manufacturing Equipment*, 2001 (withdrawn 2007).

SEMI S22, *Safety Guideline for the Electrical Design of Semiconductor Manufacturing Equipment*, 2010.

Δ **K.1.2.9 UL Publications.** Underwriters Laboratories Inc., 333 Pfingsten Road, Northbrook, IL 60062-2096.

UL 50, *Enclosures for Electrical Equipment, Non-Environmental Considerations*, 2015.

UL 62, *Flexible Cord and Cables*, 2018.

UL 248-14, *Low-Voltage Fuses — Part 14: Supplemental Fuses*, 2000, revised 2015.

UL 489, *Molded-Case Circuit Breakers, Molded-Case Switches, and Circuit-Breaker Enclosures*, 2016.

UL 498, *Attachment Plugs and Receptacles*, 2017, revised 2018.

UL 508, *Industrial Control Equipment*, 2018.

UL 508A, *Industrial Control Panels*, 2018.

UL 651, *Schedule 40, 80, Type EB and A Rigid PVC Conduit and Fittings*, 2011, revised 2016.

UL 758, *Appliance Wiring Material*, 2014, revised 2017.

UL 1004-1, *Rotating Electrical Machines — General Requirements*, 2012, revised 2018.

UL 1077, *Supplementary Protectors for Use in Electrical Equipment*, 2015, revised 2016.

UL 1682, *Plugs, Receptacles, and Cable Connectors of the Pin and Sleeve Type*, 2017.

UL 60950-1, *Information Technology Equipment — Safety — Part I: General Requirements*, 2007, revised 2014.

UL 2237 Outline, *Outline of Investigation for Multi-Point Interconnection Power Cable Assemblies for Industrial Machinery*, 2018.

UL 2238, *Cable Assemblies and Fittings for Industrial Control and Signal Distribution*, 2018.

UL 61010-1, *Safety Requirements for Electrical Equipment for Measurement, Control, and Laboratory Use — Part 1: General Requirements*, 2012, revised 2016.

K.2 Informational References. The following documents or portions thereof are listed here as informational resources only. They are not a part of the requirements of this document.

DOE-HDBK-1003-96, *Guide to Good Practices for Training and Qualification of Maintenance Personnel*, 1996.

IEC 81346-2, *Industrial systems, installations and equipment and industrial products — Structuring principles and reference designations — Part 2: Classification of objects and codes for classes*, 2009 (withdrawn).

IEC 61558-2-6, *Safety of transformers, reactors, power supply units and similar products for supply voltages up to 1100 V — Part 2-6: Particular requirements and tests for safety isolating transformers and power supply units incorporating safety isolating transformers*, 2009.

ISO 5457, *Technical product documentation — Sizes and layout of drawing sheets*, 1999, amendment 1, 2010.

ISO 7200, *Technical product documentation — Data fields in title blocks and document headers*, 2004.

UL 6420, *Equipment Used for System Isolation and Rated as a Single Unit*, 2012.

K.3 References for Extracts in Informational Sections.

NFPA 70®, *National Electrical Code®*, 2020 edition.

Index

Copyright © 2020 National Fire Protection Association. All Rights Reserved.

Sequence of Events for the Standards Development Process

Once the current edition is published, a Standard is opened for Public Input.

Step 1 – Input Stage

- Input accepted from the public or other committees for consideration to develop the First Draft
- Technical Committee holds First Draft Meeting to revise Standard (23 weeks); Technical Committee(s) with Correlating Committee (10 weeks)
- Technical Committee ballots on First Draft (12 weeks); Technical Committee(s) with Correlating Committee (11 weeks)
- Correlating Committee First Draft Meeting (9 weeks)
- Correlating Committee ballots on First Draft (5 weeks)
- First Draft Report posted on the document information page

Step 2 – Comment Stage

- Public Comments accepted on First Draft (10 weeks) following posting of First Draft Report
- If Standard does not receive Public Comments and the Technical Committee chooses not to hold a Second Draft meeting, the Standard becomes a Consent Standard and is sent directly to the Standards Council for issuance (see Step 4) or
- Technical Committee holds Second Draft Meeting (21 weeks); Technical Committee(s) with Correlating Committee (7 weeks)
- Technical Committee ballots on Second Draft (11 weeks); Technical Committee(s) with Correlating Committee (10 weeks)
- Correlating Committee Second Draft Meeting (9 weeks)
- Correlating Committee ballots on Second Draft (8 weeks)
- Second Draft Report posted on the document information page

Step 3 – NFPA Technical Meeting

- Notice of Intent to Make a Motion (NITMAM) accepted (5 weeks) following the posting of Second Draft Report
- NITMAMs are reviewed and valid motions are certified by the Motions Committee for presentation at the NFPA Technical Meeting
- NFPA membership meets each June at the NFPA Technical Meeting to act on Standards with "Certified Amending Motions" (certified NITMAMs)
- Committee(s) vote on any successful amendments to the Technical Committee Reports made by the NFPA membership at the NFPA Technical Meeting

Step 4 – Council Appeals and Issuance of Standard

- Notification of intent to file an appeal to the Standards Council on Technical Meeting action must be filed within 20 days of the NFPA Technical Meeting
- Standards Council decides, based on all evidence, whether to issue the standard or to take other action

Notes:

1. Time periods are approximate; refer to published schedules for actual dates.
2. Annual revision cycle documents with certified amending motions take approximately 101 weeks to complete.
3. Fall revision cycle documents receiving certified amending motions take approximately 141 weeks to complete.

Committee Membership Classifications[1,2,3,4]

The following classifications apply to Committee members and represent their principal interest in the activity of the Committee.

1. M *Manufacturer:* A representative of a maker or marketer of a product, assembly, or system, or portion thereof, that is affected by the standard.
2. U *User:* A representative of an entity that is subject to the provisions of the standard or that voluntarily uses the standard.
3. IM *Installer/Maintainer:* A representative of an entity that is in the business of installing or maintaining a product, assembly, or system affected by the standard.
4. L *Labor:* A labor representative or employee concerned with safety in the workplace.
5. RT *Applied Research/Testing Laboratory:* A representative of an independent testing laboratory or independent applied research organization that promulgates and/or enforces standards.
6. E *Enforcing Authority:* A representative of an agency or an organization that promulgates and/or enforces standards.
7. I *Insurance:* A representative of an insurance company, broker, agent, bureau, or inspection agency.
8. C *Consumer:* A person who is or represents the ultimate purchaser of a product, system, or service affected by the standard, but who is not included in (2).
9. SE *Special Expert:* A person not representing (1) through (8) and who has special expertise in the scope of the standard or portion thereof.

NOTE 1: "Standard" connotes code, standard, recommended practice, or guide.

NOTE 2: A representative includes an employee.

NOTE 3: While these classifications will be used by the Standards Council to achieve a balance for Technical Committees, the Standards Council may determine that new classifications of member or unique interests need representation in order to foster the best possible Committee deliberations on any project. In this connection, the Standards Council may make such appointments as it deems appropriate in the public interest, such as the classification of "Utilities" in the National Electrical Code Committee.

NOTE 4: Representatives of subsidiaries of any group are generally considered to have the same classification as the parent organization.

Submitting Public Input / Public Comment Through the Online Submission System

Following publication of the current edition of an NFPA standard, the development of the next edition begins and the standard is open for Public Input.

Submit a Public Input

NFPA accepts Public Input on documents through our online submission system at www.nfpa.org. To use the online submission system:

- Choose a document from the List of NFPA codes & standards or filter by Development Stage for "codes accepting public input."
- Once you are on the document page, select the "Next Edition" tab.
- Choose the link "The next edition of this standard is now open for Public Input." You will be asked to sign in or create a free online account with NFPA before using this system.
- Follow the online instructions to submit your Public Input (see www.nfpa.org/publicinput for detailed instructions).
- Once a Public Input is saved or submitted in the system, it can be located on the "My Profile" page by selecting the "My Public Inputs/Comments/NITMAMs" section.

Submit a Public Comment

Once the First Draft Report becomes available there is a Public Comment period. Any objections or further related changes to the content of the First Draft must be submitted at the Comment Stage. To submit a Public Comment follow the same steps as previously explained for the submission of Public Input.

Other Resources Available on the Document Information Pages

Header: View document title and scope, access to our codes and standards or NFCSS subscription, and sign up to receive email alerts.

Current & Prior Editions	Research current and previous edition information.
Next Edition	Follow the committee's progress in the processing of a standard in its next revision cycle.
Technical Committee	View current committee rosters or apply to a committee.
Ask a Technical Question	For members, officials, and AHJs to submit standards questions to NFPA staff. Our Technical Questions Service provides a convenient way to receive timely and consistent technical assistance when you need to know more about NFPA standards relevant to your work.
News	Provides links to available articles and research and statistical reports related to our standards.
Purchase Products & Training	Discover and purchase the latest products and training.
Related Products	View related publications, training, and other resources available for purchase.

Information on the NFPA Standards Development Process

I. Applicable Regulations. The primary rules governing the processing of NFPA standards (codes, standards, recommended practices, and guides) are the NFPA *Regulations Governing the Development of NFPA Standards (Regs)*. Other applicable rules include NFPA *Bylaws*, NFPA *Technical Meeting Convention Rules*, NFPA *Guide for the Conduct of Participants in the NFPA Standards Development Process*, and the NFPA *Regulations Governing Petitions to the Board of Directors from Decisions of the Standards Council*. Most of these rules and regulations are contained in the *NFPA Standards Directory*. For copies of the *Directory*, contact Codes and Standards Administration at NFPA headquarters; all these documents are also available on the NFPA website at "www.nfpa.org/regs."

The following is general information on the NFPA process. All participants, however, should refer to the actual rules and regulations for a full understanding of this process and for the criteria that govern participation.

II. Technical Committee Report. The Technical Committee Report is defined as "the Report of the responsible Committee(s), in accordance with the Regulations, in preparation of a new or revised NFPA Standard." The Technical Committee Report is in two parts and consists of the First Draft Report and the Second Draft Report. (See *Regs* at Section 1.4.)

III. Step 1: First Draft Report. The First Draft Report is defined as "Part one of the Technical Committee Report, which documents the Input Stage." The First Draft Report consists of the First Draft, Public Input, Committee Input, Committee and Correlating Committee Statements, Correlating Notes, and Ballot Statements. (See *Regs* at 4.2.5.2 and Section 4.3.) Any objection to an action in the First Draft Report must be raised through the filing of an appropriate Comment for consideration in the Second Draft Report or the objection will be considered resolved. [See *Regs* at 4.3.1(b).]

IV. Step 2: Second Draft Report. The Second Draft Report is defined as "Part two of the Technical Committee Report, which documents the Comment Stage." The Second Draft Report consists of the Second Draft, Public Comments with corresponding Committee Actions and Committee Statements, Correlating Notes and their respective Committee Statements, Committee Comments, Correlating Revisions, and Ballot Statements. (See *Regs* at 4.2.5.2 and Section 4.4.) The First Draft Report and the Second Draft Report together constitute the Technical Committee Report. Any outstanding objection following the Second Draft Report must be raised through an appropriate Amending Motion at the NFPA Technical Meeting or the objection will be considered resolved. [See *Regs* at 4.4.1(b).]

V. Step 3a: Action at NFPA Technical Meeting. Following the publication of the Second Draft Report, there is a period during which those wishing to make proper Amending Motions on the Technical Committee Reports must signal their intention by submitting a Notice of Intent to Make a Motion (NITMAM). (See *Regs* at 4.5.2.) Standards that receive notice of proper Amending Motions (Certified Amending Motions) will be presented for action at the annual June NFPA Technical Meeting. At the meeting, the NFPA membership can consider and act on these Certified Amending Motions as well as Follow-up Amending Motions, that is, motions that become necessary as a result of a previous successful Amending Motion. (See 4.5.3.2 through 4.5.3.6 and Table 1, Columns 1-3 of *Regs* for a summary of the available Amending Motions and who may make them.) Any outstanding objection following action at an NFPA Technical Meeting (and any further Technical Committee consideration following successful Amending Motions, see *Regs* at 4.5.3.7 through 4.6.5) must be raised through an appeal to the Standards Council or it will be considered to be resolved.

VI. Step 3b: Documents Forwarded Directly to the Council. Where no NITMAM is received and certified in accordance with the *Technical Meeting Convention Rules*, the standard is forwarded directly to the Standards Council for action on issuance. Objections are deemed to be resolved for these documents. (See *Regs* at 4.5.2.5.)

VII. Step 4a: Council Appeals. Anyone can appeal to the Standards Council concerning procedural or substantive matters related to the development, content, or issuance of any document of the NFPA or on matters within the purview of the authority of the Council, as established by the *Bylaws* and as determined by the Board of Directors. Such appeals must be in written form and filed with the Secretary of the Standards Council (see *Regs* at Section 1.6). Time constraints for filing an appeal must be in accordance with 1.6.2 of the *Regs*. Objections are deemed to be resolved if not pursued at this level.

VIII. Step 4b: Document Issuance. The Standards Council is the issuer of all documents (see Article 8 of *Bylaws*). The Council acts on the issuance of a document presented for action at an NFPA Technical Meeting within 75 days from the date of the recommendation from the NFPA Technical Meeting, unless this period is extended by the Council (see *Regs* at 4.7.2). For documents forwarded directly to the Standards Council, the Council acts on the issuance of the document at its next scheduled meeting, or at such other meeting as the Council may determine (see *Regs* at 4.5.2.5 and 4.7.4).

IX. Petitions to the Board of Directors. The Standards Council has been delegated the responsibility for the administration of the codes and standards development process and the issuance of documents. However, where extraordinary circumstances requiring the intervention of the Board of Directors exist, the Board of Directors may take any action necessary to fulfill its obligations to preserve the integrity of the codes and standards development process and to protect the interests of the NFPA. The rules for petitioning the Board of Directors can be found in the *Regulations Governing Petitions to the Board of Directors from Decisions of the Standards Council* and in Section 1.7 of the *Regs*.

X. For More Information. The program for the NFPA Technical Meeting (as well as the NFPA website as information becomes available) should be consulted for the date on which each report scheduled for consideration at the meeting will be presented. To view the First Draft Report and Second Draft Report as well as information on NFPA rules and for up-to-date information on schedules and deadlines for processing NFPA documents, check the NFPA website (www.nfpa.org/docinfo) or contact NFPA Codes & Standards Administration at (617) 984-7246.